The Kind of

Parent You Are

The Kind of Parent You Are

BECOMING YOUR BEST PERSON SO YOUR CHILDREN CAN BECOME THEIR BEST ADULTS

BRIAN VONDRUSKA

The Kind of Parent You Are
Becoming Your Best Person So Your Children
Can Become Their Best Adults

This book includes some personal stories involving my
children. In the interest of preserving their privacy, their names
are omitted.

ISBN: 978-0-9987511-3-9 (print)
ISBN: 978-0-9987511-4-6 (eBook)

Library of Congress Control Number: 2018901003

Publisher's Cataloging-In-Publication Data
(Prepared by The Donohue Group, Inc.)

Names: Vondruska, Brian.
Title: The kind of parent you are : becoming your best person
    so your children can become their best adults / Brian
    Vondruska.
Description: Aurora, Ohio : Aurora Park Publishing, [2018] |
    Includes bibliographical references and index.
Identifiers: ISBN 9780998751139 (print) | ISBN
    9780998751146 (ebook)
Subjects: LCSH: Parenting. | Role models. | Self-actualization
    (Psychology) in children. | Conduct of life. | Quality of life.
Classification: LCC HQ755.8 .V66 2018 (print) | LCC HQ755.8
    (ebook) | DDC 649.1--dc23

Published by:
Aurora Park Publishing
Aurora, Ohio

AURORA PARK
PUBLISHING

DEDICATION

Son and Daughter,

I began writing these words when you were very small, with the intent of delivering them to each of you when you are about to start your own families.

Please accept my warmest congratulations. You will find that caring for children is the most joyous, rewarding, and gratifying experience that life has to offer. The special moments you will share with your children as they grow and develop are as magical and abundant as they are unexpected.

Parenting will also prove to be one of life's most challenging endeavors. Your patience, feelings of vulnerability, and feelings of inadequacy will be stretched in ways you have never imagined.

There is simply nothing in life that prepares you for the feelings you will have as a parent. If you are like me, then you will feel driven to recast yourself as equal to the task. Within these pages is my best advice to help you.

Through the years I never stopped envisioning the happy, confident, well-adjusted adults you would become. I routinely studied, often in early mornings before you awoke and in late evenings after you fell asleep, the parents' role in realizing that vision. As my studies shaped my parenting style, I wrote down what I learned with the hope that it would someday be valuable to you. What began as a letter grew into books.

You might choose to use your own parenting insights to revise this book and then hand the improved version down to your children. I have taken the time to write the first edition because I love you and wish the best for all of you.

Whatever paths you make for yourselves in life, I wish for you to be happy. I wish for you to be fulfilled. I wish for you to be everything that you can be. My greatest wish, however, is that your own children bring to you as much joy as mine bring to me.

Love,
Dad

CONTENTS

LIST OF FIGURES AND TABLES

ACKNOWLEDGMENTS

Thank you to Charlie Stryker, who, as the individual entrusted to give the four-years-in-the-making first draft a read-through and assessment, assumed the role of unofficial editor. I am ever grateful for the hours Charlie invested over months to read, make annotations, offer suggestions, and discuss revisions. This book could not have grown without the help of Charlie.

This book could not have matured without Katy Hamilton, the official content editor. I have Katy to thank for one large manuscript being transformed into two books, each having a clear focus and purpose. I count myself lucky for the opportunity to benefit from Katy's editing experience, professional insight, and keen literary sense.

Thanks to Julia Kellaway, the copy editor, for ensuring the book that I wanted to write would be a book that people want to read. Thanks to Rachel Fudge for her precision proofreading.

Credit for the clean, crisp, design goes to the team at Jera Publishing. Thank you to Kimberly Martin, Stephanie Anderson, and Jason Orr for bringing this book and its companion journal to life.

WHY THIS BOOK

Becoming a parent was the best thing to ever happen to me, and I was lucky enough to have the best thing to ever happen to me happen twice. I will always remember the love I felt holding my newborn children. They were so very dependent on me, and I was so very happy to provide for them.

I just didn't know how.

Today, I am on somewhat firmer ground. I know that when my daughter confides in me about an ongoing dispute with a playmate, I want to be there to listen to her, and also provide counsel if any is requested. I know that when my son asks to use the computer before he has finished his homework, I want to let him, provided he gives assurance that he will also honor his homework commitments. I know that when my children want to take their fish along for a car ride to a friend's house using tape and Bubble Wrap to cover their fishbowls, I want to provide those materials for them and support their efforts, even if I think there is a better way. I now have underlying reasons for wanting to do all these things. But, when my children were first born, I didn't know what I should be doing or why.

I was committed to learning as much as possible. I pored over the best parenting books, research papers, magazines, websites, and forums I could find. I was confounded by the reams of conflicting advice. Equally passionate arguments were made on opposing sides of every parenting issue.

I tried to screen the advice by the motives of the advice givers. Unfortunately, motives were not always given. When they were, they were unsatisfying.

Some advice was given on the grounds that following it would help a baby fall asleep faster. Other advice claimed to help a baby stay asleep longer. Advice was given for getting children to follow instructions. Advice was given for getting children to think for themselves. Some advice aimed to aid the development of academic skills, while other advice offered to find opportunities for free play. Still more advice cited the promotion of computer literacy as a motive, or the restriction of screen time, or the encouragement of sharing, or the cultivation of self-advocacy … I could go on.

On the surface, these and countless others often seemed like good motives. The problem was that there wasn't enough substance beneath the surface. The reason for adopting an advised sleep practice may very well be so that a baby can fall asleep faster. But why is that a good thing? Perhaps so that the child is better rested. Why is that a good thing? Perhaps so that the child can better focus on his surroundings the next day. And why is that a good thing? Perhaps so that he can learn more effectively.

Some parenting resources went as much as two or three "whys" deep but then stopped. It was as if the stopping point marked the universally accepted right motive. No further exploration was attempted. But if you don't go deep enough, you will find yourself adhering to a collection of disjointed motives that will sooner or later run afoul of one another. You may end up feeling directionless or, worse, hypocritical. By asking enough "whys," a place with no further asking can be found. An "irreducible why" can be attained.

I came to realize that if I had an irreducible why, it would allow me to contextualize all the parenting advice I encountered. I could use it to distinguish the good advice from the not-so-good.

Motives that aligned under the irreducible why could be accepted. Motives that could not be reconciled with the irreducible why could then be discarded. An irreducible why would enable me to confidently negotiate controversial parenting issues. It would enable me to make difficult parenting decisions off the cuff.

If I was to provide for my children according to my best efforts, I needed to arrive at an irreducible why. A why that centered on any particular trait, ability, or facet of life—for example, politeness, athleticism, or academics—would be automatically disqualified. My why had to encompass the totality of life. It had to be big. And it had to be personal. My why had to be aligned with my core beliefs and values, which I found myself suddenly having to define.

After much contemplation, I determined that I wanted my children to live to their full potentials. Not simply as children, but over the course of their lives. I wanted them to be able to maximize the quality of their experiences, to squeeze every last drop out of what life has to offer. I wanted them to make the most of life, to make themselves as fully alive, as exhilaratingly human, as possible. I wanted them to be equipped as adults to create lives that mean something, not only to themselves but to others as well.

> My irreducible why would be to help my children to make their best possible life experiences as adults while simultaneously benefitting society.

I liked my irreducible why. It was big. It was inspiring. And it was positive. Rather than being *against* an undesirable outcome, my why was framed as being *for* a desired outcome. I could adhere to it not out of fear but through aspiration.

The wrongs of the world, the misguided direction of society, and the faults of various parenting practices are tempting distractions when setting a personal parenting direction. There are lots of resources for avoiding helicopter parenting, for addressing ailing math scores, or for tempering the egos of the "millennial" generation. Some are very good. But I believe that parenting styles based on running away from problems like these are not the best prescription for success. New problems constantly arise. Alongside each one, pundits materialize and insistently offer advice. That advice appeals to parents to steer their children away from questionable trends and developments.

I liked that my irreducible why had me steering toward something. With a positive why, I could define the direction and stay true to it, regardless of circumstances. I was not beholden to respond to every new specter that threatened my children's futures. I was in the driver's seat.

The only problem with my irreducible why was that I didn't know what it meant. The best possible life experience, as it turned out, was undefined. I needed to give it meaning for myself. In order to do so, I needed to go beyond the subject of parenting. I found myself delving into adjacent fields of study, reading up on psychology, philosophy, and even economics.

I urgently needed to know all about life and about people. Only then could I apply my irreducible why to actual situations. Only then could I begin to define what kind of parent I was going to be.

ABOUT THIS BOOK

To help me organize all the details, I wrote down what I learned. As my body of writings grew, I decided that I wanted them to be useful to more people than just me. I wanted to someday pass what I had learned on to my children when they were about to become parents. I wanted to give them a head start with raising their families. I also wanted them to be able to pass it on to their children, and so on down the line. I wanted these writings to still be relevant in a generation, and in a hundred years, and even in a thousand years. I wanted my distant descendants to be able to apply these words, no matter their countries or cultures, irrespective of their religion or creed, and independent of the fads and trends of their days.

I had to write about things that apply to people on a fundamental level. I had to uncover the common factors that influence the quality of the human experience. And I had to unify those factors under the subject of "parenting."

What I learned about the quality of the human experience became a book of its own: *The Optimal Life Experience: What It Is, Why It Matters, and How to Maximize Well-Being*. It begins with the ancient notion that virtuous behavior leads to an enriching life. It then incorporates modern research to flesh out the path. Self-beliefs and skills were determined to be the factors leading up to virtuous behaviors. When done right, the result is certain kinds of growth that fulfill human potential. Self-beliefs, skills, **virtue**, and growth may be orchestrated into a life of relatedness, competence, purpose, and **integrity**. The sole reason for writing *The Optimal Life Experience* was so that I could determine what kind of parent I was going to be—the kind who cultivates self-beliefs, nurtures skills, encourages virtue, and facilitates growth. Despite being a stand-alone book, *The Kind of Parent You Are* could not have been written without *The Optimal Life Experience*.

The Kind of Parent You Are frames parenting considerations within the wider context of the general human condition. The concepts that are presented apply universally, always linking parenting concerns back to beliefs, skills, behaviors, and growth. This makes *The Kind of Parent You Are* unique among parenting books. Parenting books typically provide specific guidance, but tend to lack a broad foundation upon which that guidance may rest. They are often built upon a foundation of the current state of affairs within a particular culture. The resulting guidance is therefore practical but narrow.

Books about humanity, well-being, and happiness typically present a broad foundation with which to buttress guidance, but tend to lack a specific domain into which that guidance may be channeled. These books often direct their guidance toward goals such as self-improvement, success, or simply living life. The guidance is broad but impractical.

Conversely, *The Kind of Parent You Are* was written to be at once practical and broadly applicable. This book contains guidance that you—whoever, wherever, and whenever you are—can use.

HOW TO NAVIGATE THE BOOK

Reflection exercises appear at the end of each chapter. These are intended to help you develop your own parenting philosophy. They are intended to be challenging. Deep thinking is required to come up with responses. You should find yourself challenging assumptions, wrestling with dilemmas, and confronting obstacles. A good barometer might be to consider whether you feel uncomfortable while probing your consciousness for responses. If not, perhaps you are not extracting as much value from these exercises as you could be.

Please resist the temptation to skip ahead to the next chapter, and instead devote sufficient time to the exercises. Doing the exercises might lead you to branch off into unprompted lines of introspection, which I would urge you to explore. Even in doing so, the time spent in between chapters will likely not be sufficient. The reflection exercises are intended to be iterative. These exercises may be done as you finish chapters, again after the book is completed, and yet again a year or so later.

In addition to the reflection exercises, there is an optional companion to this book—a journal—whose templates can be filled out daily to track your progress against objectives that you have set. The journal is organized according to months. The names of those months are to be entered by the journal user, so that you can begin at any time of the year.

A glossary is provided that defines frequently used terms. Glossary terms appear in **bold** the first time they appear in the main text.

Chapter summaries appear after every chapter. These are not designed to be synopses of full chapter content, but only reminders of the key points. It is best to read these in context, after finishing each chapter, or in order to review earlier chapters.

In the interests of gender equality, I have alternated the use of "she" and "he" in each chapter throughout the book.

ABOUT ME

This book and its precursor contain established concepts drawn from well-respected resources in the fields of parenting, psychology, philosophy, and economics. Yet I am not a parenting expert, nor am I a psychologist, nor a philosopher, nor an economist. I am a regular parent like you who wants what is best for my children.

That is why I overwhelmingly chose established concepts to write about instead of the latest studies. I base my books on expert knowledge vetted by the scientific process, not my individual experience. The advice herein is tried and true, not the personal opinion of a regular parent.

That is not to say that there is nothing new in this book. This book uses novel approaches to the subject of parenting. It includes approaches that I use for everything of importance, and have used throughout my twenty-year career in the chemical industry.

This book is original in that it is built upon a multidisciplinary foundation. As a business process manager, I learned to integrate practices from across the organization into new ways of doing business. This book, building from *The Optimal Life Experience*, integrates concepts from various disciplines into the subject of parenting.

This book takes a unique top-down approach. It presents parenting as something that flows from your carefully formulated long-term intentions. This may be surprising, but my time spent in various marketing roles crafting business strategies left me well prepared to create a parenting philosophy.

Focusing on the personal development of the parent offers a fresh perspective on the subject of parenting. Over the years, I have experimented with various ways to develop myself, usually through a journal. Whenever I learned something new, I wrote it down.

The approaches of using multidisciplinary ideas, formulating a strategy, pursuing personal development, and writing all converge in this book. There has never been a subject about which I am more passionate to apply my favored approaches than parenting.

As a ten-year-old, I wrote my first book: *Baseball's Homerun Sluggers and Fireball Throwers*. It took me all summer to complete. I used an old-fashioned typewriter—the kind where the keys needed to be pressed hard enough to stamp the ink onto the paper, and making a mistake meant starting the page over. My grandfather had it hardbound for me. I still remember the first time I held the finished work in my hand. Ever since then, part of me has been an author waiting to write *The Kind of Parent You Are*.

MY "WHY"

At its core, *The Kind of Parent You Are* is about helping people become the best they can be. It was written to help parents become their best people. It was written to help parents enable their children to become their best adults.

It can help people become their best by starting with "why?" Even though it offers a wealth of practical parenting advice adapted from well-respected resources, *The Kind of Parent You Are* is less a "how to" and more a "why to" do it. Parents who know their why, regardless of personal circumstances, will find their how.

This book may feature my personal why, but it is relevant to you because my why draws from human nature. The subject matter in this book is broad in scope. As long as you are human, you can apply what you read here to your own why. Perhaps seeing a why get fleshed out into a purpose, goals, and overarching philosophy will be instructive.

It may help you to mold your values and beliefs into your own parenting style. Because this book is also about you. It contains exercises in every chapter designed for self-examination. These exercises walk you through the process so that, one step at a time, you decide what kind of parent you want to be.

This is the book that I wish my children to have when it is their turn to become parents. We hear a lot these days about children being filled with natural goodness that just needs the right environment to unfold. I believe this to be true for all children, and that it will still hold true when those children become parents. This book was therefore not written to berate, blame, or shame parents for their shortcomings. It was written to help parents bring out what is already good in them. Everything written here is treated with the same care, diligence, and heart that I reserve for communications with my own children.

They are not yet ready for this book, so I want to share it with you in the meantime. I hope that you enjoy the content. I hope that you find it enriching. I hope that you and your children all have wonderful lives.

Starting with You

Until I became a parent, my actions had primarily influenced my own condition. When my first child was born, I suddenly became aware that I was to have a profound impact on the lives of other people. Not just any other people, but those for whom I felt indescribable love, and incredible responsibility. It was a sobering realization. The kind of person I was suddenly became important.

Becoming a parent is one of life's most momentous events, but I didn't know that being an effective parent would be so trying. Mind, body, and relationships are all tested. New roles and responsibilities are welcomed into life as others are ushered out. Having so many aspects of life in flux simultaneously is an invitation for feelings of panic for even the most ordered among us.

That an infant might inspire strong feelings may not be very surprising. It is something that people often talk about. Intense feelings of love and joy are so commonly described as to be clichéd, and so are expected by new parents. But the intense feelings of rage and helplessness do not get as much press. These feelings are just as common as joy or love, yet may be wholly unexpected by a new parent. Equally jarring is that contrary emotions seem to spawn in each other's midst. Feelings of joy, frustration, eagerness, apprehension, confidence, and inadequacy live side by side.

Unprepared for such complex emotional terrain, many new families find themselves in crisis. Many parents, their crises having compromised their abilities to care for their families or themselves, wisely turn to medical professionals for help. Others have experiences that are not as debilitating, yet still serious enough to be disruptive to their lives.

For any new family, it is easy to wonder, "*Why am I having such a hard time adjusting? Billions of people have done this successfully; what is wrong with me?*" The answer is that billions of people have had a hard time adjusting as well. It just isn't talked about very much. Having a hard time doesn't mean there is anything wrong with you. It means that you are normal.

You likely have friends and neighbors who are also having a hard time. They may be smiling when you see them at school, on the sidewalk, or in the playground. They may seem to always be able to make time for one another. Their children may be well-dressed and well-behaved.

However, they are probably not telling you about their struggles. They are not telling you about the frustration they feel that their children, for whom they give all they can, ask ever for more, refuse to listen, and seem to systematically upset their plans. They are not talking about their shifting career paths, their shrinking social lives, or their strained marriages. There seems to be a stigma associated with talking about these struggles. It is as if everyone has chosen to meet these challenges alone. Rather than calling upon confidants to ease the stress, many of us allow the tension to go untended until it builds into an eruption, or sets off an emotional breakdown.

It may be comforting, even empowering, to know that these struggles are common. They may not be openly discussed, but they are normal. It's so important to recognize that becoming a parent is an upheaval of everything life has been up until that point. Feeling overwhelmed is natural.

And it can be a good thing.

Parenting requires the best of you. If you are like me, however, then the *you* you have is not always the *you* you need. I came to realize that the challenges of parenting were bigger than I was, and

I needed to grow to meet them. I needed to make myself into some-one better. And there is still work to be done. Despite the progress I've made so far, I still find myself reprimanding when I should be coaching, keeping busy with grown-up things when I should be playing, and nursing a scowl when I should be making amends.

Becoming a parent, for me, was and is a transformative process. As it turns out, that is also normal.

When starting a family, the realization that your impact extends beyond your own life begins to sink in. The gravity of having so much influence over the life of another begins to weigh down hard. The pressure can threaten to break you. But it is possible to use this pressure to *make* you, to use it as a prompt to start asking the big questions:

- What values and beliefs do I want to survive me?
- What does life mean?
- Who am I?

These questions, no longer mere abstractions as perhaps they were before you had children, no longer a punch line as perhaps they were in your youth, must actually be confronted. The kind of parent you decide to be depends upon the answers.

It's not possible to just stumble upon these answers—they require time, effort, and intention. They require hard work. And when answers come, they must then be backed up with corresponding behaviors. That is harder work. It amounts to nothing less than a change in your identity.

Expectant parents are bombarded with resources and advice. Pamphlets, advertisements, articles, headlines, how-to videos, and books envelop the parents-to-be, giving advice on everything from diapers and safety harnesses, to allergies, milestones, and teething. As new parents become seasoned parents, the information tsunami doesn't stop but only changes. The subject matter addresses new problems, specific for toddlers, then preschoolers, next youths, and finally tweens and teens. Yet there is no mention of questioning your beliefs, searching for meaning, or transforming your identity.

TRANSFORMING YOUR IDENTITY

Transforming one's identity is not something done casually. An impetus is needed.

A new baby is a surprisingly powerful impetus. It seems a miracle that a fragile infant can motivate you to question everything, to sacrifice so much, to upend your life, to make yourself into someone better—into someone who knows what type of life to strive for, someone who can act according to deeply held beliefs, someone who can summon patience in the face of rage, and someone who can find a way when feeling helpless.

Becoming that kind of person is a major undertaking. It is something you do for your child. You transform your entire self so your child can be prepared to someday make a good life. You ask for nothing in return. It is a pure gift.

That is why the challenge of having your life upended can be a good thing: it is a prompt for you to make the conscious decision to meet that challenge. So much good comes from doing so. And it gets even better.

Your new behaviors—a product of your heightened level of self-awareness, your fresh perspectives, and your thoughtfully crafted identity—are not confined to your parenting role. You can apply them to your career, or social, marital, and other spheres. You can extend them to all aspects of your life. They become part of you. In the end, you *are* your behaviors.

Knowing who you are and backing it up with behaviors allows you to approach things with purpose. It lets you put more into life. And it allows you to get more out of life—more enrichment, more satisfaction, and more fulfillment.

The sacrifices you make on your child's behalf are ultimately reflected back to you. This new you, that you thought you created as an unconditional gift *for* your child, turns out to be a gift *from* your child.

It is worthy of marvel that a helpless infant is powerful enough to ask so much from you and get it. It is even more marvelous that he is able to give so much. I believe this is the true meaning of the miracle of childbirth.

Fulfilling the role of parent may be as momentous for the parent's trajectory through life as it is for the child's. Nascent parenthood is typically a time for an upheaval of self-concept, a reappraisal of values, a search for meaning, and an ultimate change in identity. *The Kind of Parent You Are* nourishes the naturally introspective states of mind of new and expectant parents. It aims to provide you with the background, vocabulary, tools, and most importantly the inspiration for a positive self-transformation at the time when you are most receptive to it.[1]

This book will feature advice relevant to the execution of my parenting goals, within the context of my parenting philosophy. Nevertheless, each chapter will also include background information that is universally applicable. The reflection exercises at the conclusion of each chapter will help you integrate the background information into your own philosophy.

ADOPTING THE MINDSET

A parable tells of a traveler coming across three stonecutters. He asks the first stonecutter, who is spiritlessly tending to the stones, about his work. The first stonecutter replies, "I am cutting and stacking these stones until sundown, and then I get to leave and do whatever I wish." The second stonecutter is mechanically breaking and stacking the stones, one after the other. The traveler approaches him and asks him what he is doing. The second stonecutter replies, "I am putting up a wall. That's what they pay me for." The third stonecutter is purposefully chipping away at stones, blowing away the dust, and meticulously lining them up to be flush. When the traveler asks him what he is doing, the third stonecutter says, "I am building a cathedral. It will stand here for generations to come and bring people together."

This book was written especially for expectant parents. The concepts nevertheless would also apply to aspiring parents, new parents, and veteran parents. I will offer a few guidelines to help prospective readers at any stage in their parenting journey to decide whether to take this book home.

This book is for readers who are willing to dedicate their time and energy to developing their parenting style. It is not for readers looking for a few tips, tricks, and hacks.

This book is for readers who are aiming to establish new ways to approach their lives. It is not for readers searching only for solutions to this week's family dilemma.

This book is for readers who are open to making changes. It is not for readers who are inflexible with regard to their entrenched practices.

This book is for readers who have the vision for the future, the commitment to work toward it, and the ability to adapt along the way. Parenting is hard work, done stone by stone. This book is for those who are building a cathedral.

PART I

Orienting Yourself

CHAPTER 1

Defining Your Parenting Purpose and Vision

P arenting without a purpose and vision is like hiking without a compass. You never know where you might end up. In this chapter you will have the opportunity to craft both of these key elements of your parenting philosophy. I will also outline my own parenting purpose and vision, so you can use it as a basis for drawing out your own.

THE ELEMENTS OF A PARENTING PHILOSOPHY

PURPOSE

A purpose is a reason for doing something. A thoughtfully constructed purpose helps to keep you focused on your priorities. It provides a basis for action when the right decision is not immediately evident.

Life is messy, noisy, and dynamic. Adopting a **parenting purpose** brings order to the chaos and serves as a basis for action when those things that are truly important are hindered by this chaos.

My parenting purpose is to raise adults, not kids. In other words, I believe my role as a parent is to ensure my children are prepared to create positive life experiences for themselves as adults. This purpose helps me to stay focused on the priorities of the long term while answering the many demands of life— the schedules, the mistakes, the disagreements—which always present themselves in the short term.

Your parenting purpose may be different. In this chapter we will explore what makes a parenting purpose, and then work through some reflection exercises to help you define your own purpose. Your purpose will be based upon your unique set of beliefs and values. Your beliefs and values are core parts of your identity.

BELIEFS AND VALUES

Your beliefs are things that you hold to be true, even without having proof. Your values are the principles you ascribe to for differentiating right from wrong. Your parenting purpose may be different from mine because your beliefs and values may be different from mine.

My guiding belief is that everyone has the potential to have a meaningful and enriching life. I believe that a meaningful and enriching life is not a means to any further end, but worthy for its own sake. I sign up to the principle that everyone has the right to freely pursue their own unique version of that life. I also believe that people are fundamentally good, and as such, have a fundamental desire to be good. I believe that we should strive to maximize that fulfillment by being the *most* good that we can be. I further believe that fulfilling that desire is the basis of a meaningful and enriching life. I live by the principle that any such fulfillment can only be meaningful through its impact on other people. I believe that fulfillment is never complete, but is continual and therefore the work of a lifetime.

My parenting purpose is consistent with my values and beliefs. I want to ensure my children are prepared to create positive life experiences for themselves, which I believe to be the work of a lifetime. So when I make parenting decisions, I base those decisions on the implications for their adult lives, in accordance with my purpose.

Having a purpose is necessary for any endeavor, but it is not sufficient. You also need to define an aspirational destination, known as a vision, so that your purpose has direction. Your vision, purpose, and beliefs and values should all be made to align.

VISION

My vision as a parent is of my grown children being fully equipped to make their optimal life experience, doing so with vigor and simultaneously benefitting society.

There are a few key phrases in this vision worth exploring. The first is "grown children." The vision needs to complement the purpose, and specifying grown children accomplishes that. The next phrase is "make their optimal life experience." An optimal life experience cannot be given to someone. It is something a person must make. And because of the intensely personal nature of a life experience, it is something a person can only make for herself. Because a vision is an aspirational notion, anything less than the optimal life experience and the most fulfilling life possible would be dull and listless. I hope for my children to experience all of life, and to do so "with vigor." I would like for them to have the opportunity to not simply live life, but to make themselves as wholly alive, as exhilaratingly human, as possible. And they should do so not by taking but by giving, by "simultaneously benefitting society," so that they may make lives of meaning for themselves.

Developing your own vision will take some introspection. Your vision will be the ideal result of faithful adherence to your purpose. It encapsulates what you want your whole parenting experience to mean. It can help to consider how you might feel in various future states, both good and not so good, when your children are grown. Which potential futures will make you feel joyful? Which ones will make you feel regretful?

Your vision is the future state that will make your older self the most content.

Once the elements of beliefs and values, purpose, and vision have been aligned, they need to be made executable. Practical steps known as goals are needed to map the path to the vision. Goals are the concrete actions that we take to achieve our vision, defined in line with our purpose, and in accordance with our beliefs and values. Alignment of all these elements will be discussed and illustrated in Figures 1 and 2 (see pages 13 and 14).

GOALS

To make my plan executable with meaningful **parenting goals**, three things are needed:

1) An understanding of the optimal life experience. This will give the vision clarity, and provide context for the goals. Understanding the optimal life experience entails defining it with respect to the individual experience, while also considering societal impact. Those items were addressed in my first book, *The Optimal Life Experience*, and are summarized on pages 15–21.

2) A determination of how to attain the optimal life experience. The path to that attainment will be explored on pages 21–24.

3) An understanding of the parents' role in one's adoption of that path. The bulk of Chapter Two will be dedicated to deducing this, and you will also be given background to define your own goals in that chapter.

At that point, my beliefs and values, purpose, goals, and vision will be unified and articulated in a succinct, executable **parenting philosophy**. My philosophy, by using basic concepts expressed in terms of the general human condition, has been designed to produce insights that you can use to inform your own parenting philosophy. The reflection exercises in the following chapter (pages 74–76) contain prompts to help you define your parenting goals, and incorporate them into a workable parenting philosophy. The reflection exercises at the end of this chapter (pages 26–32) provide the basis for that work, focusing on your beliefs, values, purpose, and vision.

THE COMPASS

The various elements of a parenting philosophy may be thought of as a who, a why, a how, and a what:

- Your beliefs and values are core parts of your identity. They make up the *who*.
- Your purpose, the reason for doing something, is the *why*.
- Goals, the actions taken to achieve something, are the *how*.
- Your vision is the outcome; it is the *what*.

The confluence of all these elements is represented in the compass in Figure 1 below.

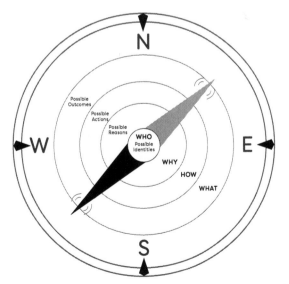

FIGURE 1. Disparate Elements of a Parenting Philosophy

Life is often messy, noisy, and dynamic. When someone doesn't understand herself, and adjusts her parenting reasons and actions to suit the randomness of life events, the outcomes she and her child experience will be subject to chance. To parent according to random circumstances is like navigating with a broken compass, the needle constantly wobbling and swinging erratically.

By contrast, parenting with a coherent philosophy is like having a True North to follow, regardless of circumstances. To parent according to one's identity, adhering to a steady purpose, in alignment with a defined set of goals, toward a predetermined destination, is to parent with integrity. Having integrity means doing something according to your self-directed patterns of behavior.

At first glance, having integrity appears restrictive in that many possibilities are precluded. But it is truly liberating, as it allows you to approach parenting responsibilities from your own core being—see Figure 2 below.

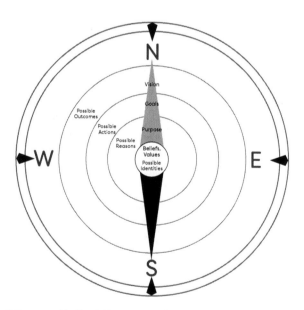

FIGURE 2. Unified Elements of a Parenting Philosophy

By parenting with integrity, you are communicating to your children what your most important beliefs and values are. You are parenting consistently, so your children will know what to expect. You are providing a stable environment for your children to grow up in. You are giving your children their best chance to become adults who live their own lives with integrity.

Living with integrity is one of the things I hope my adult children will be able to do. Living with integrity follows the same principles as parenting with integrity. It entails staying true to a course that you have mapped out for yourself. A person with integrity does not find herself at the mercy of capricious winds. She is a causal agent in her own life. She remains on course using behaviors that are integrated into her psyche (hence the term *integrity*) such that her behaviors are one with her core identity. Such integrity is required for an optimal life experience.

THE OPTIMAL LIFE EXPERIENCE

The nature of the optimal life experience was the subject of my previous book. I had to write that book to give my parenting vision meaning. I had to understand what kind of lives I hope my children will make for themselves, so that I could figure out how to parent in a way that facilitated that outcome. One of the things I learned is that the optimal life experience is available to everyone. The key takeaways from that book are summarized below, so that you, too, can envision what is possible for your own children.

RELATEDNESS AND COMPETENCE

The optimal life experience is dependent upon fulfillment of two needs: the need for **relatedness** and the need for **competence**. As recognized by self-determination theory, relatedness and competence are basic and universal human needs.[2] **Autonomy**, the third need recognized by self-determination theory, is also salient and will be discussed in Chapter Two.

Relatedness is characterized by enriching relationships with others. Those relationships are formed through repeated meaningful interactions. Relatedness is an interpersonal construct; it exists *between people*.

Competence is characterized by the full-force usage of one's capacities. Those capacities are formed by continually taking on challenges and developing skills. Competence is an intrapersonal construct; it exists *within a person*.

Relatedness provides life's most treasured interpersonal contentments. When you experience relatedness you:

- sit in the warm glow of shared laughter;
- transmit and receive unspoken messages through knowing gazes;
- interlace dialogue, expressions, and gestures in give-and-take conversations that are emotionally energizing;
- are simply there for someone as needed to assuage frailties, to dispel insecurities, and to support through misfortune, and have the same care and relief extended back to you as needed;
- enjoy peace of mind from belonging to a close circle of others who welcome each other's presence, respect each other's perspectives, and love each other despite foibles.

To experience relatedness is to feel as if you truly matter.

Competence provides life's most treasured intrapersonal contentments. When you experience competence you:

- are invigorated by ventures into challenging territories;
- feel validated by notable improvements compared with previous capabilities;
- walk landscapes, familiar and unexplored alike, with a confidence that is palpable;
- immerse yourself in cherished activities with a wholesale commitment that is enviable;

- engage your passions with a proficiency that arises as if from the depths of your very soul;
- are gratified cerebrally from sculpting your capacities according to a personally crafted theme.

To experience competence is to feel as if you truly make an impact.

Fulfilling each of these two needs results in extraordinarily gratifying states of being. Fulfilling them both marks the pinnacle of the human experience. But one who reaches the pinnacle cannot simply rest there: relatedness and competence are never realized with finality.

RANDOMNESS

Random events will always transpire that endanger the relatedness and competence you have already achieved. Circumstances change. Relationships begin and end. Alliances evolve, and associations wax and wane. Urges compel, constraints hinder, obligations materialize, and problems emerge.

In order to create the optimal life experience you need to deal with random events in two ways. First, you must treat life as a work in progress. Believing yourself to matter, you construe random events not as assaults upon your social standing, but as opportunities to foster relationships. Believing yourself to be able to make an impact, you construe random events not as conspiring to frustrate your agenda, but as opportunities to grow capacities. You can achieve and maintain the optimal life experience by adapting to changes, meeting adversity, learning from failure, and turning conflict into understanding.

The second way you can deal with random events is through integrity. At every turn, we are called upon to negotiate any number of irreconcilable demands. A well-timed opportunity for profit appears, but violates your core principles. A newly instituted rule is unjust, but the penalty for noncompliance presents an unacceptable risk. A newcomer makes flattering advances that threaten a prized companionship. Unless offset from within, these demands would rend us apart. You must have internal fortitude to weather the forces of chaos and remain whole. You must have integrity.

One who creates the optimal life experience is not at the service of every random stimuli. Her innermost qualities of beliefs, values, potentialities, **preferences**, and strengths—her identity—are what drives her. Her reasons, her actions, her aspired outcomes, though they surely serve something larger than herself, all stem from her truest self. Like a parent adhering to a thoughtfully constructed philosophy, she reacts to random events with internal consistency.

RESONANCE

For one creating the optimal life experience, internal consistency is even exercised across interpersonal and intrapersonal endeavors. Her relatedness pursuits may look different from her competence pursuits, but they are an integrated whole. This is because the critical personal qualities from which she draws, that which relates and that which develops capabilities, are one and the same.

She unifies her pursuits by orienting the best of herself toward others. By cultivating the best of herself, and doing so in service of others, she maximizes her competence. By directing that best self toward matters of togetherness and intimacy, and applying all her capacities to do so effectively, she maximizes her relatedness. She seamlessly aligns her relatedness needs with her competence needs.

When the disorder of the outside world destabilizes either her relatedness or competence fulfillment, she coordinates a holistic realignment from within. She keeps relatedness and competence in rhythm. She makes relatedness and competence resonate.

This state of **resonance** is the optimal life experience:

> The optimal life experience, or resonance, is the state of continually becoming one's best self, for purposes

> beyond oneself, while fostering closeness with other
> people who are enriched by that best self.

The optimal life experience is not a destination, but a state of becoming. It is about continual growth and continual adaptation to change. It is about personal development and relationship development. It is about complementary unification of self and others' concerns. It is about keeping them in balance despite living in a world that is messy, noisy, and dynamic. It is about positioning the best of oneself for the benefit of others. A person living the optimal life experience paradoxically masters herself in order to transcend herself, and transcends herself in order to master herself.

It can be quite alluring to imagine your children living such a life. It can also be quite daunting. As a helpful reminder, the description of the optimal life experience is intended to be a vision. It is meant to be a source of inspiration, not a cause of anxiety. It is not a measure to judge your parenting or an achievement to assess your children against.

In fact, it is not an "achievement" at all. One doesn't "reach" the optimal life experience, but instead grows toward it. That advanced stage of growth, which is available to everyone, is itself the optimal life experience. It is something undertaken for its own sake; it is intrinsically rewarding. Perhaps the most amazing part of this is that one's rewards are shared with the rest of society.

SOCIETY

In isolation, the rewards of one's endeavors would theoretically reside exclusively within. But humans are social beings, and ours is an interconnected society.

Relatedness is a shared experience. One can only reap the rewards of relatedness by creating rewarding experiences for others. Relatedness rewards cannot be taken, only mutually created.

Likewise, the rewards of competence are meaningful only in the context of others. Competence pursuits are rewarding when they are mutually beneficial. A master violinist is enriched when her music brings joy to others, but in solitude would remain unfulfilled. A homeowner may derive fulfillment from carefully arranging dinner party preparations, but not if weather conditions prevent any guests from arriving. In a highly interconnected community of others, competence pursuits set in motion a cascade of interdependencies that propagates an individual's enrichment to others while simultaneously setting the stage for others to create further enrichment.

A self-directing person acting in her own best interests—perhaps a grown child of one of this book's readers—generates her own well-being. What is remarkable is that by doing so, that well-being is transmitted across her network of social contacts and beyond, where it multiplies as it propagates. Whether by affecting the behavior of others, uplifting the attitudes of others, promoting tendencies to share good fortune, or creating the circumstances for others' fulfillment, well-being is magnified as if by magic. In the hypothetical case of the grown child, all of this will have been enabled by effective parenting. With this perspective, the leverage inherent in those small interactions of daily life—during morning routines, around the dinner table, and throughout a car ride—is nothing short of breathtaking.

One who genuinely enriches her life cannot do so without simultaneously enriching society. One who creates the optimal life experience for herself, in effect, builds the scaffolding upon which others may elevate themselves. Stated differently, in order to better society, you need only start by bettering yourself.

In the next section, the path one takes to do this will be revealed. The thought may have occurred to you that since the optimal life experience is available to everyone, it is available to you too. You may be tempted to apply your efforts to taking the path yourself.

However, positioning the optimal life experience as a personal objective can run counter to the transcendence requirement of the optimal life experience. It can entice you to excessively pursue self-focused types of enrichment, which will be suboptimally fulfilling. The moment you set out to "get" the optimal life experience, you may have already lost it. This is precisely why, in *The Optimal Life Experience*, I advise readers to apply the concepts not to themselves, but to their most precious others.

By concentrating on someone else's optimal growth, something we will focus on in Part III, you free yourself from the self-focus that can otherwise undermine your own optimal growth. Additionally, the challenges involved in earnestly facilitating others' growth can incentivize you to better yourself—which is something we will cover in Part II.

In other words, earnestly tending to the growth of others is how you can transcend yourself in order to master yourself and vice versa. By focusing your attention on someone else's optimal fulfillment, you just might find yourself becoming optimally fulfilled. That way, you get to enjoy it twice.

THE WELL-BEING CYCLE

THE PATH

The personalized nature of the optimal life experience means that it depends on a high degree of self-awareness. This generally requires a great deal of life experience. Children are therefore not yet equipped for such a rich state of being. They can, however, learn the patterns that build up to it.

Those patterns are learned not in grand endeavors but in banal occurrences: a bruised ego from a social gaffe in the playground, a new friendship kindled on the school bus, a botched puzzle, a triumphant completion of a maze. These are the humble precursors to the pinnacle of the human experience.

The path to the optimal life experience is a cyclical series of four steps. Those four steps are depicted in the well-being cycle (see Figure 3 below). Those steps are repeated over and over for a life of resonance. A parent intent on leading a child to a life of resonance therefore needs only to understand a small number of steps on a simple path.

FIGURE 3. The Well-being Cycle

Starting at the top of the well-being cycle, the first term is **matter** and **impact**. A person who construes events as opportunities for relationships believes herself to matter. A person who construes events as within her capacity to cope believes herself to be able to make an impact. A person who believes herself to matter and to be able to make an impact displays **emotional intelligence** in order to fulfill those beliefs.

Emotional intelligence is the second term of the cycle. Emotional intelligence includes abilities and traits such as impulse control, delayed gratification, empathy, and self-recognition. When those abilities and traits are used in the right amounts, at the right times, with the right people, and for the right reasons, they result in **virtuous behaviors**.

Virtuous behavior is the third term of the cycle. Virtuous behaviors are what we use to manage lower personal desires, such as those for hunger, comfort, or security, in service of the higher needs of relatedness and competence. Vicious behaviors, such as selfishness, laziness, or manipulativeness, however prevalent they may be, simply do not promote relatedness and competence. Behaviors that are generally recognized as virtuous, such as compassion, determination, and honesty, are required. On the basis of a single event, virtuous behaviors build or strengthen relationships and capabilities.

Relationships and capabilities are the fourth terms of the cycle. Those relationships and capabilities reinforce the beliefs that you matter and can make an impact. Thus, the path to well-being is a virtuous cycle.

THE BUILDUP

A person may traverse the well-being cycle through one rotation for any one event, for a single outcome. By repeating the cycle many times, the outcomes become additive. Through many rotations, a person does not simply display emotional intelligence, she *has* emotional intelligence. By using that emotional intelligence over many more rotations to perform virtuous behaviors, a person becomes attached to those behaviors and they become the person's character. The germinating relationships and capabilities that result from virtuous behaviors, over countless cycles, grow into relatedness and competence. The beliefs that one matters and can make an impact within the context of a single event, over the course of many events, evolve into beliefs on a broader scale; they evolve into a high level of **self-esteem**. The entirety of human development, which we parents have the privilege of witnessing and influencing for our children from infancy to adulthood, is a process of cycling through these four simple steps.

Well-being is the cycle's momentum. Each revolution both contributes to a person's well-being and reinforces the well-being already accrued. Years of virtuous cycle growth result in a healthy, self-sustaining level of well-being.

Each trip around the cycle, no matter how insignificant it may seem, will contribute to your well-being. Each success and failure, as long as it results in a realistic assessment that feeds into the next attempt, is progress. It is progress because it is experience. As we will see, a parent can support a child's effective acquisition of experience. When accumulated in a sufficient amount, that experience is the material through which you can thread together a story that explains your life, and weave a picture of what your life means.

Through experience, preferences are discovered, strengths are built, beliefs are formed, and values are established. We will explore how parents can help here, too. Revolution after revolution around the cycle, your identity gradually emerges. You learn what you truly care about, reflect upon your mistakes, and can articulate what you would regret not doing in your life. It is all part of the process through which you can compose a life purpose that is beyond yourself, a purpose that can keep your endeavors in alignment, a purpose that can guide you to maximized well-being.

There is no magic, no shortcuts, and no quick fixes. Small advances, made consistently and often, result in big things. Well-being is the cumulative result of a history of deliberate, hard-won, productive exertions.

When we traverse the well-being cycle, through interconnectedness we make it easier for others to do the same. To the extent that people, or even just one person, become better at finding contentment and exploiting the full power of their talents, the whole of humanity is improved. No one is better positioned than a parent to help that person find contentment and exploit talents. And there is no better time to start than at the beginning of a new life.

KEY POINTS

- Parenting with integrity requires a purpose, goals, and vision that are all aligned with beliefs and values. The coherent formulation of all these elements is referred to as a parenting "philosophy."
- My purpose as a parent is to raise adults, not kids—to prepare children to live the most fulfilling adult lives possible. The corresponding vision is of my grown children being fully equipped to make their optimal life experience, doing so with vigor and simultaneously benefitting society.
- The optimal life experience is characterized by a life of relatedness—an interpersonal construct—and of competence—an intrapersonal construct. The interpersonal and intrapersonal components are made to resonate, such that one continually cultivates the best of oneself, and fosters closeness with others who are enriched by that best self.
- The optimal life experience is not met with finality, but is instead a work in progress. Random events will always prompt more relationship building, more capability development, and a rebalancing of both.
- The optimal life experience is attained by traversing a virtuous circle of beliefs of matter and impact, which leads to displays of emotional intelligence, which lead to virtuous behaviors, which lead to relatedness and competence, which in turn reinforce beliefs of matter and impact: the well-being cycle.

REFLECTION EXERCISES

The following questions are about your beliefs, values, parenting purpose, and **parenting vision**. They are designed to help you explore your identity, pin down what you stand for, and decide what kind of imprint—one that is reflective of your core being—to leave upon the future.

Answering these questions should be uncomfortable. You should be challenging your assumptions, wrestling with dilemmas, and confronting obstacles. Writing down your responses should help you through the process.

What are your core beliefs?
A belief is something you hold as true even without proof. I have revealed that I believe people to be fundamentally good. I believe people to have great potential, the fulfillment of which is never-ending, and leads to a good life.

You may have developed different beliefs out of your own unique experiences and struggles. Someone who has lived in an unsafe environment or has been hurt by someone might believe people are inherently bad. Someone who has been helped by charity work might believe people are inherently good. Someone who has suffered under a climate of harsh laws might believe political factors to be the biggest determinant of well-being. Someone who has lived in a smog-filled city, and is intimately acquainted with the negative health or quality of life consequences, might believe humans are destroying the Earth and our future.

You may not even be fully conscious of your beliefs until you perform an honest examination of them. The prompts that follow may help you uncover your own beliefs. They are questions not about parenting, but about who you are:

- What is the pinnacle of the human experience?
- How important is the role of family?
- Are traditions important?
- What is your concept of religion? Is there an afterlife? What is it like?

- Are people fundamentally good or bad? Can people change?
- What role do others play in an individual's life: do they enhance or detract from overall happiness? How?
- Do all people deserve to be treated the same?
- What is the ideal relationship between humans and the environment?

The space below may be used to address any or all of these prompts. Alternatively, you may devise your own approach to defining your core beliefs.

What are your core values?

Values are the principles you ascribe to for differentiating between right and wrong. They make up your moral code. My values compel me to make choices that maximize human potential and goodness, such as allowing others the autonomy to make the choices they feel are best for their own enrichment. Your values should be compatible with your beliefs. Values that aim for full development of potential and full expression of goodness, for example, are consistent with the beliefs that people have great potential and are fundamentally good. The prompts that follow, which are basic ethics questions often associated with identifying one's moral code, may help you uncover your own values:

- What are your responsibilities toward others?
- Under which circumstances is it okay to interfere with another's endeavors?
- Should you strive to have a positive impact on the lives of others? Is it sufficient to simply do no harm? Is it okay to harm others in order to help yourself?
- What types of factors change the way you view your responsibilities toward another? (For example, would a person's beliefs, preferences, personal history, recent behavior, affiliations, or place of residence impact your answers to the previous questions? Do animals deserve to be treated the same as people? Do insects?)

_____

_____

_____

_____

_____

_____

_____

What are some ways those core values could be demonstrated in daily life?
Your values may be reflected in the manners you display, the company you keep, the consideration you offer others, the forgiveness you grant, the frugality or wastefulness you exhibit, the items you use, the services you enjoy, and the activities in which you partake.

_____

_____

_____

Write down some ways you could strengthen your adherence to those core values.
Specific examples include being kinder to strangers, using greater candor when dealing with clients, purchasing sustainable products, or volunteering at a local charity.

_____

_____

_____

What is your parenting purpose?
A purpose is the reason for doing something. It is an extension of your beliefs and values. My parenting purpose, for example, is to ensure my children are prepared to create positive life experiences for themselves as adults. The notion of raising adults is a direct product of the beliefs and values that people have great potential, that they should be enabled to reach that potential, and that reaching that potential is the work of a lifetime.

Your purpose may be different. If you believe in an afterlife, for example, you might wrestle with the idea of "raising adults," as I admit that I sometimes do. You might ultimately decide it is shortsighted, and your purpose might instead center on something eternal like the soul or karma. If your child has severe health issues, raising an independent adult might not be an option. In that case, your beliefs on the pinnacle of the human experience might factor heavily into what your purpose is. Your purpose might be to make your child feel loved. If you believe people are fundamentally bad, you might have a purpose geared toward protection. If you believe the political climate to dictate your happiness, your purpose might be to provide your child an environment that offers more opportunities than you had. If you believe the Earth is dying, your purpose might be to make the world a more hospitable place for your child.

A parenting purpose reflects what you will like to have accomplished after having fulfilled your chief parenting obligations. It may be helpful (if not uncomfortably morbid) to consider what kind of upbringing you would hope your child to have if something were to happen to you. Would you be able to provide helpful direction to your surrogate in ten words or less?

_____

_____

_____

What is your parenting vision?

A vision is an aspirational destination. It is the anticipated result of adhering to the purpose. It gives direction to a purpose, and offers a target for the goals. My vision of the optimal life experience is a sensible aspiration to pair with the purpose of raising adults to have positive life experiences. In the next chapter, goals will be presented that enable an optimal life experience. If your purpose is religious in nature, then your vision might be of heaven or the next reincarnation. Your goals might reflect values largely borrowed from religious texts, like forgiveness or compassion. If your purpose is to make your child feel loved, then your vision might involve a sense of belongingness, with goals centered on the types of care and attention you know your child needs. If your purpose is to protect, then your vision might be of a safe and secure adult. You may formulate goals designed to inoculate your child against manipulations or assaults. If your purpose is to provide your child with more opportunities than you had, then your vision might describe the kind of society that facilitates that. Your goals might be to prepare for a relocation and integration into such a society. If your purpose is to make the world a more hospitable place, you may have a vision of a sustainable planet, with goals involving a carbon footprint or some similar notion.

_____

_____

_____

What is your fundamental reason for parenting according to your stated purpose?

_____

_____

_____

What is your fundamental reason for parenting toward your stated vision?

_____

_____

_____

Does answering the two previous questions allow you to restate your purpose or vision with greater clarity or depth? Asking enough "whys" with respect to your purpose and vision should ultimately lead you back to your beliefs. For example, I want to raise adults because I want to prepare my children to create their fullest lives, which I believe to be the work of a lifetime.

_____

_____

_____

Are your parenting purpose and vision consistent with your core beliefs and values? How? If not, you can either revise your purpose or reconsider your beliefs.

_____

_____

_____

CHAPTER 2

Creating Your Parenting Goals

n Chapter One, I challenged you to pull together your parenting purpose and vision. You now need an accompanying action plan. The objective of this chapter is to define clear parenting goals in order for you to move forward with a coherent parenting philosophy.

Throughout the chapter I will punctuate parenting research with my own personal experience and goals. It is my hope that you will be able to extract something from my story, regardless of your own purpose and vision. The reflection exercises at the chapter's conclusion will further help you do so.

By the end of the chapter, your purpose, vision, and goals should gel into a coherent parenting philosophy. The remainder of the book will then be dedicated to the practical application of the goals and how they can help you achieve your parenting purpose.

PARENTING STYLES

Unfortunately, an adult's attainment of the optimal life experience currently has no scientifically validated correlations to the parenting style with which he was raised.[i] Fortunately, we have a progression to the optimal life experience—the well-being cycle—whose terms *can* be linked to parenting styles. The well-being cycle offers insight into the general human condition, as explored in depth in my previous book, *The Optimal Life Experience*, and summarized in Chapter One. We are using it here for assessing parenting guidance. The parenting guidance we ultimately extract will therefore be undergirded by a broad humanistic foundation.

There are many models of parenting styles. We will examine three of them, and ultimately synthesize an integrated model that adopts the best features of each. We will start with the most well-known: the Baumrind model.

BAUMRIND PARENTING STYLES

Supported by a vast database of studies, this model has produced insights that can be linked to every term on the well-being cycle. Diana Baumrind, a developmental psychologist, initially characterized three dominant parenting styles and recorded their outcomes.[3] Baumrind's three parenting styles are: authoritarian, permissive, and authoritative. Social development researchers Maccoby and Martin updated the Baumrind model to include an additional style called neglecting.[4]

Maccoby and Martin also updated the model by defining two dimensions: **demandingness** and **responsiveness**. Demandingness refers to parental control, supervision, and maturity demands. Responsiveness refers to parental warmth, acceptance, and involvement.

The authoritarian parenting style is high in demandingness but low in responsiveness. Authoritarian parents expect rules to be

---

[i]   A notable study, cited below, is consistent with the eventual conclusions offered in this chapter, but the research landscape is otherwise sparse: Dominguez, M. Melinda, and John S. Carton. "The relationship between self-actualization and parenting style." Journal of social behavior and personality 12, no. 4 (1997): 1093–1100.

obeyed without question, and often under threat of punishment. The needs of the child are not considered in authoritarian homes.

The permissive parenting style is low in demandingness but high in responsiveness. Rules are generally not enforced in permissive homes. Permissive parents indulge the whims of the child.

The neglecting parenting style is low in both demandingness and responsiveness. Rules are not enforced, and the child's needs are not considered.

The authoritative parenting style is high in both demandingness and responsiveness. Rules must be followed in authoritative homes, but the reasons for rules are explained and the specific needs of each child are considered. Children are encouraged by authoritative parents to learn and think for themselves and to develop a sense of autonomy. As will be illustrated, the authoritative parenting style produces the best outcomes among the four.

As an example, let's say a child has strewn toys about the living room and now it is time to clean the room. The authoritarian parent may lay down the law and command the child to do it under threat of punishment. The permissive parent would probably assume the role of toy cleaner, while the neglectful parent, if present at all, would just ignore the mess, as well as the child.

The authoritative parent would instruct the child to clean the room and give the reasons why. Perhaps the family is expecting guests later, or the toys are a trip hazard to someone, or they risk being broken by the vacuum cleaner that is about to pass through. If the child protests, the parent might respond by asking the most important question in family dynamics: Why? The parent may learn that the child doesn't know where to start and needs some instruction which can then be provided. Or the child may complain that cleaning is not fun. In that case the parent may decide to get creative and come up with a cleaning game, or may just decide to impose fair consequences by limiting future toy use until good cleanup habits are established. Or the child may explain that some of the toys are involved in play still in progress, and then the parent can decide whether it is acceptable to have everything cleaned up except for the building blocks, at least until the castle is finished.

For a parent wishing for a clean home relatively free of conflict, the authoritative approach is certainly the more difficult route; it would be quicker for parents to adopt the authoritarian or permissive parenting styles. And for parents willing to sacrifice a clean home, the neglectful approach may be adopted as the easier option. However, the most expedient ways to get what you want in the short term often do not produce the best long-term outcomes.

These four parenting styles have been linked with countless child and adolescent outcomes over the years. For the purposes of this book, the only outcomes we will explore are those that can be mapped to the terms of the well-being cycle: self-esteem (matter and impact), emotional health (emotional intelligence), good behavior (virtuous behavior), social skills (relationships), and school grades (capabilities). A summary of the relative rankings for each of these five outcomes against all four parenting styles, and how they map to the terms in the well-being cycle, appears in Table 1.

There are, of course, a lot of complexities underneath the simple-looking entries in this table. Like any evolving area of study, there are research papers with conflicting conclusions and interpretations. For example, there are unknown effects of having two parents utilize different styles with their child. There are potential differences between the outcomes for boys and girls. There are questions about the effect of changing parenting styles during a child's development. There are disagreements about what constitutes optimal results in different cultures.

However, this level of detail is not within the scope of this book. Table 1 therefore presents a high-level view of the correlations because, in this case, simplified results are the right tools for the job.

Matter and impact
Self-esteem is the attitude toward whether one believes in his competence to have positive interactions with others, to form healthy relationships, to manage negative interactions, to develop the capabilities to meet challenges, and to deal with adversity.

PARENTING STYLE AND DESCRIPTION	Relative Child and Adolescent Outcomes				
	SELF-ESTEEM[5]	EMOTIONAL HEALTH[6] (FREEDOM FROM ANXIETY, TENSION, AND DEPRESSION)	GOOD BEHAVIOR[7] (FREEDOM FROM MISCONDUCT, DELINQUENCY, AND DRUG USE)	SOCIAL SKILLS[8]	SCHOOL GRADES[9]
Authoritarian: Rules must be obeyed without question and under threat of punishment. No consideration is given to the needs of the child.	−	+	+	−	+
Permissive: Rules are generally not enforced. The whims of the child are indulged.	+	+	−	+	−
Neglecting: Rules are not enforced and no consideration for the child's needs is given.	−	−	−	−	−
Authoritative: Rules must be followed, but the reasons for rules are explained and the individual needs of the child are considered. Children are given the opportunity to develop autonomy.	+	+	+	+	+
Maps to Well-being Cycle Term	Matter and Impact	Emotional Intelligence	Virtuous Behavior	Relationships	Capabilities

TABLE 1. Baumrind Parenting Styles Outcomes

Self-esteem encompasses the beliefs that one matters and can make an impact. The self-esteem outcomes in Table 1 therefore map to the matter and impact term of the well-being cycle.

Children raised by authoritative and permissive parents are likely to have higher self-esteem. Children raised by authoritarian and neglecting parents are likely to have lower self-esteem.

Emotional intelligence

Some presumptions are in order here because the current literature landscape lacks comprehensive studies linking emotional intelligence to Baumrind parenting styles. In the research cited, it wasn't emotional health that was actually measured but *lack of* emotional health. Specifically, signs of anxiety, tension, and depression were measured. These are exactly the type of outcomes that people with high levels of emotional intelligence are inoculated against. So we can presume that people with higher incidences of these conditions possess less emotional intelligence, and those with lower incidences possess more emotional intelligence. Using these presumptions as a guide, children raised by neglectful parents are less likely to have emotional intelligence than children raised by authoritarian, permissive, or authoritative parents.

Virtuous behavior

Good behavior is an indirect measure of virtuous behavior. An indirect measure is necessary because there are not yet reliable methods of measuring virtue, let alone studies linking any such measurements to parenting styles. In fact, it was bad behavior—such as cheating, tardiness, theft, weapons possession, drug use, and trouble with the law—that was actually measured. Presumably, those with higher rates of bad behavior did not achieve those scores by exhibiting virtue. Conversely, those with lower rates of bad behavior were presumably more likely to have cultivated and exhibited virtuous behavior. Using these presumptions as a guide, children raised by authoritarian or authoritative parents are more likely to exhibit virtuous behavior than children raised by permissive or neglectful parents.

Relationships

Social skills include measures of popularity, number of friends, and the ability to make friends. Having better social skills, children raised by permissive or authoritative parents are likely to be better equipped to build relationships throughout life than their peers raised by authoritarian or neglectful parents.

Capabilities

School grades were selected because the modern scholastic environment provides a wide range of opportunities for children to express capacities and experience continual growth. And school consumes more of many children's time and attention than any other single endeavor. It makes sense that those who excel in this environment are more likely to build capabilities throughout life. In fact, that is one of the things the education system is designed to do: expose children to the range of things most likely to serve as the foundation for how they will express capacities as adults. Be that as it may, academic success is still a relatively narrow measure when compared to other domains in which competence may be exercised. For this reason, I believe academic success to be a suboptimal measure to link to the capabilities element in the well-being cycle, but it is the best one available at this time. Using academic success as a guide, children raised by authoritarian or authoritative parents can be presumed to be more likely to build capabilities than children raised by permissive or neglectful parents.

Summary

Taking all five outcomes into view, the overall assessment of parenting styles favors a combination of high responsiveness and high demandingness (see Table 2 below). The neglecting parenting style, with low responsiveness and low demandingness, correlates with poorer outcomes across all the areas linked to the well-being cycle. The authoritarian and permissive parenting styles, each a mixed bag of responsiveness and demandingness, result in a mixed bag of outcomes. The authoritative parenting style, with high responsiveness and high demandingness, is the only one that correlates with the better outcomes in all five areas.

	Low Responsiveness	High Responsiveness
HIGH DEMANDINGNESS	Authoritarian	* Authoritative *
LOW DEMANDINGNESS	Neglecting	Permissive

TABLE 2. **Baumrind Parenting Styles Summary**

High responsiveness and high demandingness appear to be the key parental characteristics that enable a child to traverse the well-being cycle and create an optimal life experience. But there is a problem. While the authoritative category includes parenting practices that foster good outcomes, it also includes parenting practices that do not. In other words, the Baumrind model gives us an overall indication of where to find favorable parenting practices, but it is not precise enough. We need to carve out the "parenting sweet spot" from the authoritative quadrant. For that, we once again turn to self-determination theory.

SELF-DETERMINATION THEORY PARENTING STYLES

As noted by Bart Soenens and Maarten Vansteenkiste, two psychology researchers prominent in the field of self-determination theory, there are two types of parental control:[10]

1) *A harsh type of control.* Practitioners of this harsh control seek to modify not only the child's behavior, but also his thoughts and feelings. This type of control is exercised through various degrees of manipulation and coercion. Examples of harsh control include: belittling, humiliating, chastising, withholding attention, restricting freedoms, and inflicting physical punishment.

2) *A kinder, gentler type of control.* Practitioners of this type of control seek to modify the child's behavior while respecting his thoughts and feelings. This type of control is exercised by structuring the environment. Examples include: setting clear expectations and furnishing constructive guidance.

The research cited in the previous section does not distinguish between these two types of control. As a result, the authoritative quadrant of the Baumrind model includes parenting practices that utilize harsh control. Even spanking can be considered as authoritative parenting, provided it is used sparingly in an atmosphere of parental warmth.[11]

This is a problem because, although harsh control can conform to the definitions of high demandingness and high responsiveness, it is negatively correlated with all the terms on the well-being cycle. Harsh control has been linked to lower self-esteem,[12] lower emotional health,[13,14] more behavioral problems,[15,16] more social difficulties,[17,18] and poorer academic capabilities.[19]

To be clear, harsh controls are not standard practices of authoritative parents. Nonetheless, they exist within the definition of authoritative parenting when accompanied by parental warmth and involvement. Furthermore, Diana Baumrind has endorsed punishments, including spanking, as authoritative techniques that are effective when used prudently.[20] But what are they effective at accomplishing? According to Baumrind, harsh controls including spanking are effective at modifying behaviors in the short term. Yet, she concedes that spanking alone does not achieve long-term goals such as competence and character development.[21]

This is the value of having a parenting purpose and a vision. My purpose is geared toward the long term. My vision is of competent adults of character. Using these aspects of my parenting philosophy as guiding lights, I cannot adopt authoritative practices wholesale. I am only interested in those parenting practices that can be independently linked to a child's flourishing.

Such practices have been identified by researchers in the field of self-determination theory. They posit three parenting dimensions along which positive outcomes, and the children themselves, flourish. Those dimensions are aligned with the three basic needs of relatedness, competence, and autonomy. They are: involvement, **structure**, and autonomy support.[22]

Involvement

Involvement concerns being a vital and benevolent figure in a child's life. A parent exhibiting a high degree of involvement is present and engaged in a child's activities, commits means and effort to support the child, demonstrates warmth and caring in interactions with the child, and fosters a general atmosphere of love. This dimension is well-aligned with the responsiveness dimension of the Baumrind parenting styles. It is also consistent with existing conceptions of parental warmth, and thus has a rich history in research literature.

It is already established that parental involvement is correlated with relatedness and social skills.[23,24] A high degree of parental involvement has also been correlated with a child's greater belief in his own competence,[25] better emotional control,[26] fewer behavioral issues,[27] and a higher level of competence demonstrated in school.[28] Thus, involvement is positively connected with every point on the well-being cycle.

Structure

The dimension of structure is a relatively newer concept. Although the data set associated with structure continues to grow, it is not as abundant as that associated with involvement. Nonetheless, the research on structure is enlightening.

Structure involves setting up a child's environment so that competence can blossom. A parent using a high degree of structure communicates boundaries, including rules and expectations, to their child, explains the consequences of going beyond those boundaries, provides objective information about the child's impact on his environment in real time, and emphasizes the self-improvement aspects of growth rather than using comparisons to other children. A parent using a low degree of structure does not create such an ordered environment, but instead allows disorder to reign.

More structure is better for a child: it will enable your child to perceive direct links between his actions and his circumstances, and to thereby develop a sense of competence. Parental structure has been correlated to a child's belief of his competence as well as academic performance.[29]

The structure dimension is roughly aligned with the demandingness dimension. Notably absent from the description of structure, however, is any form of harsh control—that is included on a different dimension, to be discussed next. Structure incorporates only the kinder, gentler type of control. This is a key difference between the structure and demandingness dimensions.

We now have two self-determination theory parenting dimensions that we can visualize as overlaying on Baumrind's dimensions: involvement can be superimposed onto the responsiveness dimension, and structure onto the demandingness dimension. A high degree of involvement and a high degree of structure would be completely contained within the authoritative quadrant, eliminating harmful practices while offering greater specificity on beneficial ones. To identify parenting practices that are optimal, however, or as close as we can get using current research, we have one more dimension to cover, and that is autonomy support.

Autonomy support
Exercising autonomy is crucial for developing the relatedness and competence that characterizes the optimal life experience.

Living optimally entails acting in accordance with one's core self—including one's beliefs and values—and volitionally pursuing the relationships and capabilities that are most reflective of that self. Doing so as an adult is facilitated by being exposed to autonomy supportive environments as a child.

Autonomy support involves empowering the child to author his actions and to own the outcomes. A parent providing a high degree of autonomy support allows choices, respects his child's interests, encourages self-advocacy, supports volitional activities, gives reasons for expectations, and takes his child's viewpoint into consideration. A parent providing a low degree of autonomy support is directive and controlling, using harsh measures such as excessive criticism or mockery.

The autonomy support dimension is interactive with both the structure and the involvement dimensions: while the involvement and structure dimensions describe *what* parents do, the autonomy support dimension describes *how* they do it. Thus, autonomy support is unique and can be independently studied.

More autonomy support is better for a child: it has been correlated with higher self-esteem, greater self-regulation and more advanced executive function,[ii] both of which have elements of emotional health and behavior, better social outcomes, and greater academic achievement.[30] It has been linked to better emotional regulation,[31] longer delayed gratification and impulse control,[32] and fewer incidences of depression.[33] Autonomy support is correlated with every point on the well-being cycle.

An outcome of autonomy support is that children develop internal motivations, or inner drives reflective of the true self, that guide behavior. A lack of autonomy support supplants an inner drive with something else. Parents exhibiting a low degree of autonomy support, for example, might use material rewards and punishments. These represent an external drive that motivates the child to behave in certain ways, but is less consistent in its effectiveness and less fulfilling for the child.[34]

[ii] Executive function is a collection of mental, emotional, behavioral, and self-control skills.

There are also more insidious means by which parents can supplant a child's internal motivation. Parental conditional regard, a form of harsh control, is a prime example. Parental conditional regard involves extra attention, appreciation, and affection being given for approved behaviors, and withdrawn for disapproved behaviors. Parental conditional regard amounts to using love as a reward and punishment system. This form of manipulation is decidedly low in autonomy support. It is also common practice, and associated with many underappreciated dangers.

In effect, parental conditional regard implants the parent's will into the child's psyche. This is different from external behavior modification techniques like material rewards and punishments, because its impact is *within* the child. Yet it is also different from other internal motivations. Rather than having his authentic inner voice guiding his behaviors, the child is moved to action by what amounts to an imagined cajoling or judgmental affect from his parents. This intrusion may be imagined, but it represents a real assault on critical autonomous processes. It drowns out the child's own inner voice, and results in real psychological damage. Children subject to parental conditional regard are more likely to suppress emotions, less able to regulate emotions, less able to recognize emotions in others, and less likely to share emotions with others.[35]

Autonomy is recognized within the Baumrind parenting styles as important for child development. Yet, within the definition of authoritative parenting, autonomy support may still be dispensed on an exception basis, either for expediency or for perceived necessity. With self-determination theory, however, autonomy support is essential and indispensable. This is the key distinction between the two models.

The optimal parenting practices of self-determination theory can be presented graphically, much like we did with the Baumrind parenting styles. Autonomy-supportive practices could be exercised in any quadrant, but are utilized optimally when contained within the limits of high involvement and high structure, as shown in Table 3.

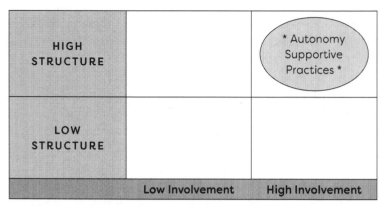

	Low Involvement	High Involvement
HIGH STRUCTURE		* Autonomy Supportive Practices *
LOW STRUCTURE		

TABLE 3. Optimal Self-determination Theory Parenting Styles

Being autonomy-supportive means offering explanations and guidance in a way that is meaningful for the child and nourishes his development. This requires understanding the child's motivations, thoughts, and feelings. As noted by Richard Ryan and Edward Deci, the co-developers of self-determination theory, it requires that "interactions between parent and child begin with *empathy*...."[36] And empathy takes us to our third model of parenting style: the model developed by Dr. John Gottman.

GOTTMAN PARENTING STYLES

Dr. John Gottman, a psychology researcher known for his studies on family dynamics, has defined and studied a model of parenting styles. Like the Baumrind model, Gottman identified four main parenting styles.[37] Unlike the Baumrind model, which encompasses the role of parenting in a broad sense, Gottman's four styles focus only on emotional aspects of the parent–child relationship.

Gottman's four parenting styles are: disapproving, dismissive, laissez faire, and emotion coach. Disapproving parents actively disapprove of their child's negative emotions, resulting in insecure children having limited emotional control. Dismissive parents attach no importance to their child's negative emotions, also resulting in insecure children having limited emotional control.

Laissez faire parents accept but do not co-manage negative emotions, resulting in their child having limited emotional control, limited self-control, and limited social skills. Emotion coach parents accept and co-manage negative emotions, resulting in their child having emotional control, self-control, and social skills. Table 4 below summarizes Gottman's descriptions of each parenting style as well as the child and adolescent outcomes he reported as correlating with each style.

PARENTING STYLE	DESCRIPTION	CHILD AND ADOLESCENT OUTCOMES
DISAPPROVING	Children's negative emotions are viewed as irrational, trivial, devoid of substance, manipulative or generally bad, and therefore unimportant. Because negative emotions are believed to come from weakness or flawed character traits, they are treated with harsh judgment and criticism. Conformity to a state of emotional homeostasis is demanded, and enforced via punishment.	Because feelings are believed to be wrong or invalid, these children think that they are flawed as people. They may show a lack of emotional control.
DISMISSING	Children's negative emotions are viewed as irrational, trivial, devoid of substance, manipulative or generally bad, and therefore unimportant. The child must "get over" their emotional storm, but without parental guidance because resolving such problems is not viewed as worthy of the parent's time and effort.	Because feelings are believed to be wrong or invalid, these children think that they are flawed as people. They may show a lack of emotional control.

PARENTING STYLE	DESCRIPTION	CHILD AND ADOLESCENT OUTCOMES
LAISSEZ FAIRE	All emotions are okay. Comfort is given but there is no guidance, no limits, and no parental assistance. Children are allowed to "ride out" emotional storms.	Children have difficulty regulating emotions, focusing on tasks, and making friends.
EMOTION COACH	Children's negative emotions are met with awareness, patience, and respect, and viewed as an opportunity to develop intimacy. Children are guided through emotional storms with listening, empathy, identification of feelings, limit setting on behavior, and assistance with problem-solving. Specific solutions are not mandated, and "should-be" emotions are not dictated.	Children are comfortable with their feelings, display emotional control, and solve their problems. They have high self-esteem, high learning aptitude, and an ability to form friendships.

TABLE 4. **Gottman Model of Parenting Styles**

Both Baumrind's and Gottman's models of parenting styles fall within ranges of responsiveness and demandingness: responsiveness to the child's needs, responsiveness to the child's emotions, demandingness to follow rules, and demandingness to resolve problems, as shown in Table 5.

Imagine the toy cleanup scenario again, and the child is upset and crying because he doesn't want to tidy up the toys. A permissive laissez faire parent's heart may melt when seeing their distraught child, and they may pick up the toys themselves while offering comfort such as "There, there, you poor thing" without acknowledging the source of the child's distress. By contrast, the authoritarian disapprover will become irritated and may threaten, "Pick up those toys and you had better stop crying before I give

HIGH DEMANDINGNESS TO FOLLOW RULES (High Demandingness to Resolve Problems)	Authoritarian (Disapproving)	Authoritative (Emotion Coaching)
LOW DEMANDINGNESS TO FOLLOW RULES (Low Demandingness to Resolve Problems)	Neglecting (Dismissive)	Permissive (Laissez Faire)
	Low Responsiveness to the Child's Needs (Low Responsiveness to the Child's Emotions)	High Responsiveness to the Child's Needs (High Responsiveness to the Child's Emotions)

TABLE 5. **Combination of Baumrind and Gottman Models of Parenting Styles**

you something to cry about," without offering guidance to help the child deal with his intense emotions. The neglectful dismisser may say something like, "It's just a few toys, there is nothing to cry about," completely invalidating their child's feelings. The authoritative emotion coach will start by exploring the issue with questions such as "You seem upset. Can you tell me what is bothering you?", thus helping the child to label his feelings and then to overcome the problem. The authoritative emotion coach is accepting of both the child's needs and the child's feelings, and takes them into consideration when setting expectations for the child to meet. While those expectations are high, they are attainable as the parent and child navigate challenges and emotional difficulties together.

The pairings of Baumrind and Gottman styles are somewhat artificial.[iii] The real value in overlaying the two models is to contrast their representations of the whole child. While Baumrind-centered studies focus on how the parent operates and what the child does, Gottman's work centers on the parent–child bond and how the child feels. When reading descriptions of the Baumrind parenting styles, I feel as if I am probing data in order to characterize a child's behavior. With Gottman's definitions, I feel as if I am peering out from behind the child's eyes. I have personally found this change in perspective to be enlightening; you may do so too.

Gottman adds life to the clinical-sounding dimensions of responsiveness and demandingness. He adds vulnerability, promise, despair, and hope. Parents would do well to infuse those sentiments into their thinking when considering which parenting style to adopt.

I find that doing so naturally draws me to autonomy-supportive practices. Ryan and Deci were right about beginning with empathy. When I read about disapproving, dismissive, and laissez faire parenting styles, I feel inadequate and ineffectual as a parent. And that must be exactly what children raised by authoritarian, permissive, and neglectful parents feel at times. When I read about emotion coaches, I feel like I matter and can make an impact. And so it is with children raised with an autonomy-supportive, authoritative, emotion coaching parenting style.

[iii]   The Baumrind model is scoped to include general conditions of the parent–child dynamic, while Gottman's model is confined to the emotional domain. It is plausible that a parent could exhibit high demandingness in one domain like academics but low demandingness in the emotional domain. So authoritarian parents are not always disapproving parents, and so forth.

It is therefore not surprising to see different correlations between the two models. The study referenced using Baumrind typologies showed one inferior style and three superior with regard to emotional intelligence, while Gottman's results showed one superior parenting style and three inferior ones. But overall, the authoritative and emotion coaching styles, both sharing the same quadrant in the matrix, are associated with the best outcomes.

I can share a pivotal example from personal experience. When my son was two years old, he was misbehaving. I don't remember the behavior, but I do remember that he was intransigent. I decided to administer a "time-out." It was a standard parenting tactic, and highly recommended by many parenting authorities.

My son refused to go to the time-out chair. After many failed attempts at diplomacy, I picked him up to move him to the chair. He protested more vigorously, thrashing in my arms. I'll never forget the words he shouted as he resisted: "Don't take me." He delivered those words—to his own father—with a mixture of fear and hopelessness. He was still resistant, yet resigned to my will. This made a deep impression on me. Is this what a child says to someone who empowers him, enables him, cares for him, and loves him—"Don't take me"—or is this what a child says to someone who represses him, controls him, and takes from him?

Would you feel like you matter to someone who imposes their will upon you, physically forcing you into a place you do not want to be? I wouldn't, and I don't think a child would, either. I think a child would feel like an object, an expendable possession of the parent.

Would you be made to feel like you can make an impact, when you are being "taken" against your will, against your most ardent protests? Do you think a child would? I think a child would feel powerless, impotent against the irresistible force of his parent.

In that moment, I became anti-time-out. I never again attempted to issue a punishment to one of my children. Back then, I did not know about harsh controls or self-determination theory. All I had to go on was how I thought my son must have felt. All I had to guide me was my sense of empathy. My empathy guided me to practices that happen to be autonomy-supportive.

You may also find your empathy to be a useful source of guidance. I urge you to pay attention in those times when practicing a standard parenting method doesn't quite feel right. It could be your "empathy alarm" going off.

Have there already been instances where your empathy alarm has sounded? If so, what do you think it was trying to tell you? Might you approach similar situations differently in the future?

THE OPTIMAL PARENTING STYLE

We can now explain why those who use effective parenting styles advance their children through every point on the well-being cycle. These parents have an access point on their child's well-being cycle. They make their children feel like they matter and can make an impact.

Every time parents are responsive to their child's needs, emotions, and interests, demonstrating warmth, involvement, and benevolence, they are sending the signal that their child matters. Every time they provide structure by explaining contingencies to help guide their child, by verbalizing their observations on their child's efforts, and by communicating expectations to follow rules and resolve problems, they are sending the signal that their child can make an impact. The most effective parents do these things with empathy, in ways that empower the child to express his individuality.

I have pulled together an integrated model that identifies the optimal parenting style (see Table 6 on the following page). We can designate parents who practice that style as autonomy-supportive authoritative emotion coaches.

Autonomy-supportive authoritative emotion coaches regularly impress their influence upon the matter and impact term of their child's well-being cycle, providing little pushes, transferring momentum every time, creating the conditions for their child to form positive beliefs about his own self-worth. The resulting matter and impact beliefs are crucial to well-being development. A child who believes he matters has better social skills, and is better equipped to live a life of relatedness. A child who believes that he can make an impact has better grades in school, and is better equipped to live a life of competence.

What differentiates the autonomy-supportive authoritative emotion coaches from other parents is that they convey the notion that the whole child is of positive personal worth. They make the child feel big, whereas practitioners of the other parenting styles make the child feel small. The way a child feels has a profound effect on his future.

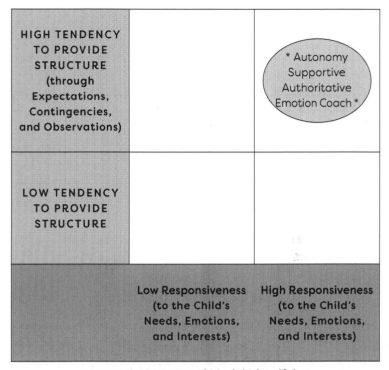

	Low Responsiveness (to the Child's Needs, Emotions, and Interests)	High Responsiveness (to the Child's Needs, Emotions, and Interests)
HIGH TENDENCY TO PROVIDE STRUCTURE (through Expectations, Contingencies, and Observations)		* Autonomy Supportive Authoritative Emotion Coach *
LOW TENDENCY TO PROVIDE STRUCTURE		

TABLE 6. An Integrated Model Identifying
an Optimal Parenting Style

Unlike adults, who are capable of forming independent self-assessments, young children derive their sense of self-worth almost entirely from signals received by their parents. This is a critical point, because people behave according to their beliefs about themselves. The matter and impact signals received from parents set the tone for the kind of person the child will make himself to be. And so parents who send signals that their children matter and can make an impact are more likely to have children who develop high self-esteem, and who make lives of well-being.

We can now follow a parent's influence on a child's well-being cycle through all the terms. We can then look at formulating parenting goals (page 59).

EMOTIONAL INTELLIGENCE

The literature on the relationships between emotional intelligence, behavior, relationships and capabilities, self-esteem, and well-being, although extensive, provides little in the way of definitive causation. There is a great deal of overlap between causes, effects, and contributing factors. I believe this to be because many of the correlations work both ways, which is illustrated in the cyclical depiction. Any point on a circle connects through any other point and then eventually back to itself, making it hard to know whether something is a cause or an effect, or something else.

Emotional intelligence, for example, correlates with every point on the cycle. In *Raising an Emotionally Intelligent Child*, Gottman cites behavioral outcomes such as greater protection from succumbing to social ills, such as youth violence, antisocial behavior, drug addiction, premature sexual activity, and adolescent suicide as correlates of emotional intelligence.[38] He includes capabilities such as greater aptitude at focusing attention, improved problem-solving, and greater academic success. Relationship outcomes such as better ability to relate to other people and better friendships with other children are also included. Gottman also links higher emotional intelligence to higher self-esteem. Gottman not only credits emotional intelligence for these outcomes, but makes an overarching linkage back to parenting style.

When children are treated by their parents as though they matter and can have an impact, they have a reason to devote their attention to developing the skills needed by people who matter and can have an impact. They develop emotional intelligence to ready themselves for the opportunities available to the kind of people they believe themselves to be. Virtuous behavior then emerges from a child's emotional intelligence, provided he does not choose to abuse his developing skills, for example, by manipulating others to suit his own ends.

VIRTUOUS BEHAVIOR

From Gottman's point of view, it is parenting style that encourages children to use their burgeoning emotional intelligence for good behavior. More specifically, it is the strong bond with the parent created by the parenting style that channels emotional intelligence into good behavior. Gottman indicates that children who feel supported, loved, and respected within their families are motivated to live by the family code; that it is through their emotional connections to family members that they adhere to the family virtues; that, ultimately, they behave well because they want to.[39]

Children raised with an autonomy-supportive authoritative emotion coaching parenting style behave well without threat of physical abuse, without bribes, and without fears of harsh punishment, getting yelled at, or being isolated from loved ones by way of the "time-out." These tactics, utilized by the other parenting styles explored earlier, do not imbue children with emotional intelligence but instead leave them to carry various types of emotional baggage. As a result, those other parenting styles do not promote behaviors that will equip their children to form relationships and build capabilities.

RELATIONSHIPS AND CAPABILITIES

The relationships and capabilities point on the well-being cycle is where a lot of parents are misguided. Wanting so badly for their children's relationship and capability attempts to translate into signals of matter and impact, parents attempt to "stack the deck." They use a variety of means to do this.

They may convince a child that a struggling relationship is not the child's fault. They may provide the child with a handy excuse for why a friend refuses to play with the child anymore, such as "He still likes you; he is just busy with schoolwork."

They may interfere on behalf of the child to smooth over the rocky relationship by speaking to the parents of the other child in order to moderate a reconciliation. When efforts to salvage the friendship fail, they may distort reality by consoling their child with something like, "The whole thing must be his fault anyway."

But a child does not need to receive matter and impact signals from every endeavor. Rather, a child needs a genuine understanding of his effect on the world, even when that effect is unfavorable to him. A trusted parent can help him achieve that genuine understanding by making observations that are factual and objective. For example, "It sounds like your friend is angry with you. What happened the last time you two played together?" The parent can then coach the child as he negotiates challenges and failures, by explaining how his efforts can make a difference going forward. These are the things done by parents who provide a high degree of structure.

Parents who try to stifle the world's unfavorable signals from reaching their children are low in structure. They may instead try to manufacture favorable matter and impact signals, or manipulate and misrepresent negative matter and impact signals coming from the real world. Parents low in structure may make excuses for flawed capabilities and unsuccessful attempts. They say things like, "You should have won but the other player got lucky." Or they may flagrantly bend rules to unfairly favor their child over others in order to effect the outcome they want. Or they may prevent mistakes by correcting the child's every homework assignment. Or they distort reality to accommodate failure, meeting a poor performance with something like, "You actually really did well," and meeting a mediocre performance with praises of "Good job." These tactics do not present a solid framework upon which the child can build.

What these parents are trying to do is comparable to helping a chick hatch from its egg. Hatching happens according to a protracted process that is far more involved than a chick simply breaking through its shell. Through impatience or misplaced compassion, one may rush to rupture the egg so that the chick may come out. But doing so bypasses the natural physiological progression necessary for the chick's preparedness to face the world.

MATTER AND IMPACT

The chick needs to work through the process of hatching like a child needs to work through the generation of self-esteem. A chick can't simply be given passage into life. The chick must arrive at it according to the prescribed processes. In the same way, a parent can't simply supply a child with self-esteem; the child must earn it organically by building beliefs of matter and impact. He must generate relatedness and competence by cultivating relationships and capabilities in the rough and tumble of the real world.

Evading a harsh reality just surrenders the valuable lessons of reality. It may provide temporary assurance of relationship skills, but ultimately compromises the development of inner qualities that cultivate relationships. It may improve short-term morale over a particular capability, but at the long-term expense of inner qualities that build capabilities. By interfering with the natural signals flowing from relationships and capability development, parents contaminate a child's self-development process.

The child so raised may at best develop "pseudo-self-esteem." Pseudo-self-esteem is a term coined by psychotherapist and author Nathaniel Branden. Instead of being measured through a conscientious evaluation of one's true worthiness, pseudo-self-esteem is measured through an evaluation of something else more likely to give a self-affirming result,[40] such as a parent's empty commendations.

In order to maintain his pseudo-self-esteem, the child then carries forward the techniques to falsely construe events that he learned from his parents. He masters all kinds of mental acrobatics, such as distortion of facts, denial of feelings, and pursuance of false matter and impact signals. Like the chick "rescued" from the egg, the child exonerated from failure is not given a fair chance to be everything he can be.

As he grows, a child will set his sights on an evolving land-scape of relationships and capabilities. In his early years he may have harmed a relationship because he mistook a social cue on the playground, or may have missed a soccer goal because he failed to practice enough. He may succeed in adult endeavors, not in spite of mistakes on the monkey bars and on the soccer field, but because of them. Through the lessons of childhood mistakes and failures, he will have developed the capacities to overcome adversity, to rebuild from a deficit, to redirect energies, to accommodate new interests, and to tackle his dreams.

Parents must let signals from the world reach their children intact, and actually provide authentic matter and impact signals only from the source over which they actually have dominion: themselves. The well-being of children, seeded by their parents, then builds and builds. As the child grows, the influence of the parents diminishes. The majority of matter and impact signals received by the children then come from their independently cul-tivated relationships[41] and capabilities. As long as the early signals received by the parents were in sync with reality, the grown child will have developed a repertoire of techniques for managing such signals. At that point, the cycle has become self-sustaining. It perpetuates on its own, ultimately propelling children to become adults at their full potential: adults who create resonance, who cultivate their best selves, for purposes beyond themselves, and foster closeness with others who are enriched by their best selves.

WELL-BEING

A healthy self-sustaining level of well-being is the cumulative result of all of the efforts exerted by both parent and child. A parent's influence on the well-being buildup is enormous.[42,43,44] Although parents catalyze the buildup, the child is ultimately responsible for his own destiny. The pinnacle of well-being—the resonance of interpersonal and intrapersonal experiences—is an independent, intrinsically motivated experience. It is this experience for which the parent's efforts are preparing the child.

Those early matter and impact signals can be delivered through an effective parenting style. Those signals may promote a developing child's well-being to a level modest enough to warrant a parent's assistance, yet high enough for the child to launch himself. The parents take the child all the way up to the breakthrough point.

FORMULATING PARENTING GOALS

It could be rested upon here that my parenting goals are to let my children know that they matter and that they can make an impact. But these charges are rather vague, and therefore unsatisfactory.

We know that matter and impact signals come from parental practices of responsiveness, structure, and autonomy support. Responsiveness means responding to a child's needs, emotions, and interests with warmth, involvement, and benevolence. Structure means communicating expectations with regard to rules and problem-solving, explaining contingencies, and making observations on your child's efforts. Autonomy support involves empowerment and empathy.

So, being highly responsive and providing a high degree of structure, both in an autonomy-supportive way, are also candidates for parenting goals. However, when it comes to practical application, these are somewhat vague and unwieldy; they are descriptive rather than prescriptive. Something is needed that combines the various elements into concrete actions, yet is simple enough to be called to mind when under stress.

In order to achieve this, I surveyed the landscape of parenting techniques by searching, studying, discussing techniques with other parents, and filtering out any conflicting advice, according to both parenting purpose and parenting vision:

- Parenting purpose: guidance was adopted when geared toward the adult that the child will become. All other guidance, such as that geared solely toward immediate behaviors, parental convenience, or judgments from others, was disregarded.

- Parenting vision: guidance contributing to a child's optimal life experience, by sending matter and impact signals through autonomy-supportive responsiveness and autonomy-supportive structure, was adopted. All other guidance, such as that conforming to authoritarian or permissive parenting styles, or that being low in structure or autonomy restrictive, was disregarded.

I arrived at four actions that can serve as concrete parenting goals:

1) Build awareness.
2) Give decisions.
3) Solve problems together.
4) Exemplify virtuous behaviors.

I will now introduce each of these in turn and explore how they interrelate.

BUILD AWARENESS

By helping children build awareness of their needs, emotions, and interests, parents are being involved with their children, assuming their children's viewpoint, and being responsive. By helping children build awareness of the expectations, parents are providing structure. And by helping children build awareness of the world at large and their effect on it, parents are providing structure and guidance that enables children to autonomously pursue interests and resolve problems.

GIVE DECISIONS

By giving decisions that convey the scope of the rules and communicate the possible outcomes, parents are providing the structure and guidance for their children to autonomously live up to expectations. By incorporating their child's needs, emotions, and interests into the design of those decisions, parents are demonstrating responsiveness.

SOLVE PROBLEMS TOGETHER

By solving problems together with their children, parents are reinforcing expectations to resolve problems. They are also encouraging their child's initiative to devise and try his own solutions. Furthermore, working together allows the parents to stay involved, to offer guidance, and to exercise real-time responsiveness.

Building awareness, giving decisions, and solving problems together lets children know that they matter and that they can make an impact. When practiced continually, these three things feed the virtuous cycle shown in Figure 3 (page 22). Having awareness, decision-making abilities, and problem-solving skills are as applicable on the basis of a single event as they are on the basis of an entire lifetime. And because they are both simple and prescriptive, they can be recalled even in the heat of the moment, and used as guidance.

On the basis of a single event, a healthy level of awareness allows for more complete consideration of the risks and rewards involved in social interactions and other types of endeavors. Good decision-making abilities help one to translate those risks and rewards into wise actions. And problem-solving skills allow one to reach the target outcome.

On the basis of an entire lifetime, these three things enable the optimal life experience. The optimal life experience is the state of continually becoming one's best self, for purposes beyond oneself, while fostering closeness with others who are enriched by that best self. In order to become one's best self, one first needs to know exactly who he is. In order to act for purposes beyond oneself, one needs to know what he truly cares about. For these two things, a deep level of awareness is required. In order to become his best self, decisions about which challenges to pursue need to be made. In order to foster closeness with others who enjoy that best self, decisions about which relations to pursue need to be made. Therefore decision-making skills are vital. Along the way, problems will also arise from random events and from dealing with people having different perspectives, desires, and motivations. Therefore the ability to problem-solve is necessary.

EXEMPLIFY VIRTUOUS BEHAVIORS

There is a second access point on the cycle where parents have an influence: parents transfer momentum not only at the point of matter and impact, but also at the point of virtuous behavior. Parents, through their actions, set examples for their children's behavior. Parents therefore need to adopt behaviors that are worthy of being a model.

If Gottman is correct, then the parent–child bond itself encourages virtuous behaviors. So this bond must be protected, especially in emotionally trying moments when it is the most fragile, such as when anger flares, when sadness consumes, or when confusion reigns, so that the right behaviors may emerge. Those who make the most out of life are those best equipped to live it. In order for us as parents to equip the people most important to us—our children—to make the most of life, we must lead them along the right path. We can only lead our children along the path to a wholly fulfilled life by simultaneously walking the same path. As parents, we must exemplify virtuous behaviors.

INFLUENCING THE WELL-BEING CYCLE

A healthy, self-sustaining level of well-being is the result of years of hard work exemplifying virtuous behaviors, building awareness, giving decisions, and solving problems together. Practicing these four actions consistently, despite having less strenuous methods at your disposal, can work miracles for your children's development. The initial efforts accomplish very little, and may even seem to be unnecessary expenditures of energy for such negligible effect. But in time, persistent efforts pay off huge dividends in the form of emotional intelligence, character skills, relatedness and competence, self-esteem, and well-being.

The final well-being cycle is shown in Figure 4 below. All four goals are represented. Exemplify Virtuous Behaviors describes parental behaviors that influence a child's behavior. Build Awareness, Give Decisions, and Solve Problems Together are parental actions that send signals of matter and impact. Together, and with each event, they transfer just a little bit of energy to a child's well-being cycle.

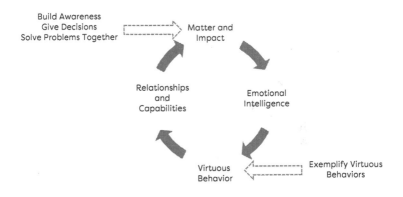

FIGURE 4. Influencing the Well-being Cycle

I have found that with almost any parenting conundrum, if I look to building awareness, giving decisions, and solving problems together, and with an eye toward exemplifying good behaviors, I can figure out what to do. These four things are prescriptive enough to be actionable, yet provide enough leeway so that the execution is customizable to any given situation.

DEFINING THE PARENTING PHILOSOPHY

A philosophy defines the approach one takes. Based in beliefs and values, it is the consummation of your purpose, vision, and goals. It serves as a practical guide for when the appropriate action is unclear.

You can define a philosophy by starting with your purpose, incorporating your vision, and linking to your goals. As an example, my parenting philosophy can be succinctly summarized in a paragraph:

> When facing a parenting choice, I ask whether each option is geared toward the child or toward the adult that the child will become. Options geared toward the adult that the child will become are consistent with the purpose of raising adults not kids, and warrant further consideration. For such options, I assess the agreement between their anticipated outcomes and the vision of my resonating adult children. Only when advancement toward that vision is facilitated may a parenting option then be translated into actions. Those actions are to be consistent with the goals of building awareness, giving decisions, solving problems together, and exemplifying virtuous behaviors.

STAYING THE COURSE

Parenting often seems like an endless series of dynamic situations to manage: getting kids off to school on time amid a myriad of distractions and hindrances; preparing meals for tastes and appetites that change daily; cleaning messes when least convenient; strapping squirmy kids into car seats when already late for an appointment; giving baths to screaming little ones who loved water yesterday but inexplicably hate it today; answering questions about why the car is faster than a dog while trying to pay the bills; and trying to get kids to bed on time while they are trying to stay up as late as possible.

I am reminded of a time I was running late for work, and needed to take the kids to school on the way. When it was time to leave the house, I called for the kids to come down the stairs. My daughter, then four years old, came down wearing her pajamas.

Why, I demanded to know, was she *still in her pajamas*? She was taken aback by my accusatory tone. Her feelings hurt, she left a piece of paper on the table and ran back upstairs. I picked up the paper.

It was a page from a coloring book. The picture was of a little cat kicking a soccer ball, with the words "Love Dad" scrawled in pencil underneath.

She hadn't changed into her clothes yet because she was coloring a picture for me. While I was thinking about getting to work, she was thinking about me. Reflecting on this later, I asked myself two questions:

1) If I had been a couple of minutes later to work that day, in the long run, would it have mattered to anyone?
The answer is of course not. In twenty years, or in one year, or even in a week, no one will have remembered that I showed up to work a couple of minutes later than usual.

2) If I had taken the time to get down on one knee, comment on her choice to combine yellow and red to make the sun, and ask what it felt like to color that bright orange bow on the cat's head, in the long run, would *that* have mattered to anyone?
Of course it would have. It would have mattered to that little girl, and to the grown-up she is to become. And sharing that moment with her would have mattered to me, too.

Life can get in the way of those little moments. Sometimes it's unavoidable, but sometimes we *let* life get in the way. It's important to take charge, and make time for these little moments.

If you forget to step back from the moment to see the bigger picture, you will find yourself at the mercy of your immediate needs and what you want your child to do. These things are often incompatible with the big picture. You will be too engrossed in the details of life's demands to do what is really important, and you will teach your children to be the same way.

Living this way is like having your course dictated by the vagaries of chance. Having an overarching parenting philosophy is like charting your own course. You can stay faithful to your charted course using a vision as the aspirational destination, a purpose that sets the direction, and goals as steps along the way.

With a defined parenting philosophy—a purpose, a vision, and goals—you will be able to navigate through unfamiliar territory and quickly react in situations for which you feel either unprepared or ill-equipped.

In my case, with a purpose of raising adults, the emphasis is on the child's long-term interests over the pressures of the moment. The needs of the moment, of expedience, comfort, and pride, must be stripped out of the assessments of parenting choices. Preconceived notions about a child's future regarding success, achievements, or goals, and how that possible future affects or reflects upon me, must also be discarded. The focus belongs not on me, my present, my future, or even any designs I may have on the child's future, but on the child and his future.

Raising adults means that if goals can be implemented in a manner expected to build well-being and result in adults who resonate, then they are implemented no matter how difficult or inconvenient they are in the moment. Raising adults means that if the goals can be implemented only in a manner expected to inhibit well-being, then they are rejected no matter how expedient or socially acceptable they are in the moment. With a defined philosophy, sifting through confusing parenting guides and contradictory opinions becomes doable and is often simple.

Parenting may be simple at times, but it is never easy. It involves difficult choices. Choices often involve either doing something easy in the short term yet off the long-term course, or doing something hard in the short term that keeps you on the long-term course.

The autonomy-supportive authoritative emotion coaching approach takes more time and energy than the other styles in the short term, and is certainly more mentally taxing, but it produces the long-term results most aligned with my purpose and vision. It is so important to resist focusing on immediate needs or taking the easy way out.

This optimal approach actually yields favorable results in both the short and the long term. Consider again the toy cleaning scenario. The autonomy-supportive authoritative emotion coach might explain to her child the reasoning for cleanup, empathize with the child's desire to keep playing, allow five more minutes for the child to finish playing and maybe even play along, and offer feedback about how well the cleanup is going and whether other family members might trip over the piece that was mistakenly left out. This approach will not only get you a clean and peaceful house, it will also help your children develop into adults who know that their decisions impact their condition as well as the condition of others. They become adults who are aware that their needs and their feelings are considered important, and have learned to consider the needs and feelings of others to be important. They learn to solve problems, and they learn to compromise when needed.

By contrast, adults having been raised with permissive or neglecting styles may perceive their decisions or their feelings to be insignificant and inconsequential, which will limit their endeavors in multiple facets of life. Adults raised with the low structure or the authoritarian style may know only how to meet challenges with anger or apathy. Or they may only learn to comply with orders unquestioningly, which is not the most flexible of relationship skills. It will certainly leave them poorly equipped to deal with an authority figure who instructs them to do something unethical or illegal.

Spanking

The difference between short-term and long-term concerns is illustrated by studies involving the harsh practice of spanking. Gottman discusses spanking in *Raising an Emotionally Intelligent Child*. He points to the abruptness and destructiveness of the practice, to be summarized separately in the following two paragraphs, as its flaws.[45]

Spanking results in immediate behavior corrections, hence its abruptness. Despite making spanking seem effective, this immediacy is problematic. It represents a relinquishment of opportunities to thoughtfully explore why a particular behavior is off-limits, and to consider alternative options for the future. Another problem with the abrupt nature of these behavior changes is that any new child behaviors will have their foundations in short-lived fear, instead of in an enduring emotional intelligence skill set. As a result, the behavior changes will not be permanent.

Spanking is destructive on two fronts. First, it is an assault on the child's self-esteem, and second, spanking places a wedge between parent and child. A child may feel degraded by the treatment, reduced to being the subject of someone else's domination. For a child, suffering such an abasement of character at the hands of his parents is destructive to the most influential relationship in his life. It is therefore destructive to the parents' very influence.

Parenting involves a lot of difficult moments. It is easy to forget our priorities and get lost in the moment, focusing on how we can make things more convenient for us. But difficult moments can be used as teaching moments that help our children develop into happy, well-adjusted adults, and help us grow closer to our children. The key to doing this is stepping back from the moment, and instead of thinking about short-term concerns such as the behavior of the child, thinking about the long-terms concerns such as the adult that the child will become.

It may be hard to think about long-term concerns while you are juggling three tasks and your child is insistent that he needs to know right now why a car is faster than a dog. Dismissing such questions may be easier for you in the moment, but it may also teach your child that his questions are not worthy and that he should not trust his thoughts nor have confidence in himself. So answer all your child's questions about the relative speed of dogs and cars, but not just so your child can learn about dogs and cars. Answer questions so that your child learns that his questions are valid, worthwhile, and deserving of a response. Answer questions so that your child learns that curiosity pays off, and earns him a more informed position to do whatever he feels he needs to do. Let your child know that he matters and can make an impact so that he may learn to manage himself and his relationships, and make his path to maximized well-being.

SETTING REASONABLE EXPECTATIONS

Simple as any philosophy may be, it may still seem like a lot to remember. Being a good parent will not be easy. You are bound to fall short at times no matter how hard you try or how steadfast your commitment. The enterprise of parenting is generous in its lessons of just how terribly imperfect you are. So for the sake of your own sanity, set reasonable expectations for yourself and allow yourself to make some mistakes.

One time I was talking to a friend and fellow parent, and shared that I was feeling bad because I had lost patience earlier that morning and basically failed to follow my own advice. I was worried about the effect on my child. "Don't worry," he said. "It's hard to do them any harm." This is somewhat true. Children are forgiving of your mistakes. They can be resilient to your minor failings.

The converse is also true, however, that it is hard to do them any good. They can be resilient to your teachings. Being a parent requires consistency, sacrifice, and persistence. You may encounter a difficult situation a thousand times before your child finally chooses to assimilate that critical belief or internalize that key behavior. Keep trying. Let your mistakes be your teachers as you discover new and better ways to communicate with your child. Over time, your continuous efforts will compound like the interest in a bank account, accumulating returns far greater than the deposits.

Starting from infancy, you nurture, you teach, you love. Using virtuous behaviors, you build awareness, give decisions, and solve problems together. You watch your baby become a toddler, and you keep nourishing, keep accepting, keep respecting. More awareness, more decisions, more problem-solving. The toddler grows and becomes a teenager, and still you coach, still you trust, still you love. That teenager, having awareness, decision-making abilities, and problem-solving skills of his own, becomes an adult of virtuous character, an adult having meaningful relationships and strong competencies. Seeing such a child, once a fragile infant, take the reins of his destiny to become all he can be is like watching a wheel that once seemed immovable having been spurred to break through and rotate in a way that comes to appear unstoppable.

ENABLING YOUR CHILD TO BECOME HIS BEST ADULT

Effectively implementing a parenting philosophy opens a vast horizon of possibility for your child, but that which carries no promises. Your child is ultimately responsible for his own destiny. Your grown child must choose his own destination and then use his faculties to drive himself to it. His is a personal journey, an independent, intrinsically motivated experience that cannot be pushed upon him from the outside. Knowing this is a reminder that even though parenting is first about involvement, sacrifice, and persistence, it is also about reducing dependence and encouraging autonomy. It is your child's own longing for relatedness, competence, creativity, and expression that will impel him to his destiny for his own well-being and to the enrichment of the world.

While it is ultimately your child's job to define what his full potential is going to be, your job is to provide the environment in which he can equip himself with the tools he needs to drive himself to it. That means enabling your child to build a strong foundation on which to build a lifetime of solid competencies and fruitful relationships where triumphs, defeats, and all of life's unexpected turns can be shared. It means letting your child acquire the awareness to envision the best path for his resonance, helping him grow the ability to decide the best way to achieve it, and incubating his faculty to navigate obstacles and his perseverance to endure setbacks along the way.

These adult-sized abilities do not simply materialize when one becomes an adult. The seeds need to be sewn in childhood and cultivated continually so that they grow with the child's growth and strengthen with the child's strength. The nourishment of those skills needs to be baked into your parenting style.

As you define your parenting style, try to imagine you are standing where a road splits into two paths. The first path has an even downhill slope. Down this path may be such things as coercion, disapproval, permissiveness, and dismissiveness. It seems like the easiest route, but this path is fraught with unseen hindrances and dangers. The child led down this path becomes an adult who is troubled, unfulfilled, and maladjusted. Along the second path may be such things as communication, consideration, respect, and autonomy. With a steady uphill slope, this path looks like it will be a lot of hard work, and it will be. But it will also be the more rewarding journey. The child led along this second path becomes an adult who is happy, confident, and well-adjusted. These two very different children, one having heavier burdens to carry and the other having grander mountains to conquer, are the same person but for having been led down different paths.

BECOMING YOUR BEST PERSON

The right path helps not only your child, but you as a parent as well. You cannot lead another along the right path without walking it yourself. I can claim from firsthand experience that embracing the role as a parent also helps the parent make the most of life. The way my children look at me and the way my efforts help their development let me know that I matter and that I can make an impact. It makes me want to be the best dad I can be, and always strive to be better still. Being the best dad I can be and trying to enhance the well-being of my children has unequivocally enhanced my own well-being.

Well-being is not zero-sum, but multiplicative. The net effects of the interconnectedness of people in society may be unquantifiable, but they are unarguably great. To the extent that people, or even just one person, become better at finding contentment and exploiting the full power of their talents, the whole of humanity is improved. By becoming fully human, we get to be multipliers of well-being. We get to make a difference.

You make the biggest difference with the people over whom you have the greatest influence. There is no better place to do this than the home, no better place to make the most out of Life with a capital L than with the relationship between you and your children. What greater gift could be given to someone with a new life than to help them learn how to use it to its fullest?

Parenting is about helping small people become big people. What better place for building a strong foundation for your little people to turn into big people, what place with more abundant opportunities to do so could there be, than the trusting and loving environment of the family unit? The difference you can make is immeasurable when you only set out to let your children know that they matter and that they can make an impact. And the best way to start making the difference, in fact the only way to start, is with yourself.

KEY POINTS

- Autonomy-supportive authoritative emotion coaches describe the parenting styles associated with children who excel along every term of the well-being cycle.
- The common denominators of effective parenting styles are high levels of responsiveness and structure. These two parental characteristics, when used in an autonomy-supportive way, essentially transfer momentum to a child's well-being cycle. High responsiveness conveys to children the interpersonally oriented belief that they matter, while high structure conveys to children the intrapersonally oriented belief that they can make an impact.
- Parental behavior serves as a model for children's behavior. Parents may also transfer momentum to a child's well-being cycle at the virtuous behavior term.
- Four goals have been formulated to help parents advance their children through the well-being cycle, and create optimal life experiences: build awareness, give decisions, solve problems together, and exemplify virtuous behaviors.
- A coherent parenting philosophy allows a parent to factor long-term considerations into short-term decisions.

REFLECTION EXERCISES

List the three most important things you can do to make your children feel like they matter.
Be specific. Acts of parental warmth, involvement, and benevolence may be included.

_____

_____

_____

List the three most important things you can do to make your children feel like they can make an impact.
Be specific. Ways to set expectations, explain contingencies, and offer observations may be included.

_____

_____

_____

List the three behaviors you would most like to see your child exhibit.

_____

_____

_____

Can you find creative ways to use the well-being cycle to formulate your own parenting goals?

_____

_____

_____

_____

_____

_____

What are your parenting goals?
Goals are concrete actions that map the path to a vision.

_____

_____

_____

_____

_____

_____

What is your parenting philosophy?
A philosophy is a coherent executable statement that unifies a
purpose, a vision, and goals.

_____

_____

_____

_____

_____

_____

Characterize your ideal parenting style.
Your ideal parenting style should be perfectly compatible with
your parenting philosophy. It may be expressed using the dimensions of responsiveness and structure, in terms of autonomy, a
combination thereof, or in terms that are uniquely your own.

_____

_____

_____

_____

_____

_____

PART II

Becoming Your Best Person

CHAPTER 3

Exemplify Virtuous Behaviors

Virtuous behavior represents an access point on a child's well-being cycle where parents can transfer momentum. By serving as a model, parents can influence their children's adoption of virtuous behaviors; like begets like. Those virtuous behaviors will spur the development of relationships and capabilities for both parent and child.

By consistently exemplifying virtuous behaviors, parents go a long way toward influencing the adults that their children are to become. They fulfill the purpose of raising adults. They make it possible for their children to live lives of meaning, and to become everything they are capable of becoming, to make the vision of resonance a reality.

The example that you set as a parent is like a stone dropped into a pond. Like concentric wave patterns rippling across the entire surface, your circle of influence begins with the people closest to you and reverberates outward. Each of those people then carries something from you across the expanses of their own circles of influence. Your example makes a difference.

Wanting to make a difference is human. Knowing to start from within is wise, as rabbi and philosopher Yisroel Salanter came to realize:

"I tried to change the world and I could not. I tried
to change the city where I live, and without success.
Finally I tried to change my neighborhood, also without success. Until I concluded: I changed myself and
my light will change others around me …"[46]

The behavior that you model ultimately traverses humanity
and cascades through the generations. Of all the people you will
ever influence, however, your children are the most impressionable and attentive. Of all the people your children will be
influenced by, the strongest influence is that of their parents.
Your children are where the stone meets the surface of the pond.
They have an imitative instinct.

MIMICRY AND FORMATION OF HABITS

Children learn what to do largely by watching others. In fact, they
are built to imitate what they see. The human brain is populated
by numerous systems of what are called "mirror neurons."[47] These
mirror neurons reflect back what we perceive someone else to be
doing, producing a strong impulse to mimic that action. Children,
absent of the self-control that most adults have cultivated over
years of character development, lack any meaningful defense
against these impulses and are likely to indulge them.

Once they have mimicked an action, children have laid the
groundwork to repeat that action. Once they have repeated the
action, they have begun to form a habit. In *Social Intelligence*,
Daniel Goleman related a metaphor used by hypnotherapist
Milton Erickson involving freshly fallen snow to describe how
this works.[48] As a child, Milton would head to school early after
a snowy night. He liked to trench his way through the undis-
turbed snow so that the other children would use the path he
left behind. He enjoyed experimenting with indirect routes to see
whether other kids would still walk in his boot prints. Because
walking his trail was easier than clearing a new one, they always

did. However meandering his path, each successive child would follow it, widening and deepening the passage, and making it the established pathway.[49]

Formation of a neural circuit in the human brain works like the children tracking through the snow. The connections in a neural sequence become stronger each time that sequence is followed. With enough repetition, a new circuit is created and following those neural pathways becomes automatic.

As an example of an action being mimicked and becoming habit, emotionally distant parents tend to have emotionally distant children.[50] Children who are constantly beset with demeaning remarks instead of affection, who are disregarded instead of nurtured, who are dismissed instead of accepted and understood, and who harbor resultant feelings of insecurity are more likely to take an attitude of detached passivity toward the world. Such children have been conditioned to take an emotionally distant approach to relationships, and to feel general anxiety about themselves. So detachment begets detachment.

For a very powerful example of how behavior is mimicked, let's return to the issue of spanking, first discussed on page 41 as a harsh control measure. As noted by Gottman in *Raising an Emotionally Intelligent Child*, aggression begets aggression. Parent–child aggression begets child–child aggression, which grows with the child's growth to become adolescent aggression, then adult aggression, before finally completing the cruel cycle when parent–child aggression begins anew.[51] Whether the abuse is physical, verbal, or emotional, the potential exists for such a vicious cycle.

Sadly, such violent patterns of behavior can result in neural circuits forming or strengthening in both parent and child. One bout of aggression can be the basis of a new habit for the parent, an example to be followed for any witnesses, and a model for how to interact for the child. Thankfully, such extreme examples are the exception, not the rule. Nonetheless, it is important to be cognizant of the potential impact.

But the potential also exists for virtuous cycles. Abraham Maslow said, "Give people affection and security, and they will give affection and be secure in their feelings and behavior."[52] When children are given affection and treated by their parents with compassion and responsiveness, the children treat others with affection in return. When children are nurtured in this way and given security in their position in the home, they feel secure. When confronted with unfamiliar places, situations, and people, that sense of security makes the difference between perceiving threats or opportunities. It translates into a positive outlook with which children confidently explore their world, knowing they have a "secure base" to which they can return.[53] Just as detachment begets detachment and aggression begets aggression, so affection and security beget affection and security.

The imitative instinct operates not only on behavioral and attitudinal levels, but also on emotional levels. Researcher Tiffany Field has found that depressed mothers have babies who often emulate their sadness, disengagement, and anger.[54]

THE NEURAL LINKAGE

Emotions are actually contagious. Goleman described in *Social Intelligence* how this applies to persistent emotions such as those associated with depression, as well as fleeting emotions such as from a happy laugh. He related how the mirror neurons operate within an integrated nervous system designed to connect us to those around us.[55]

Subconscious neural circuits play a central role. Working from within the brain's primitive limbic system, they coordinate the facial expressions and body language between social participants. This mutual interplay occurs through cascades of hormones that translate the perception of another's emotions as one's own.[56] Our nervous systems respond to the signals from others in what Goleman calls a "neural ballet," such that happiness begets happiness, sadness begets sadness, anger begets anger, and love begets love.

A person's emotions, attitudes, and behaviors are not only self-reinforcing, they are also communicable to some degree through these shared neural connections. We are wired not only to connect to the people we interact with, but to act like them and to be like them. Children, with budding neural pathways like a blanket of snow uncluttered by footprints, are more impressionable and receptive to the examples of others.

Your behavior sends a message, much more powerful than your words, that "This is okay to do." In the very early years when children view their parents as being flawless, the message is even stronger: "This is the exact right way to do things." As a parent, you can never forget just how powerful your example is. Children can imitate what they perceive you to do and then with repetition or reinforcement, encode some of those behaviors into their own personality.

PERSONALITY AND ENVIRONMENT

NATURE AND NURTURE

A child's personality is dynamic, taking shape as the child simultaneously discovers and invents herself. As her personality unfolds, it begins to set. Like paths cut into the snow by a steady procession of determined boots, key personality traits get established. Circumventing the established pathways in favor of blazing new trails takes great effort. The earliest pathways taken by your child are therefore the most important. They are the central highways in vast neural networks as yet unbuilt.

As the people with the most influence over how that personality development unfolds, it is instructive for parents to have an understanding of just what personality is. Personality encompasses the attitudes and behaviors that make a person unique, and drives how they think, feel, and act. It is the coaction of two interdependent elements: the predominantly innate element of temperament and the predominantly learned element of character.

Temperament arises from our preferences. Preferences are the raw materials given to us that govern how we perceive and approach the world. They are nature. Whether someone is private or outgoing, methodical or spontaneous, logical or sympathetic, decisive or deliberative, realistic or visionary, is all in the realm of temperament. These characteristics are neither good nor bad, they just naturally *are*.

Character is the habitual component of personality. It is derived from our behavior. It is the part of personality that is under individual control. It is nurture. Unlike temperament which is given to us, character is what we make it, and may be either good or bad. A person's character may be described as compassionate or selfish, honest or deceitful, fair or unfair, optimistic or defeatist, determined or lazy, conscientious or careless.

Rather than being two distinct and competing facets of personality, temperament and character are intimately intertwined. Our preferences shape our behavior choices. How our behavior is received by our environment, in addition to either reinforcing or discouraging that behavior, is fed back to then guide the discovery and harnessing of our preferences.

There is no right temperament except the one that feels most comfortable for your child. A parent need only provide an accommodating environment in which the child may discover it; an environment that provides the child opportunities to use her natural gifts free from meddlesome disapproval and discouraging dismissiveness. Temperament will be discussed in detail in Chapter Five (page 169).

Children accumulate perceptions of their environment, particularly the behavior of others. Early character creation involves imitating some of those behaviors in ways they find comfortable. As they grow, children adopt some of these imitations into their behavioral norm.

But we human beings are not mere reproductions of our surroundings. We are thinking individuals. Some observed behaviors we reject outright, some we simply disregard, and some we imitate. On each behavior we imitate, we add our own personal imprint. The resulting character identity is a complex mosaic influenced by many but unique unto the self.

SHAPING THE ENVIRONMENT

A good environment acts as nourishment and allows a child to use her temperament to its advantage, helped along by good character traits. A bad environment acts as a toxin. It leaves a child consumed by what she perceives to be her temperament's liabilities, and burdened further by negative character traits.

The role of the parent is to provide a nourishing environment. Of course, no one can create an entire environment. The world exposes a child to an entire ecosystem of influencing factors, such as friends, family, teachers, coaches, caregivers, clergy, video screens, books, and many others. To try to shield a child from those influences would leave her unprepared for the world and its challenges. What parents can do instead is shape the environment where practical, provide the proper context when needed, and most importantly serve as a role model by consistently demonstrating good character traits.

You may not be able to completely control all of these influences, but in many cases you can make informed choices about them. You can select your schools, activities, and friends. You can choose which books, television channels, and electronic devices are in your home. You can set rules around which types of activities are appropriate and which are off-limits. You can encourage enriching activities by making opportunities available, and by participating yourself. And you can read to your children as much as possible.

When you trust they have your child's best interests at heart, you can shape many of the interactions your child will experience with influential people. In other words, you can influence the influencers. You can stay engaged in your child's activities and remain connected to her friends, teachers, coaches, and caregivers. You can let them know what some of your most important values and practices are, and that you expect those to apply even when you are not there. For example, your young child's friend may have older siblings who like to play violent video games that you consider to be age-inappropriate. You can ask that friend's parents to restrict your child from participating in those games. If your child is to attend a campfire, and your family does not eat pork, you can equip your child with gelatin-free marshmallows so she can still make s'mores. Conversely, you can reinforce in the home whatever worthy values are being emphasized to your child outside the home.

You also have the power to limit how much time your child is exposed to many of these influences. You can prune attendee lists to functions that you host. You can select your family activities to be spent with good influences, while steering clear of bad influences to whatever extent is practical.

Where it is not practical to limit your child's exposure to questionable influences, you can minimize their impact by discussing the bad influences with your child. If a friend or family member says something that is not aligned with your values, then you can use that as an opportunity to clarify to your child what your values are, and why you do not support the comments in question. If your child chooses unsavory friends, you can explain how you view those friends' behaviors, what the potential consequences of those behaviors are, and what alternative behaviors are available.

PARENTAL INVOLVEMENT

The best thing you can do to benefit your child's environment, however, is maximize your involvement in your child's life. Your behavior is the only part of your child's environment over which you have complete control. You can shape some of the aspects of your child's environment, and you can provide context to other aspects, but your abilities to do so are limited. Concentrate your energy where you have the most control and can make the greatest impact: with your own influence.

Recognize that your influence will gradually diminish. As your child gets older, she will crave more independence. That may happen as the teen years approach, or even sooner. So strike while the iron is hot and maximize your involvement while your children still want you to be involved.

There are many ways to maximize your influence by maximizing your involvement. If you have work to do, you can let it wait until after your child's bedtime. If she wants to accompany you somewhere but you know that will slow you down, you can let her accompany you anyway. If your child is watching television, you can watch it with her. If you can afford to outsource chores like housework or yard work in order to spend more time with your children, then you may choose to do so. And when you are with your kids, you can be there mentally as well as physically. If you are trying to read an email instead of paying attention to your children, you will find yourself irritated whenever they "interrupt" you and it will not be good quality time. Try putting down your phone and really staying engaged with your children.

You won't be able to do all of these things all the time. I still find myself writing that one last sentence when I should be listening to what my child is trying to tell me. But when you make an effort to be aware of how you can still improve, you are putting yourself on the right path.

One of the hardest parts about maximizing your involvement with your children may be balancing your family with your career. They are, after all, related: you need money to take care of your family. There will come many opportunities to improve your income. You may be able to work evenings, weekends, and holidays for increased pay. You may become eligible for promotions that entail longer hours and more travel. You may wish to enhance your upward mobility through evening and weekend educational sessions. Whether to take any of these opportunities can be a difficult decision for any parent.

When faced with these types of decisions, I have found it helpful to do some imaginary time travel. In my imagination, my older self has taken whatever opportunity is under consideration. In this possible future, I am now retired with independent adult children. I have at my disposal a sum of incremental money as spoils from the opportunity. I am then presented with a magical offer to relive my past evenings, weekends, and holidays with my family instead of earning the incremental income. Instead of working late, I could be having dinner with my family. Instead of traveling, I could be listening to my daughter tell me about a problem she is having with a friend at school. And instead of being at the office on the weekend, I could be playing Frisbee with my son. All I have to do to accept this offer is give up the sum of money.

TECHNIQUE: IMAGINARY TIME TRAVEL

Envision the long-term outcomes of any choice that sacrifices quality (or quantity) time with your child. Then, from the perspective of your future self, ask whether you would trade the spoils of that choice to get back the lost time with your child. How you think you would answer then is how you should choose now.

Reframing the situation in this way brings some helpful perspective. Someone who has chosen money—and has a disconnected, rebellious, or resentful adult child because of it—might be remorseful. Such a person might choose to trade in the money to get their time back. But they can't, because this deal is imaginary and never actually comes. There is only one chance to decide, and it is right now. How you think you would respond to that deal later is how you should choose now. Not only would most parents benefit from recovering that lost time, but so would their children benefit from the additional parental involvement.

THE POWER OF YOUR EXAMPLE

I now want to take some time to highlight the power of parental examples in six virtuous character traits: compassion, honesty, fairness, optimism, determination, and conscientiousness. This is not a complete list of valuable character traits. I have chosen to illustrate these six because I believe them to be the basis for relationships and capabilities—the point on the well-being cycle immediately following virtuous behaviors.

VIRTUOUS INTERPERSONAL CHARACTER TRAITS

Compassionate, honest, and fair behaviors are the basis for relationship success. They are interpersonal behaviors. These behaviors are, in my estimation, the essence of the Golden Rule. The Golden Rule states that we should treat others as we would like others to treat us. A form of the Golden Rule may be found in virtually every culture, religion, and philosophy. In the New Testament, for example, it is stated as "Therefore whatever you desire for men to do to you, you shall also do to them."[57] The pervasiveness of this principle is a testament to its validity as well as its importance. Behavior according to the Golden Rule is the universal platform upon which good relationships are built.

To some degree the Golden Rule is self-fulfilling. People are inclined to treat us like we treat them. They are, in fact, designed to reciprocate our conduct toward them through the imitative instinct. Followers of the Golden Rule, by treating others with compassion, honesty, and fairness, are recognized by others as being worthy of compassion, honesty, and fairness. They are recognized as being worthy of reciprocal acceptance, respect, trust, and love. People are induced to relate to, to cooperate with, and to create terms of mutual influence with followers of the Golden Rule. Other people want to be around those who follow the Golden Rule; compassion, honesty, and fairness beget compassion, honesty, and fairness.

A very young child is first exposed to compassionate, honest, and fair behaviors by her parents. The child may imitate those virtuous interpersonal behaviors in the relaxed setting of the home, with the people she is mimicking. Her reciprocation of virtue will help strengthen the parent–child bond, which stokes the belief that she matters. This belief will entice her to repeat the virtuous behaviors.

As her emotional intelligence matures, she may be emboldened to apply those behaviors in more tense situations. She may begin to willingly make sacrifices in order to maintain favored behavior patterns. For example, she may choose to honestly express an opinion, even if she knows doing so will not win the regard of popular peers. And she can gradually exhibit these same behaviors in more advanced settings. She will be able to approach other people with the benevolent attitude to which she is accustomed.

She can establish these behavior patterns with an expanding circle of associates and in a broad array of contexts. As her behavior solidifies into character, and her relationships flourish into relatedness, a growing sense of self-worth can fuel continued virtuous behavior. Thus a self-reinforcing cycle is created, making possible a lifetime of good relationships with colleagues, friends, family, her spouse, and someday her own children.

Compassion

You begin modeling compassion the day your child is born. Birth may be difficult for you and your spouse, but it must be downright terrifying for your child. After nine months of solitude in the muffled and relatively static atmosphere of the womb, your baby will endure a brutal introduction to a world filled with intense lights, colors, sounds, sensations, temperature variations, and smells.

All the things she will perceive will have no discernible relationship among them, and will probably feel like a wild assault on her senses. Your baby's lungs may burn as they first fill up with air, and her back might fill with pain as her spine straightens for the first time. She will no longer be fed continuously and must space her meals out every few hours, not understanding this new feeling of hunger or if it will ever go away. She will have no control over her own movement, vocalizations, or feelings. She will have no sense of identity, no notion of where she ends and everything else begins. Everything is yet to be learned. She will experience discomfort from soiled diapers, being hot or cold, and wanting to move. She will experience tiredness, lonely feelings, overstimulation, the desire to be swaddled, and the desire to suck. She will be confused by all she is experiencing, and helpless to change her situation. Until she learns what is happening, what it means, and how to respond, she is completely dependent upon loving adult caregivers.

How you answer your crying baby is her model for how to treat someone under duress. Whether she needs to be fed, to be comforted back to sleep, or to be changed, how you approach her plight makes a difference. Indifferent or cruel parents who feel burdened by the weight of their parental responsibility risk raising children indifferent to the concept of helping others. Compassionate parents recognize that without their intervention, their baby would be powerless to help herself. Compassionate parents who embrace their ability to solve their baby's problem, and who see her through her predicament with love and understanding, are positioning themselves to raise compassionate children.

As parents of infants, in response to the hard work and grueling hours involved in taking care of a new baby, we often shift into survival mode. We might not devote the energy to treating the baby with the compassion she deserves because we are overtired and overwhelmed. We might think that because babies are resilient, taking emotional shortcuts is okay.

We might rationalize this choice by concluding that how we parent at this early age won't affect the child anyway. And we might presume that when the child is old enough to understand things better, we will change our approach—only we won't. In fact, as the child grows and learns, she will develop opinions and have motivations, some of which will be in direct opposition to those of her parents. The level of emotional friction will increase and the level of compassion, if anything, will decrease.

Lifelong compassion toward your child therefore requires a baseline to be established in infancy so that it can be built upon later. Taking care of your infant is your first walk through the snow as a parent. Take the route now that you envision using later, because the opportunity to start a new route later will never seem to materialize. You can *make* the opportunity later, but it is much easier if you arrange it so that you don't have to. If you are compassionate when you hear your infant crying at 2:00 a.m., then you can be compassionate when at two years old she breaks a beloved toy through carelessness, or at four years old when she suffers through wet shoes after deciding to jump in puddles.

Whether an infant utterly dependent on adult help or a toddler needing to be shown how to help herself, a struggling child offers you a chance to truly make a difference in the life of another human being. A child having a hard time needs to be accepted, understood, and comforted. She may not know why she feels bad, or that the bad feeling will come to an end. Show your child compassion when you are lucky enough to be called upon. The compassionate approach is far more fulfilling, for both parent and child, than resentfully slogging through your parental duties, cursing your lost sleep under your breath as if being forced into hard labor through the manipulations of a devious child. A "difficult" child is not a laborious duty, a task to be carried out with drudgery. A struggling child is a shooting star, a fleeting opportunity to let someone know that they matter, that their anguish is warranted and accepted.

Speak to your troubled child softly when you let her know that you are there for her, and look deep into her eyes. Fixing your attention on the eyes opens up advanced levels of communication. Transmissions of thoughts and feelings are subconsciously sent and received through subtle directional cues, dilations, moisture, and muscle movements of and around the eyes. As you attune to her emotional level and she to yours through eye contact, you send her the message that she matters and she is important enough to draw and hold your attention.

As Daniel Goleman points out in *Social Intelligence*, you also provide a model for how relationships are managed. The complex emotional back-and-forth between parent and child—with both taking turns providing a stimulus and a response—is practice for even more advanced forms of communication. Conversations that weave dialogue with the gauging of emotions, the reciprocation of sentiments as appropriate, the timing of responses, and the initiation of topical shifts, are built on the foundations of these early parent–child give-and-take communications.[58]

A baby who does not receive this sort of attention misses out on the practice as well as on the affection. If you withdraw emotionally while you wait for your child to soothe herself, your child will register your emotional distance even within the physical closeness of your embrace. A baby can sense your commitment, or lack of commitment, to her in that moment.

So many parents do not appreciate the precious little time they have with their young children. I don't know how many parents I have heard lamenting the work their young child demands of them, even portraying it as if it were thrust upon them by malicious and unfair means. They accuse their children of "being bratty," "looking for attention," or "causing trouble." They long for their child to grow out of their troubles, saying things like, "Things will be easier when they are out of diapers," or "I can't wait until kindergarten starts and I can have my time back," or "As soon as high school is complete, my job is finally done." Before you know it, your child will become a teenager. And sooner than you realize that teenager will become an independent adult. Things can't get better later; things are already wonderful right now. Cherish the moments you have, for one day you may long to have them back.

Whenever I found myself challenged to savor a moment with a struggling or defiant child, I would once again use my imagination to reframe the situation (see box on page 88). I would envision a time in the future when my children had grown up and moved out. I, in my imaginary retirement, no longer lived sleep-deprived and hectic days of getting children ready for school, working all day, and then coming home to homework, piano lessons, and brushing little teeth. Rather, I passed the time looking through old videos of my daughter singing "Twinkle Twinkle Little Star" and of my son climbing on the playground equipment. I longed for the sounds of little feet running through the house, the pealing laughter of my children at play, and the perfect love in my small children's hugs, now all just a memory. And then I would reenter reality. As if by magic my wishes were granted and I was brought back to the time I had missed so dearly.

If the preciousness of the moment is not appreciated by you, you will let the opportunity slip through your fingers to the potential dismay of your older self. Too often parents start to feel time ticking away in the teen years, and attempt to spend their child's late adolescence and early adulthood tending to the unfinished business of building relationships. But it is often too little, too late. You only get one shot, and it will be over in a flash whether you resent it or treasure it. If you approach trying situations with understanding and a compassionate smile, you may get the same in return. If you approach difficult times with anger and conflict, your child will give you anger and conflict in return.

How you behave in these situations starts with how you think about them. Behaviors truly are born in your thoughts. Compassion is not already within you waiting to be called, but is something you choose to create.

It is worth emphasizing, however, that sometimes you will choose not to create it, because you are human, and perhaps you just need sleep. The behaviors in this chapter are described as idealized versions to aspire to. But we should recognize that life is not ideal, and we are imperfect. It may be a helpful reference point for you to know that I feel like an effective parent if I can adopt a compassionate mindset toward distressed or uncooperative children 80 percent of the time. For the other times, I record my actions in my journal, and consider ways I can do better the next day.

Many parents think of soiled diapers, hungry children, tweens arguing to change the rules, and teens openly defying them as "have-tos," the part of the parenting job they wish they could skip. They love the hugs and smiles, but dread the cries and wails. They do not realize that the cries and wails are really "get-tos." Those are the moments when parenting really happens, when you get to define what kind of parent you are and your child gets to define in her mind who you are. Those are the moments she will remember most about you. It is when you get to learn all the quirks about your child's personality: what she likes; what makes her laugh; how she responds to stress; and what comforts her. It is how you get to know her, and she you. It is where you get to model compassion for your child, and where your compassion toward her earns you countless unsolicited hugs and smiles when circumstances are calmer. If you do not go to your child for the cries and wails, your child will not come to you for the hugs and smiles.

TECHNIQUE: "GET-TOS"

Reframe parenting duties—those things you "have to do"—as things you "get to do." Consider the contribution to your child's long-term well-being you are making through those duties.

It all starts with how you frame these types of situations in your own mind. Whether you view a distressed child with a positive outlook or with dispirited dejection, your mindset goes a long way toward defining how you set your example as a parent. So watch your thoughts, for it is said that thoughts become words. Words then become actions; actions become habit; habit becomes character; and character becomes destiny.[iv]

Honesty

Dishonesty is seductive. It is easy to rationalize telling a lie, to be convinced that it will offer a simple and convenient solution. To further justify telling it, the severity of the lie is mentally downgraded. "It's just a harmless little fib," the inner voice says.

It is hard to get children to leave the park when it is time to go home, so some parents tell them that the park is closing. Parents want their children to eat their vegetables, so they tell them that the eggplant tastes yummy. Visiting the doctor is less stressful without fuss, so parents tell their children that the doctor will not hurt them. Parents throw away an old toy, and tell their child that it must have gotten lost. Leaving the house to run errands can

---

[iv] Adapted from a saying often attributed to Lao Tzu.

be challenging, so some parents tell their children they will only be gone for a minute. Parents are tired during bedtime stories, so they skip ahead a few pages and as long as the child doesn't notice, it's okay, right? When these "harmless little fibs" are reinforced by seeming to work, we can repeat them and make them habit.

Telling a lie of convenience is like taking a high-interest loan. A high-interest loan will settle this month's obligations, but add even more debt for next month. When next month's bills come due, a bigger advance will be needed. After bargaining oneself into this pattern, escape is difficult, if not impossible. In the same way, the benefits of dishonesty today will be outweighed by the costs tomorrow.

The costs of a lie may be as numerous as they are unpredictable. When a child hasn't learned how to leave the park before she is ready, the parents find themselves repeating the lie that the park is closing the next trip to the park. When this happens, the child does not learn how to quell the urge to play. The scenario must be played out in various settings and circumstances to the pleasure of no one. As the child grows older and smarter, the parents need to make the lie more elaborate. They may even up the ante by threatening to leave the park without the child. Threatening a child with abandonment may hasten the walk out of the park, but it will also make her believe that her parents view her as expendable, and that can be crippling to her confidence.

The child eventually discovers that it was all a lie, though, at which point trust between parent and child is lost. Moreover, the child has been taught that using lies to get what she wants is okay. That child may think it is okay to tell her parents she has already brushed her teeth when she simply does not want to do it. She may see nothing wrong with falsely reporting to her parents that the teacher assigned no homework this weekend. She may convincingly tell Mom and Dad that yes, of course her friend's parents know about the party and will be there the whole time. Each of these untruths would open the door for greater troubles down the road.

No matter how good your example is, however, children will still experiment with dishonesty. They do this for many reasons.

Very young children haven't yet learned the difference between truth and lies and therefore lack an ethical foundation on which to base their behavior. Children who do understand the concept of honesty may have good intentions but will appear to lie if they conflate their imagination with reality. Children may be sneaky or untruthful to avoid angering or disappointing their parents, the two people they are intently focused on pleasing. They may be tempted to cheat at games because they haven't yet learned how to accept losing. Or they may simply want to take something that isn't theirs and have a weak resistance against their impulses. When a child behaves dishonestly, it is important to explore her reason so that you can patiently offer guidance in a way that is developmentally and situationally appropriate. The child who falsely claimed to have brushed her teeth out of convenience, for example, can be shown pictures of cavitied teeth. Her parent might explain that they don't want her teeth to end up like that because they love her. They might also explain that they will always tell her the truth, because they value honesty. In addition to guidance and patience, your example can eventually steer children toward honest behaviors.

A child with dishonest parents may have a distorted sense of ethics to factor into her behavioral decisions. She might be more inclined to choose the path of dishonesty. When her parents berate her decision, she might be unable to comprehend the inconsistency. The parents might even tell her that lying will make her nose grow like Pinocchio. The irony of such a proclamation may be lost on the parents, but not the child. She may come to begrudge the hypocrisy of her parents. The parents have discredited themselves and must now attempt to communicate from a position of weakened credibility. A dishonest example triggers a downward spiral of the bad behaviors, damaged relationships, and poorly raised adults.

One time I was at an outlet mall. There were coin-operated rides for children stationed around the premises. There I saw a child asking to go on one of the rides, but his dad told him the sign said out of order. The child was not old enough to read, but old enough to discern that there was no sign. The child knew he was being deceived. Lacking the language skills to mount any meaningful counterargument, he protested with a noisy temper tantrum. The father hoisted the wailing child onto his shoulder and said, "Out of order means out of order," as he casually hauled the boy away.

This was a man who decided not to say "no" to his child, probably for purposes of expediency. Granted, rationalizing with a toddler is an energy-intensive undertaking, but destroying trust by using lies and forcefulness is an unwise alternative. This man could have simply told his child no and given the reason. Maybe there was somewhere else to go and not enough time for rides, or maybe the man didn't have any coins to use. Being truthful and then helping the child cope with his frustration would have taken more time, but it would have helped the man avoid the long-run costs of the behavior he actually modeled that day. It would have helped him preserve trust.

Honesty should be used in all situations. In addition to providing truthful information, truly honest communicators also volunteer relevant helpful information when its omission could have gone unnoticed. They operate without pretenses, hidden agendas, or undercover maneuvering. They communicate directly and overtly. You are aware that your child might not like eggplant the first time she tries it, so why pretend otherwise? You can let her try it and decide for herself whether she likes it without making her feel manipulated. You can offer a candid explanation that you want the child to at least taste the eggplant before she rejects it because kids generally have to taste strange new foods ten or twenty times before they like it. If you know that your child will be weighed, measured, examined, and inoculated at the doctor's office today, then you can tell her about it. Help her get mentally prepared for the visit and let her know that you will be there for her the whole time. If you need to take away a dangerous toy, you can explain why. Tell your child if you accidentally stepped on it and exposed sharp broken edges, that you are sorry, and that you love her too much to risk her safety by keeping the broken toy around. If a page has been accidentally skipped during a story, point it out. Then you can go back and read it. If you are leaving the house for an hour, then tell her you will be back in an hour. You can let her choose to come with you or not, but make it clear that there are no toys to play with where you are going and no additional purchases will be made, regardless of how many candy aisles you walk past. And if she chooses not to come with you, make sure you are back in an hour. A child may interpret "I meant to be back in an hour, but unexpected circumstances intervened" as a lie.

Being honest is simple in concept but can be tricky in practice. Your child may ask about the age of an elderly friend. In situations like this, understand that you don't have to respond to everything in graphic detail in order to maintain integrity. You can tell the truth—that it is impolite to talk about that sort of thing, and that many adults do not like other people to know their age.

When my son was four years old, he uneasily asked me if he would still get Christmas presents even if he did not behave. I was tempted to indulge his fears in exchange for some good behavior. Instead, I told him yes, he will get Christmas presents even if he breaks the rules, but that I expected him to follow the rules anyway.

When my daughter was two years old, I took her to see the doctor. When we arrived, the nurse told me that there were no inoculations scheduled for that visit. So I told my daughter she could relax, there would be no needles today. Then the doctor came in and told me that the flu was going around, and it would be unwise to skip flu shots this year. I had already given my word that there would be no shots. I decided that my daughter's trust was more important than a bout of the flu that, while inconvenient for her and me, would be inconsequential in the grand scheme of her life. So we skipped flu shots that year.

Your authenticity will enhance your influence. When a child has faith in the sincerity of her caregivers, she can build upon what they tell her. Using what her parents tell her as a starting point, she can focus on making sense of the world around her. If her mind is clouded by mistrust, she will be unable to build on any teachings of her parents, instead being preoccupied by doubt. This is completely understandable. How can a child be comfortable with the world around her and all the new things she learns, how can she ever feel she has a firm foundation on which to build if her own parents are lying to her?

Honesty should be modeled not only in interactions with your children but with everyone, so that your children may be exposed to someone practicing an honest lifestyle. For example, if you promised another adult something in front of your child, then you can allow your child to observe you following through. If you are late to your child's dentist appointment, don't fabricate stories about traffic. Instead, you can apologize for being late and if anyone asks the reason for your delay then respond truthfully, even if it shows you in a slightly unfavorable light. If while visiting friends you complement somebody's new hairstyle, then on the way home you can say nice things about that hairstyle.

There is a fine line between tact and disingenuousness. Your example in commenting neutrally yet tactfully on things like strange new hairstyles can later be used to buttress coaching sessions. For example, you might help your child to develop strategies for accepting unwanted presents. Your child may learn that saying, "Oh, it's a new board game. Thank you so much!" is a viable alternative to "But we already have this one!"

One of the most demonstrative times to model honesty is when no one else is watching. If you have been given extra change by a cashier, you can point out the mistake and return the overage. If your barely-three-year-old child can get into the pool for free by claiming to be two years old, then you can report her age as three and pay the entry fee. If you accidentally tore a page from a library book that you borrowed, you can report the damage when you return the book. In any such case, you can take the time to explain to your child what you just did and why, and entertain her questions about it. When you rise to the ethical standard of behaving even when you can't be caught, you have grounds to expect your child to follow rules even when you are not watching.

You are, however, human. Just as your child will sometimes do the wrong things, so too will you. When you have done something wrong, you can use it as an opportunity to show your child how to correct course. The man from the outlet mall, for example, can return there especially for his child to take the rides. Don't let the shame of your misdeed induce you to cover it up with even more wrongs. You can come clean to whomever you've wronged with an apology, and make the situation right again to whatever extent is possible.

You can also allow your child to do the same. When you know her to have done something wrong, don't make her double down by having to lie about it. Attempting to entrap her by asking leading questions with a threatening posture and a rising volume—for example, "Did you!?"—will only scare her into digging a deeper hole for herself. Rather, coax out the truth by being inquisitive instead of accusatory, and be graceful in your forgiveness. You might begin by asking open-ended questions about motives, feelings, and actions, and then following up with more inquiries until you have the complete picture. The deed may still have consequences, but those should be focused on course correction rather than being punitive. When faced with an admission, let your compassion guide your response. By modeling compassion while encouraging honesty, you "get to" help your child cultivate two character traits at the same time.

Fairness

Fairness is easily misunderstood by a small child. She may perceive anything preventing her from fulfilling every desire as being "unfair." As she grows from an egocentric child into a socially adept adult, she will come to understand that other people have thoughts, feelings, and perspectives that are different from hers. She will understand that nobody, including adults, gets everything they want. She will develop an accurate concept of fairness, provided some parental guidance is given along the way. Your consistent practicing and teaching of fairness will help your child to understand and embrace the concept.

We can make an analogy to competitive games here. Fairness is having the rules declared before the game is played, having the same rules apply to all the players, and having impartial hearings for accused rule breakers. You have the unenviable position of being a coach, a rule-maker, a referee, and a player in the game.

Remaining fair amid your conflicting interests is a precarious balance, but one you must keep in order to demonstrate fairness.

You have the responsibility of making sure the rules and expectations are clear to your child. She cannot be expected to follow unpublicized rules or to meet unspoken expectations that to you seem like common sense. You have to provide explicit instruction. In that respect, you are like a coach openly discussing the procedures and consequences.

The corollary of that is that you also have the privilege of setting some of those rules. In your capacity as rule-maker, you may introduce new rules spontaneously to adapt to changing circumstances. But those new rules should not be applied retroactively, only to future gameplay.

If the rules are to be an effective backdrop for gameplay, they must be thoughtfully formulated. As an example, we once created the rule that milk must be kept in its cup until consumed. If the milk was instead poured onto the dinner plate, then there would be no milk refills for that meal. This rule was imposed specifically to address my one-year-old daughter's eating habits, which often resulted in milk puddles on the floor.

We explained the new rule to her while we were cleaning up the milk. I calmly pointed to her fresh cup of milk and repeatedly instructed her to keep her milk inside, and she understood. She complied with the rule, but not how we expected.

She adopted the practice of taking the food from her plate and plopping it into her cup piece by piece, and then consuming both food and drink from the cup. While unappetizing for us to observe, it was consistent with the rule as stated. So it would have been unfair of us to chastise her at that point for putting food in the cup, even though at first blush the seemingly willful disregard for the spirit of the rule felt mildly insulting. Berating her creativity would have been retroactive enforcement of a new rule.

What we could have done, however, was amend the rule for the future to require that food also be kept in its original serving container until consumed. While tempting, we opted not to do that. Although my daughter was not capable of articulating her motives, it was clear that she was not creating messes just for her own amusement as we suspected, nor was she displeasing us for attention.

She just liked her food to be softened by her beverage. She liked turning dinner into a milky soup, almost like cereal. She was preparing her meals the way she wanted them. And with the modified method that she created, there was no spillage. So she got what she wanted in a way that allowed us to have our way as well. So long as her inventive circumvention of the milk-in-cup rule didn't impose on other members of the family, we ultimately decided that it was her prerogative to eat the way she preferred.

Like adults, children find imaginative and ingenious ways to contrive freedoms from within a set of rules. For that reason, be sure to think through the rules before you declare them. Envision ways they may be adhered to, and ways they may be bypassed.

Also consider how the various rules interact with each other, and clarify what happens if any rules appear to conflict with one another. For example, if you've told your child she can spend her own money as she wishes, but there are house limits on candy, what happens when she buys her own candy? When you have a well-constructed code of conduct in place, your newly instituted rules will be meaningful, respected, and amenable to consistent enforcement. And through your example as coach and rule-maker, your child will have a blueprint for organizing activities within her social group, such as creating games or proposing methods to take turns.

If you instead have a set of rules full of loopholes and contradictions, you will be forced to improvise. You may appear to be vacillating among an indiscriminate set of confusing decrees. And, by your example, you will be teaching your child to arrange the rules to her advantage regardless of whose rights they infringe. She may follow your lead by improvising a set of shallow rules among her playmates that are always favorable to her while disadvantaging others. And in the process she will have created a whole set of unnecessary social issues to maneuver through.

One key consideration when setting rules is that you will be expected to follow the rules as well. In this respect you are one of the players in the game. If the television is to be turned off at mealtimes because that time is reserved for conversation, then don't pick up your smartphone during dinner. If politeness is required in your house, then be courteous and model apt usage of words like "please" and "thank you" when speaking to family members. If your child is not allowed to interrupt you, then do not interrupt her. If children are expected to clean up their own clutter, then keep an organized house. If you will be unable to follow your own rule, then you should either adjust your behavior or reformulate the rule.

Despite what you may perceive, your child does desire to please you by listening to you. But she has an even stronger desire to be like you. Problems arise when you act in contradiction to your declared rules, because that sets these two desires in opposition to one another. Your inconsistency will make it impossible for your child to both listen to you and be like you. Her desire to be like you may prevail. She might perform imitations of your behavior that are greeted by reprimands. She may interpret the discrepancy as hypocrisy and come to resent you for it. When you instead practice what you preach, you make it easier for your child to adhere to the rules. You also prevent your relationship with your child from bearing needless stress.

There are some nuances that may be particularly difficult to convey to a small child. For example, some types of privileges may be earned non-uniformly by different players. These types of privileges may be earned on a responsibility-dependent, a development-dependent, or an ability-dependent basis. Rules containing these types of nuances are fair because they extend the same opportunities to all players. The catch is that they do not guarantee the same outcome for all the players. So you as the parent may at times be perceived to be playing by an unfair set of rules when in fact you are not.

Responsibility-dependent privileges are those that are granted commensurate with a player's demonstrated level of responsibility. For example, you have the privilege of choosing for yourself a later bedtime than that of your child. Adults are expected to choose a bedtime that does not interfere with their punctual waking, their next day's obligations, nor their disposition. Additionally, adults have more tasks they need to accomplish in a given day, and therefore need more waking hours in which to do them. When your children have grown, you can explain, they will have the same privilege to choose a later bedtime, and the same responsibility to complete their duties with sufficient rest. For now, it is your responsibility to ensure they get enough rest and therefore your privilege to choose their bedtime.

When my son turned five he argued that his 8:30 p.m. bedtime was too early, and that he was ready for the privilege of choosing his bedtime. At least the first part was true; he was no longer able to fall asleep at bedtime. So we granted him the privilege on a probationary basis, pending his successful management of responsibilities. The experiment lasted a few weeks, and was characterized by 10:30 p.m. bedtimes. It was also peppered with more emotional meltdowns than usual, which were traced back to inadequate rest. We ultimately reclaimed the bedtime-choosing privilege on the grounds that he was not ready for the responsibility. We did, however, concede to a 9:00 p.m. bedtime, which worked out for everybody.

Development-dependent privileges are those that vary based on growth. Larger children may enjoy larger meals to match to their appetites. Smaller children may be allowed to jump on furniture until they grow enough to cause damage. Having these disparate set of permissions is not playing favorites. It is fair because the concessions become tailored to suit the individual as they change. You as the parent, for example, have the privilege of operating all of the kitchen equipment because the equipment is made and arranged for people of larger size. More importantly, adults generally have greater dexterity than children and are far less likely to injure themselves while preparing a full meal. As a safety measure, adults have the privilege of running the full kitchen.

Ability-dependent privileges allow some to perform at a higher level than others. In a footrace, everyone has the same opportunity to win but that does not mean that everyone should take turns winning. The swiftest runner has the privilege of more victories by virtue of being faster. It would be fair if that player won every race.

That does not mean, of course, that you should trounce your child in every competition simply because you can. That would be no way for a child to develop a zest for competition. Nor should you lose every match, as that would be no way for the child to develop a realistic sense of her capabilities. Trust in yourself to know the right amount of competitive energy to inject into a game. It is a delicate balance, and the right balance may be different for every child. The important thing is that you get to model sportsmanship whether you win or lose. So win humbly and lose graciously so that your child may know to do the same. This is applicable in games as well as in more serious matters, such as household disagreements.

You are more knowledgeable and intellectually superior to your child, at least for a while. By virtue of these advanced abilities, you will win most of the disagreements you have with your child. Win humbly. When you lose, you can verbalize how the child made a solid argument and based on that, you have either changed your mind or have come to appreciate a different perspective. This lets your child experience victory so she knows she has some control over her destiny. It can give her the confidence to further develop such critical life skills as persuasion and negotiation, and provide her with a model for losing graciously.

It takes an even hand to judiciously apply the "equal opportunity but not necessarily equal outcome" axioms. Be careful not to misuse the nuances of responsibility-dependent, development-dependent, and ability-dependent privileges. As the authority in the house, you have the privilege of setting the rules and the corresponding responsibility for doing so in an equitable fashion.

Your equitable nature will again come into play when rule breaking is suspected, in which case you play the role of referee. Everyone, including children, deserves impartial and fair hearings. So be sure to withhold judgment until you get the whole picture. In other words, do not simply accuse your child or assume her to be at fault unless you witnessed an infraction firsthand. Instead, give your child the benefit of the doubt and ask open-ended questions.

When your child leaves the dinner table with sticky hands, for example, and you hear her opening doors and rummaging through things against your specific instructions, you might say, "Your hands are sticky and I told you to wash them before touching anything, but that's not what you are doing. Why?" You might learn that the towel had fallen on the floor and the child had the foresight to get a fresh one before starting to wash. Or the floor was wet and she was getting paper towels with which to dry it so she could stand in front of the sink without getting her socks wet. Or the soap was depleted and she needed to get more. These would all be valid reasons that you would never get to hear if you took a confrontational approach and bowled your child over with your superior language skills. You could instead lose credibility and respect with your child, while leaving her feeling helpless, depressed, and spiteful. Your child has valid perspectives that incorporate information that you may not have. Your child's perspective deserves to be heard. And when you grant her that, she can learn to guard against premature judgment whenever she suspects others of misdoings.

Your authority to officiate over disputes, however, is not an obligation to do so. When children are in disagreement with one another, sometimes they just need to work the differences out for themselves. You may decide to offer some informational feedback relating to feelings, tactics, and potential outcomes, but directly involving yourself in a resolution is by no means a requirement. Let the children try out different approaches to understand how they may work or not. They will, at times, implement unfair solutions, and will be able to see firsthand the damage caused. They will know that being unfair causes sadness, anger, and loneliness. This will help them to internalize a notion of fairness. When they learn to do the right thing this way, they will know *why* they are doing the right thing—and it won't be simply to avoid parental wrath.

When intervention is needed, you can put some of the execution in the hands of the children. For example, rather than correcting the offending child yourself, you may coach the victimized child to tell her playmate that she is not yet finished playing with a disputed toy. Some children may need to hear "She's not finished playing with that" from an authority figure a few times on their behalf before they are comfortable enough to start asserting their own rights. By observing your fairness in this and other situations, the child can eventually begin displaying fair behavior herself.

Compassion, honesty, and fairness are the basis of good relationships. Good relationships let us know we matter. They provide a sense of belonging. People know they matter when they are accepted, trusted, respected, and loved for who they are at a very base level. Not for how they look, or for what they have, or for what they can give, but for their unique expressions of self.

When people have established good relationship terms with your child, the Golden Rule adherent, they will be willing and pleased to present her with opportunities. She will be offered opportunities to be on a playground kickball team, to join student clubs, and to interview for jobs. She will have opportunities to make an impact.

VIRTUOUS INTRAPERSONAL CHARACTER TRAITS

Making an impact means making a difference. It requires effective self-management. It requires the virtuous intrapersonal behaviors of optimism, determination, and conscientiousness, which are the basis for capability development. With a sense of optimism comes the notion "I *can* do it." Determination is the mindset that says "I *will* do it." A conscientious attitude says "I will do it *right*." These are the skills that allow us, once presented with that opportunity to have an impact, to make the most of it.

This is another virtuous cycle that can be set in motion by the parents in the home. If a parent demonstrates behaviors that are optimistic, determined, and conscientious, the child can then mimic these virtuous intrapersonal behaviors and experience favorable outcomes. The child can believe herself to have an impact, and seek more opportunities to make a difference.

As her emotional intelligence develops, she can apply these behaviors outside the home, across an expanding horizon of opportunities. Her behavior can solidify into character, her capabilities can flourish into competence, and a growing sense of self-worth can fuel continued virtuous behavior. As an adult, she can be driven to seek the most rewarding challenges the world has to offer her—and meet them.

Optimism

To protect our children, we parents frequently use negative and disallowing language. We tell children, "No, you can't go into the street," and "No, you can't pet strange dogs." We also use phrasing that limits ourselves, as in, "No, I can't pick you up right now because I'm busy cleaning the floor."

Children hear "no" and "can't" so often that they are some of the first words they understand. "No" is usually one of their first spoken words, wielded skillfully and frequently. Similarly, "can't" becomes their fallback response to challenges. Children claim that they can't get dressed because they can't find any clothes to wear, they can't catch the ball because it is too difficult, and they can't wash their hands because the sink is too tall. A declaration of "can't," like a well-placed "no," is often an imitation of the parents' typical responses.

By switching to positive language, you can reverse this unintentional training in pessimism. Instead of "You can't run into the street," try "The street is dangerous. Stay in the yard and on the sidewalk." Rather than "You can't just run up to that dog and start petting it," use "First ask the dog's owner if the dog likes to be petted." And instead of "I can't pick you up right now, I'm cleaning the floor," try "Please wait until I've finished cleaning and have both hands free, and then I can hold you." In each of these examples, both pairs of expressions convey the same message, but the latter ones lack the inherent tone of defeatism that characterizes the former. Instead of centering on restrictions, the latter statements focus on the possibilities. When your child imitates your style and uses "can" thinking instead of "can't" thinking, she will approach difficulties with more hopefulness, concentrating her mental energy not on the limitations but on the attainable.

In cases when your child still does report that something is outside of her capabilities, you may coach her through some "can" thinking tactics. For example, rather than declaring inability using "I can't," you can encourage her to practice positive inquiry using "How can I?" Perhaps the child is faced with a task that is too complicated, like picking one outfit from her extensive wardrobe. When she poses the question "How can I?" to herself, if she doesn't devise her own solution, she can be coached on how to break it down into smaller manageable tasks. A closet full of choices can be systematically narrowed down to a less daunting set of options. Long sleeves can be eliminated in favor of short sleeves, stripes in favor of solids, and green in favor of blue.

Or perhaps she is not practiced enough to perform a task yet, like catching a ball. Her "How can I?" question can be answered with techniques to gradually enhance her performance. A ball will be made easier to catch if it is first thrown from a closer distance or if a larger ball is first used, before progressively returning to the original conditions.

If she is truly unable to do what she is trying to do, like reach a tall sink, then a better question to encourage is "How can *we*?" Asking for help is an acceptable and powerful tactic. Many people can often accomplish together what one cannot accomplish alone. Those who learn how to work in teams generally enjoy greater success in multiple facets of life. If the parent lifts the child up, for example, the child will then be able to reach the sink to wash her hands.

In order for a child to adopt positive inquiry as her standard mode of grappling with challenges, coaching sessions will not be enough. She will also need to be exposed to her parents' firsthand modeling of this approach. So, in the example of the parent whose hands are occupied cleaning the floor instead of holding the child, another approach would be for the parent to sincerely and inquisitively ask, "How can I pick you up when

I'm cleaning the floor?" By verbalizing this challenge, the parent is recruiting the child to help think through mutually satisfying ways to attain both of their goals. The parent is inviting the child to make an impact. The child may suggest cleaning faster, to which an obvious response is "How can *we* make this job go faster?" The child's involvement in formulating a solution such as helping to clean, and then actually implementing that solution, allows her to enjoy a sense of accomplishment when she is eventually welcomed into her parent's arms. Her taste of success will fuel her "can" thinking and drive her hunger for future challenging endeavors.

Optimism starts with a positive outlook, but that by itself is insufficient. A child needs to taste success before she will truly believe that she "can." How will she ever believe she "can" if she never "has"? Optimism results from a combination of a positive outlook and past experience.

As parents, we are left with the puzzle of how to facilitate a small child to drive herself to meaningful successes using her limited set of skills. Success cannot be meaningful if it was too easy or if the expectations were too low. If the expectations are too high, on the other hand, then the child will only develop feelings of powerlessness and inadequacy. The essence of the puzzle, then, is in setting expectations that are both high and attainable. The solution is that the expectations need to be high not with respect to adult standards, but in relation to the child's specific abilities. The minimum acceptable performance in a given task should be set to match a child's abilities and gradually raised with her growth. Cleaning the floor as well as her skills allow would be an example. The expectations are therefore aligned with the child's maximum ability, and occasionally may even be set slightly above her ability as aspirational goals. Parents can then inspire their children to meet these high expectations by acknowledging efforts, providing feedback, and recognizing improvements.

In order for your child to accept the notion that expectations are high and being continually raised, you of course should hold yourself to the same ideal. Your child should be accustomed to seeing you performing up to your advanced ability, free from shortcuts, half-hearted attempts, and careless efforts. It is also helpful to call attention to improvements you are making in your performances, be it cooking a new dish, playing a new game, or using new software. When high and increasing expectations are viewed as normal, children will naturally desire to perform to their ability and continually improve.

Hard as it may be to leave imperfect results uncorrected, performances that are at the child's capability level should be accepted. This may mean living with a bed that is not made completely smooth, words that aren't spoken completely clearly, and floors that aren't swept completely clean. Consider that a child's rudimentary fulfillment of tasks is often not a sign of sloppiness or laziness, but rather a placeholder for results not yet within reach. In the floor-cleaning example, the parent may see crumbs and streaks that are unnoticed by the child. If the child has the coordination and strength to leave the floor with a polished glow, then it is best to call attention to the crumbs and streaks—after acknowledging the progress already made—and allow the child to complete the job and rightfully earn her parent's embrace. But if the child has already performed up to her developmental level, and the parent offers only criticism, or negates her efforts by personally rectifying the deficiency, then the child's feeling of triumph could instantly become a feeling of inadequacy.

By focusing on limitations with "can't" language, parents can unknowingly transmit a pessimistic outlook to their child. And by demanding performance beyond their child's abilities, they can diminish her confidence and discourage her desire to have an impact.

By using "can" language for yourself and your child, you can help your child develop a positive outlook. And then with properly placed expectations, your child will contribute at her level and have a meaningful impact on herself and on the family. She can build an ever-growing base of knowledge and abilities. Her successes can fuel her to seek out and attain more successes, because she will know that she "can."

Determination

Enjoying successes is not always a one-step journey, and often involves setbacks or failure along the way. These difficulties, even if they do not detract from optimism about pure ability to succeed, may still wear down a child's will to continue. Determination means continuing despite difficulties, overcoming not only the external adversity but also one's own weakened resolve.

Parents often feel compelled to push children into persevering until a job is completed. However, the external pressure of an interfering parent will not effectively give a child the strength of spirit to succeed. Parental intrusions, harassments, threats, and bribes may indeed instill in the child strong determination, but it is a suboptimal kind of determination. I think of it as "push" determination because it is thrust upon the child, driving her to advance through sheer exertion of force.

This push determination falls short because it is often short-lived, misdirected, or emotionally harmful. Push determination is short-lived in the sense that the child may produce an artificial display of fortitude, the facade of which will crumble when the parent is absent and the child is free to direct her own agenda. Push determination is misdirected when the child resents the invasive tactics and focuses her motivation on resisting her parents instead of on productive endeavors. Push determination is emotionally harmful when the child's doggedness is rooted in fear and insecurity.

Because weakened resolve is an internal inhibition, the most effective motivation to move past it is also internally generated. There are different types of internal motivation. Edward Deci and Richard Ryan, the developers of self-determination theory, refer to the purest type as "intrinsic motivation."[59] I think of this intrinsically driven motivation as "pull" determination. With pull determination, the child perseveres of her own volition, using her faculties to their full capacity to draw herself to a goal.

Its effectiveness is due to its long-term, goal-directed, and emotionally healthy nature. Pull determination is long term in that it is a skill that the child may call upon when needed for the rest of her life, regardless of whether the parent is present. Pull determination is goal-directed, with energies being concentrated on the task at hand because completing that task is personally endorsed as worthy. Pull determination is emotionally healthy because it is rooted in confidence, the belief that the child has the competence to reach the goal. *Genuine* determination is pull determination.

Determination is a product of autonomy.[60] When a child is granted autonomy—the agency to govern her activities, to express her individualism through her actions, and to purposefully exercise her influence in the world—she becomes intimately invested in her endeavors. By having charge over the course of her activities, she has a personal stake in their eventual success. She becomes engaged in her efforts, knowing that they are the proving grounds for her own ideas. She discovers that making her methods work is both desirable and pleasurable. She develops a feeling of ownership over her tasks.

Autonomy is not to be confused with absolute sovereignty. A child does not simply do anything she pleases without limitation, but rather is granted independence within the framework of the expectations set by her parents. The parents set the overarching structure and the child figures out how stay within that structure. The child defines specific goals and determines how to reach them, when to ask for help, what kind of help to accept, when to take a break to regroup, and when to declare completion. Her sense of ownership is derived from the freedoms she enjoys within the constructs of the larger framework.

For example, parents may set the overall expectation that a child work up to her ability level at school. The child then decides how to meet that requirement, like which classes to take and how to distribute her time and energy among those classes. She sets specific targets for herself that may include acing a math test, finishing homework by a certain time, or understanding a subject well enough to explain it to a fellow student. The parent can comment on how well the child must have applied herself to learn that tricky math concept. Alternatively, the parent can give feedback on how slacking off on reading assignments today can limit the child's choices in the future.

In another example, parents may offer transportation and financial support for one extracurricular activity from a curated list of options. The child then has a wealth of opportunities to choose from. She may decide to play an instrument, to join a sports team, to compete in individual sports, to pursue dance, or a martial art, or theater, or cooking, or painting, or something else, or nothing at all. She can decide where to enroll in these activities and when to schedule lessons and practice sessions. Her skill level targets will be the product of her own desire to fulfill her passion for that activity. The more choices left entirely to the child, the more opportunities she will have to experiment with plowing through setbacks. She will explore, experience, and discover ways to achieve her goals. She will do so because she has formulated the goals herself. She is the sponsor of her efforts, and therefore feels responsibility for their successful completion.

For the child, exercising her autonomy produces ownership of the goal and pride in the performance; for the parents, granting that autonomy produces some degree of risk. Developing a sense of ownership over something may take the child weeks or months, and events leading up to it may not unfold as the parents had hoped. There is a level of uncertainty associated with the handing over of control that makes parents uncomfortable. But handing over control is ultimately what parenting is about. In the end, the output of all parenting efforts is an adult.

Parents who utilize autonomy to raise adults eventually get engagement and self-direction from their child, skills that will serve the child well as she steers herself through life. Parents who use coercion to raise kids get immediate compliance, but that may never develop into adult determination.

Genuine determination, having been mastered in pursuit of endeavors that are stimulating, can then be applied to activities that are far less invigorating. Determination is used to complete tedious work when it would be easier to just leave the job unfinished, like when a child rakes leaves. Determination is why people continue to make attempts despite disappointingly slow progress, like a child learning how to draw her favorite cartoon character. Determination is what drives people to relentlessly press forward against heavy resistance, such as a child completing an assignment despite time constraints.

With an optimistic outlook coupled with an autonomous atmosphere, the stage is set for your child's determination to thrive. But don't simply take the chance that determination will flourish because you have invited it. Show your child what determination is supposed to look like. Exhibit determination in your daily life. Be determined.

You can make your struggles "public" so your child can see how you approach difficulties. When saddled with the mundanity of doing taxes, you can express both your boredom and your firmness of purpose to get it done. Your child may have difficulty relating to your struggles. You can explain the similarity between your tax filing and her leaf raking, how both jobs require doing something that one does not want to do. After you have finished your taxes, you can emphasize how hard you worked and how proud you feel because of that work. It explicitly demonstrates your determination.

While making home repairs that require more trips to the hardware store than expected, you can staunchly insist to yourself aloud that you will complete the job, and then do so. You can draw parallels between a home repair project that is tricky to complete and a cartoon character that is tricky to draw. When your initial attempts are unsuccessful, you can note that those setbacks are temporary and surmountable much like cartoon hands that don't look right. You can explore why setbacks happened and what you learned from them. You can verbalize "I'm not quitting," even when you have to start over from scratch, like crumpling up a piece of paper and starting fresh. You can take inventory of what you have learned so far and how far you need to go. You can reflect on your eventual success and how you got there as a result of some failures. Your narrative of the home improvement project may make an impression on your child. It can help make the process of learning through failure seem natural, impersonal, and necessary.

When facing headwinds, you can be an example for how to remain steadfast despite the strong resistance. Some of your strongest headwinds will come from your child herself, in the form of defiance. There will be times when her opposition to your authority will be justified and worthy of consideration. But there will also be times when there is no room for negotiation, when rules must be enforced without debate, and you must stand your ground. In these circumstances you get to demonstrate consistency and persistence.

There is a tone of voice that you can develop for these types of situations, and when used correctly it will be incredibly powerful. In order for it to work you must convince yourself that the child will comply, and gently but firmly make your statement. Your words will demonstrate your position, and the way in which they are delivered will demonstrate your seriousness. Look directly into your child's eyes and speak with conviction. Speak with absolute self-assurance and certitude, as if your words were a stake that you have just pushed into the earth. Mastering the right tone of voice will take practice. It says "I mean what I say, I intend to follow through, and I love you." When done right, your child will feel the weight of your words and the finality they represent. And she will learn how resoluteness sounds, how it feels, and what it looks like, so she can eventually be able to deliver it.

My five-year-old son delivered it after a lengthy dinner that did not end until bedtime. I told him that there was no time for piano practice. He found this idea to be unacceptable. He wanted to have the boxes checked off for his piano practice log. I argued that I would not help him with his practice because I was busy cleaning the kitchen, and Mom would not help him because she was busy getting his sister ready for bed. These reasons were not good enough for him. He balled up his fists and said with words as solid as a brick wall, "I will not go to my piano lesson on Saturday without all my checks," and then walked to the piano and began playing scales all by himself. I can't be certain whether he was pushed to the piano bench by the prospect of a completed practice log or pulled there by his own desires, but he earned his checks that night.

A determined child will find a way to persist through the drudgery of raking a yard full of leaves. She will flounder while drawing that cartoon character, yet continue to practice and discover for herself the best techniques to use. She will work against resistance to meet her commitments, like resolutely completing piano practice assignments.

As her determination flourishes, she can learn how to apply it to her long-term goals. In the field of psychology, and as popularized by Angela Duckworth, long-term determination is referred to as "grit." It is characterized by the courage to set long-term goals, potentially spanning years, and the stamina to see them through to completion, no matter the headwinds, delays, and setbacks.[61] Long-term determination involves doing difficult things that require prolonged effort without regular feedback. It requires a combination of zeal and persistence of motive.

As your child's determination grows with her growth, so should your example. So, do difficult things. Exhibit grit. You have high expectations for your child, so it is only fair that you also set high expectations for yourself. Set long-range goals and then work to meet them. Learn a language, or learn how to play an instrument, or earn a degree, or tackle a major home improvement project, or save coins for a sizable purchase, or write a book, or anything else that will excite and challenge you. Talk about your enjoyment of doing things that are hard, and the exhilarating feeling of gratification when you make improvements. Publicize your struggles, failures, and eventual attainment of your expectations. Do this exactly as before, only on a longer timescale.

The high expectations that you set for yourself and for your child are a form of optimism. They are implicit statements of belief. Every so often, however, they should be made explicit. A child should know that her parents have faith in her abilities. A well-placed "You can really make lifelike drawings when you put your mind to it" can do wonders. Your optimism will rouse her own optimism and help stoke the flames of determination. This concept is captured by the company Avon, who state in their core values that belief empowers people to be their best: "Believe in someone—and show it—and that person will move mountains to prove you're right."[62]

A determined child will use all that she has, leaving nothing on the field. She will stay up late, skip meals, and try over and over again if that's what it takes to meet her objectives. She will pour her entire self into an effort, and she will get it done.

Conscientiousness

Now that she has tackled challenges, it is time for your child to get the details right, too. A task done with conscientiousness is a task done with orderliness and carefulness. Being orderly means working with deliberation and organization. It requires pre-task planning. Being careful means being thorough about details and vigilant regarding progress. It requires post-task checking.

With the knowledge that the task is to be bookended by planning and checking, the actual doing of the task will be carried out differently. The act of planning beforehand sets performance expectations. A task well planned is therefore a task done with attention to detail, so that those performance expectations may be met. Knowing that the task will be checked afterward starts a mental status meter, allowing one to keep the progress on track. Meeting expectations can result in the expectations being raised for the next time. If the performance is below expectations, then the task is redone, making this an iterative process.

In business management, this process is called the "control circle." The control circle is an iterative cycle comprising the four steps of plan, do, check, and act. Each of the four plan-do-check-act operations are intended to be explicitly implemented. For children, the two explicit steps of planning beforehand and checking afterward are enough to remember.

Bear in mind, though, that even two steps can be complicated for a small child to remember. For this reason, the walk-before-run approach is recommended for instilling conscientiousness. Planning can be modeled in some situations, and checking can be modeled in others, before combining them in any given undertaking.

Let your child observe you using planning tools. The tactile experience of using physical planning tools can be more instructive, even though electronic options are available. Use such tools frequently and involve her when possible. When she asks you questions about what you are doing, take time to answer.

Keep calendars. Post a calendar in a common area like on the refrigerator or on a countertop. Mark an important date like a family vacation and count down the days together.

Make lists. Write down the things that need to be packed for the vacation. Allow your child to contribute items to the list. Take the list to the store and have her help you pick up the items that you do not already have. Cross off the items on the list together as you pack them.

Use maps. Trace out the vacation travel route on a road map. Show her how to use the map along the way to monitor progress, count miles, identify landmarks, find gas and food, and anticipate rest areas.

Organize schedules. Schedule a busy vacation day. Verbalize how the pieces of the day's activities fit together, including where the dependencies are, what drives the order of doing things, and how logistical decisions are made.

Make age-appropriate planning tools available to your child. Blank paper, lined paper, and graph paper all have different functions. Keep copious stocks of different kinds of paper. Replenish writing utensils as needed. Pencils, pens, crayons, and markers can all be kept available. Place them in the home, in the car, and in coat pockets. Have folders, binders, and calendars at her disposal. Make sure she has her own clock or watch. Some of these things may sit idle for long stretches. That's okay. When she is ready to use them and asks questions about any of these items, entertain them to her satisfaction.

Let your child observe you checking your work after it has ostensibly been completed. When the result is unsatisfactory, let her see you redo the work. And let it be known when you are satisfied with your work product.

Scan the floor after you and your child have put a game away. If there is a stray game piece, then reopen the box, place the piece in its designated compartment, close the box, and put it away properly. Take a moment to admire the neatly stacked games.

Do a room-by-room inspection after vacuuming. Pick up large pieces of lint, crumbs, and scraps of paper that the vacuum may have missed. Offer commentary while you do it, and enlist your child's help. Express satisfaction when the floors are spotless, and that they will be at least as spotless next time.

After years of planning and checking activities performed separately in many scenarios by both parent and child, the child will perceive these operations as normal. Such a child can then be expected to use planning and checking together when it becomes developmentally appropriate for her to do so. At this point it will not be an overextension of her faculties, but a natural extension of behaviors she has already normalized.

So help her to put it together. Do things conscientiously, with planning beforehand and checking afterward. Be conscientious.

Show her how to deep clean her room. Start with a simple plan, such as taking everything out of the room, cleaning the empty room, and then restoring everything to its proper place. Then build out the finer points of the plan. Where will everything go when it is moved out of the room? In a hallway? In boxes? Do we have boxes? Or should the room be tackled piecemeal so the clutter can be shuffled to one quadrant of the room while another is being worked on? Will the room be reorganized? Furniture rearranged? Toys reassigned? Maybe lesser used items can be relegated to a basement or garage, or given away or sold. Piles may need to be created to classify the items while the work progresses. After the planning is completed, you can help with the actual work, or at least provide general oversight.

Check the quality once the job is complete. There may be small paper scraps in between furnishings and the wall that need to be removed. Make sure those scraps are cleared out. Some items may have been scuttled into the closet. See that those items are tended to by having the whole operation redone on the closet scale. The desk may be organized into neat stacks of papers, but the stacks themselves may be in disarray. Provide file folders so that it may be made right. Once she has been shown how to conscientiously clean a room, she can do it without help next time.

Without optimism and determination, there cannot be conscientiousness. Conscientiousness is therefore an advanced skill. It is important that the lessons of conscientiousness are not expected to be absorbed too soon, and that the types of activities that can build conscientiousness are not thrust upon the child before she is ready.

The activities a child does are rarely themselves the point, anyway. The floor will get more crumbs on it. The clean room will become messy again. The cleaning was never important in and of itself, but for how the child uses these types of activities to make her character. From the cleaning, she may better herself, she may instill herself with conscientiousness. Once a child has developed conscientiousness, she may take it with her through life. She may apply it to the activities that actually are important, as determined by her. Unlike the organized room and the painted walls, the character she builds will not fade over time but strengthen.

The six illustrative character traits presented here may be exemplary, but they do not make a comprehensive or absolute list. There are scores of virtuous character traits that would be beneficial for a child to have. To flood one's mind with the particulars of them all, and then to try to model the right one, in the right way, for the right situation, would be a futile exercise for a parent. I have tried to streamline the information by identifying the most illustrative character traits for helping little people become the best big people they can be.

You can lay the groundwork for your child's well-being, and you can start from birth. The imitative instinct provides you the opportunity to show your children behaviors that will return signals that they matter and can make an impact. You get to guide your child through that critical first walk through the snow. You get to guide her as she leaves her first footprints, and as you leave yours as a parent. Good character begets good character. Gearing your example toward the benefit of your child will shape her direction through life and, you will find, your own as well.

FIRST FOOTPRINT QUESTIONS

Providing a good character example is simple in concept but not necessarily easy in practice. Once becoming a parent to impressionable children you may find yourself, as I found myself, struggling to be a better person than you had been for your entire life previously. Cutting a new path for yourself is a great undertaking. But it is achievable, for through your children you have great motivation. When you find yourself questioning whether any contemplated behavior or parenting tactic is fitting, regardless of whether it is directly related to the six specific character traits already addressed, a simple "first footprint" question can help you come to an answer. By selecting a question like the ones in the box below, or any such question that strikes a chord with you, you will find the answer in your heart and will know what to do.

TOOL: FIRST FOOTPRINT QUESTIONS

Use this list of questions to explore how your behavior may be perceived in other contexts, and how it may be repeated by your child in other contexts.

Would I want my child to behave the same way—like me—toward me, my spouse, or my family?
For example, you feel frustrated because your child is trying to learn a new game and you have explained the same rule multiple times, but she still doesn't get it. You want to raise your voice and say, "No, no, no! I already told you to only take one card! Can't you understand that?" Well, would you want your child to talk to you in that way? Certainly not. Because it is hard for a child to articulate her thoughts, she will frequently experience the frustration of being misunderstood by others, including you. You probably don't want her default attitude to be indignant impatience whenever

this happens. So find another approach to teaching your child the game and dealing with your own frustration.

Is that how you want your child to treat her siblings or her friends?
For example, your small child has reached onto your night-stand and taken your glasses, and you are worried that she will break them. Your first thought is to wrench the spectacles from her hand. But is that how you want your child to react when she sees her sibling playing with a prized toy of hers? If you would like your child to have conflict resolution strategies more advanced than raw aggression, and a notion of justice beyond "might makes right," then this first footprint question will probably tell you to think again.

Would I like my child to repeat the behavior in other settings?
For example, you are driving down the street and are cut off by another car. Your child blurts out, "That knucklehead needs driving lessons!" Would it be okay if your child resorted to name-calling when one of her classmates in school answered a question incorrectly? You may find humor in those words when they come from the mouth of a small child, but the first footprint question will likely lead you to the conclusion that instead of laughing you should start modeling more respectful attitudes toward other drivers and be more forgiving to other people in general.

The first footprint questions can provide clarity with regard to tactical approach, disposition, communication style, and even tone of voice. An example situation is when your child is persistently asking questions. If your inclination is to answer her with "Not now, I'm busy" or "You wouldn't understand," then the first footprint questions would help bring the perspective that to follow through with that kind of response would be to teach your child to take a dismissive attitude toward her playmates, siblings, or parents. A first footprint question would probably lead you to find different words and use them with a different tone of voice. It would help you choose a response that accomplishes your immediate goal while also modeling good character.

We should acknowledge here that the thought of maneuvering through the nuances as you model even one good character trait can be intimidating. Please remember to consider the descriptions of exemplary behaviors in this chapter to be idealized aspirations. It wouldn't be healthy to pressure yourself into trying to meet impossible standards, but it would certainly be enriching—and entirely possible—to continually progress toward them.

As an example, I was that dad who would raise his voice in frustration as he repeated the board game instructions. I taught myself not to do that anymore, but I still get impatient when we play games. My children see my eyebrows pulled down and my jaw clenched, they hear my calmly but curtly given corrections, and they know that I have run out of patience. I don't like that I am modeling that kind of behavior for them. Yet I take comfort in the fact that I am a better role model than I was, and find inspiration in the idea that I am not as good a role model as I am going to be.

I like to imagine what it would be like if everybody raised their children by serving as a positive role model. We are each born with the capacity to be happy, to make meaningful connections to others, to discover ourselves, and to maximize our impact. Yet not all of us fully realize this potential. Consider the human experience, and how much of its failure and success rests on parenting. I think of all the helpful words unspoken, the hatred unrestrained, the accomplishments unattempted, and the creative passions unstirred but for positive parental examples. I imagine how many miscommunications could be bridged, how many conflicts could be resolved, how many opportunities could be exploited, and how many talents could be brought to bear through the aggregate effect of better upbringing. Parenting done well can change the world.

KEY POINTS

- Patterns of behavior originate in childhood, and are strongly influenced by the imitative instinct.
- Learned behaviors (character) combine with innate preferences (temperament) in the context of the environment to form a child's personality.
- Parents may encourage good character by shaping their child's environment: selecting and coaching good influences, and explaining bad influences.
- Parents may also encourage good character by modeling good character. Children learn the most from their parents' behavior. They follow your example. Modeling good character utilizes the "virtuous behavior" access point on the well-being cycle.
- Model the Golden Rule behaviors of compassion, honesty, and fairness as the foundation for building good relationships, the establishment of which reinforces to your child that they matter.
- Model optimism, determination, and conscientiousness as the foundation for developing capabilities, which your child will use to demonstrate to themselves that they can make an impact.
- Use first footprint questions to help you find suitable modeling behavior.

REFLECTION EXERCISES

How do you want to use your life to make a difference?
In order to answer this question, it may be helpful to consider the following related questions:

- How do you want to be remembered after you are gone?
- What ideas, values, or effects would you like to survive you?
- How will the world be different in a hundred years because of something you did?
- If you just learned that you had only a day to live, what would you regret not having done?
- If you just learned that you had only a year to live, what would you start doing?

_____

_____

_____

_____

_____

_____

Which behavior patterns are important to you?
These are the behavior patterns needed for your life to make the difference you described while answering the previous question. For example, if you want to use your life to inspire others, then enthusiasm may be important to you. If you want to help the poor, then generosity might be your most valued behavior. If you want to teach, then you might choose patience.

_____

_____

_____

How can you cultivate those behaviors in your home, for your children to emulate?
Consider the role of those behaviors in everyday situations.

_____

_____

_____

What challenges will you face as you cultivate those behaviors in interactions with your children?
Consider how your own personality, experiences, and circumstances factor in to your ability to execute those behaviors.

_____

_____

_____

How will meeting those challenges help you improve other facets of your life?
Consider both the immediate and long-term effects of being better able to apply those behaviors not only at home, but across all of life's domains.

_____

_____

_____

CHAPTER 4

Exemplify Virtuous Behaviors in Hot Moments

T he virtuous behavior term on the well-being cycle is an access point through which parents can transfer momentum. Perhaps the most opportune time to model virtuous behaviors is under stressful conditions. This is because the experiences that have the greatest influence on your child are the ones that are associated with heightened emotions, especially negative emotions. Those powerful experiences can be referred to as "hot moments." Hot moments are the critical learning experiences when a child gradually learns to separate emotions from behaviors. But hot moments are volatile, and the potential for learning can easily be wasted.

The environment set by us as parents determines whether these moments are constructive or destructive. Without a patient, composed, and respectful parent, hot moments may be too emotionally overwhelming to allow a child to take control of his behavior. He may find himself weakened by the stress.

In comparison, with a patient, composed, and respectful parent, hot moments are constructive and become opportunities for a child to cultivate his own virtuous behaviors. Hot moments are opportunities for your child to forge the steel of his character, and set the stage for an optimal life experience in adulthood.

Hot moments may be as trying for parents as they are for children. As it turns out, they may be just as impactful. They are opportunities for parents to practice their own virtuous behaviors, and forge the steel of their own character. They are opportunities for both parent and child to advance through well-being cycles.

Hot moments should therefore be welcomed as the highly impactful experiences that they are.

MAKE-OR-BREAK MOMENTS

THE IMPORTANCE OF HOT MOMENTS

For a child with limited tools and vocabulary at his disposal, such as with toddlers, the only recourse for an emotional setback may seem to be whining, screaming, crying, or thrashing. This is because young children lack the ability to separate emotions from behaviors. They lack the virtues of patience and composure.

In *The Happiest Toddler on the Block*, Dr. Harvey Karp compares toddlers to little cavemen in this regard.[63] Unsure of what is happening and what to do about it, children employ crude coping mechanisms for emotional upheavals. In time, according to Karp, they will learn the rhythms of emotional upheavals so that they can eventually discover how to predict them. Then they may learn how to react to them using increasingly sophisticated behaviors, continually under development as their growing cavemen brains transition from prehistoric to modern functioning levels.

A level of mastery can only come through trial and error, concurrent with their natural psychological evolution. A child needs years to develop the ability to display measured behaviors amid emotional chaos. Such refinement can only happen through experience. There must be hot moments.

THE VOLATILITY OF HOT MOMENTS

For a busy parent, a child's heightened emotional state presents an intense environment. It seems as though everything else grinds to a halt during a child's emotional meltdown. This can be frustrating.

From a parent's perspective, the child may appear to have malicious intentions. A parent may imagine the child is being purposefully irritating. He may seem to be using emotional leverage to hold his parent's attention captive.

It can also feel as though a child's emotional meltdown will last forever. This can amplify a parent's frustration. Anger can build as the seconds pass. A minor turn of events can easily catalyze feelings of rage.

For a child, his heightened emotional state is an especially intense environment. This is because the strong feelings are relatively unknown to the child. He may use his imagination to fill his knowledge gaps.

He may imagine his anguish is caused by parents having malicious intentions. To understand how this could be so, it helps to try to see the world through the eyes of a child.

From a child's perspective, parents are like giant magical superbeings whom he loves dearly. His very survival depends on the benevolence of these loving superbeings. But sometimes they seem to arbitrarily withhold their powers, or use them for malicious purposes.

For example, a one-year-old screaming from discomfort might need diaper cream, but not be immediately treated. Unbeknownst to the child, the superbeings may simply not understand what the child really wants. Or a situation's remedy may be beyond their abilities, for example the instant healing of a skinned knee. They can change diapers, why not heal a knee? Maybe they use their powers to confiscate a piece of shiny broken glass picked up off the ground by the child, thwarting the child's curiosity. Or they may refuse to provide crayons from a high shelf because the child has expressed a desire to color the furniture.

In any of these scenarios the child, having limited understanding of the real underlying motives, may interpret the superbeings' actions or inaction as a relinquishment of love. With the love of these magical beings gone, outright abandonment is imminent.

From one denial of crayons, the child feels alone and as though his very survival is at risk.

A child may also imagine that the bad feelings will stay forever. The feelings then become amplified by fear. A seemingly minor turn of events can therefore catalyze waves of negative feelings, sweeping a child up in a torrent of emotions he doesn't understand and hasn't yet learned to master.

When your child encounters such intense distress, your patience will be tried. And if you lose your composure, then your child's negative emotions, already a disorientating flood, will escalate further. Heightened negative emotions, regardless of where they originated, may spread among family members and multiply. Hot moments can easily spiral out of control.

PARENTS SET THE ENVIRONMENT

With so much tension built up between parent and child in these moments, someone needs to take the initiative to exercise the virtues of patience and composure. Someone needs to be an example and separate emotions from behaviors. That responsibility falls to you as the parent.

Parents, or "twenty-first century ambassadors" in Dr. Karp's terms, can coach their children throughout the modernization of their cavemen brains. They can inspire their children to exhibit behavioral control. And while doing so, they can remember to always demonstrate respect for the child.

This environment sets the stage for two things:

1) The parental patience and composure provides an atmosphere conducive to learning. The child may develop his own character, using his parent's example.
2) The parental respect positions the parent as an ally. It strengthens the parent–child relationship.

Within the stable emotional environment created by the parent, the child learns to be comfortable with his feelings. When he is comfortable with his feelings, his exploration and discovery of better ways to express them will be accelerated. The child will be able to focus on his actual behaviors instead of some frightful fantasy.

We parents will often respond to a distraught child by dictating behaviors, sometimes in a heavy-handed or derogatory manner. "Calm down" and "Stop that whining" are fairly common directives. We want to restore the emotional tone back to "normal." We want the behaviors to address the root issue and expect extinguishment of emotions to follow. But whatever has provoked those emotions has been overridden by the emotions themselves.[64] The emotions have become the issue. Behavior coaching must be suspended for the moment. Emotion coaching, to be discussed in the next chapter, is more appropriate. In order to enable that, we as parents must regulate our own emotional pressure.

This is why remaining calm during an emotional storm is of primary importance. Remaining calm begins with self-awareness, some tools for which will be shared later in this chapter (see pages 145–149). Exhibiting poise takes precedence over any discussions of coloring books or furniture maintenance. A child cannot be expected to feel loved or respected, or to focus on problem-solving, when his difficulties are met by unaccommodating parents bubbling over in fits of rage.

It should be stressed that remaining calm is not suppression of emotion. Whatever emotions you have, however dark and selfish they may seem, are worthy and valid. They are not in need of censorship. It is merely your expression of those emotions that needs to be managed. It is strictly external; it is behavioral. Retaining patience and composure means having calm words and actions *in the midst of* explosive thoughts and emotions. It means acknowledging negative emotions and expressing them in a nondestructive manner.

ACCEPTING AND WELCOMING HOT MOMENTS

Emotional storms are the make-or-break moments. A child's character is forged in the fires of hot moments, as is a strong child–parent relationship. Rather than being dreaded, these moments should be accepted and welcomed.

As a reality check, we should recognize that even though these moments *should be* accepted and welcomed, they won't *always be* accepted and welcomed. You are human, and have many conflicting demands placed upon your time, attention, and energy. Though we may strive to accept and welcome every single hot moment, that is really too much to ask of any parent. Nonetheless, stay aware that each time you do so, it is beneficial.

It is possible to accept and welcome hot moments when they are understood to be natural occurrences. It is possible when they are viewed as normal parts of your child's learning process. It is possible when they are treated as the powerful moments that they are.

Hot moments are natural occurrences. A family is comprised of multiple people having different knowledge, different ideas, different ways of thinking, different priorities, different motivations, and different capabilities all living under the same roof and needing to function as a unit. There are bound to be misunderstandings and disagreements leading to heightened emotions. It would be unreasonable to expect otherwise.

Hot moments are normal parts of the learning process. A child needs to learn to develop good behaviors alongside rough emotions. Unless he has the freedom to experience his emotions in an accepting environment, the child will not have the chance to do so. Your child's negative emotions are just as valid as yours. Inappropriate behaviors should be discouraged, but never the emotions that spawned those behaviors. However unsophisticated his expression of feelings may be, a child has a right to feel anger, disappointment, or frustration.

Hot moments are powerful. Any time you share a moment with your child when one of you is overcome by anger in the face of a disagreement, frustrated by unmet expectations, saddened by a failure to communicate, consumed by fear of a perceived danger, or agonizing over a fresh injury, you are playing a pivotal role in a potentially momentous occasion in your child's life.

Attempting to forgo hot moments is not only futile and counterproductive, it is also irrational. Wanting to avoid hot moments is wanting your child to have character skills but not wanting him to learn them. It is wanting a strong relationship with your child but not wanting to build it. Welcome the situations with heightened negative emotions for what they are: valuable opportunities for forging the steel of character and relationships.

POTENTIAL FOR GREAT DAMAGE

When emotional storms are treated by parents as shameful episodes to be avoided or cut short, their unrealistic expectations showing in exasperated facial expressions, aggressive tones of voice, harsh words, or physical aggression, then the child will view the parent as an adversary. Hemmed in by the cause of the hot moment, his own inner turmoil, and his parent's displeasure, the child is unable to choose a focal point. He may frantically hurl forth ill-conceived behaviors in the hope that something will miraculously work. Alternatively, he may smother the emotional storm into silence for fear of losing his parent's love and respect. As a result, emotional storms will remain scary and may be forever dealt with in a state of shame, frustration, and ineptitude.

Parents can make disastrous mistakes in the heat of the moment. Words can be spoken that can never be taken back, actions can be taken that can never be undone, and attitudes can be expressed that, to an impressionable child, can never be forgotten. Even though we can never be perfect stewards of hot moments, we parents must remain vigilant against their destructive spiraling out of control.

As you read these words, somewhere there is a small child huddled under his blanket, trembling for fear of retribution from his parents over some inconsequential offense; a child who, with a pervasive motive to avoid being caught in the next eruption, will grow into an adolescent voluntarily disconnected from his own parents; a child who will become a man heavy with anger, carrying through life vivid memories of his mistreatment, yet sparse recollection of any infractions that triggered it. For this child, experiences under heightened emotions are producing tragic outcomes, subtracting daily from the person he is capable of becoming.

POTENTIAL FOR GREAT BENEFIT

But where there is potential for great damage, there is potential for great benefit. Like metal exposed to the heat in a furnace, your child may either lose potential or draw strength from experiences under the heat of his heightened emotions.

The difference between a child losing potential and gaining strength is a good parental example. Character skills, like steel, are often forged under high temperatures and pressures. Hot moments provide the fires, while parents provide the guidance.

With calm parental guidance through the hot moment, a child can focus. Undistracted by flights of fantasy and inflammatory parental behaviors, he can address the root cause of the hot moment. He can weave his emotional intelligence skills into virtuous behaviors.

You and your child are also using the fires of hot moments to forge lifelong bonds between you. Your perspectives and motives may be in direct opposition to one another, yet through your unwavering support the relationship gains strength. Being there for your child through an emotional storm, listening without judgment, supporting without criticism, and helping without condescension are the behaviors that build lasting bridges of trust and respect. You get to position yourself as the home base, as the place your child can go to in moments of doubt to be accepted, listened to, and understood; the place where he feels that his viewpoints and opinions are valued; the place where he feels important, and where he receives confirmation that he matters. It is how your child learns that you can be counted on in times of trouble. It is also how your child learns the types of behaviors that go into building a healthy relationship.

BE THE MOLD

You are like the mold that supports and guides the molten steel. Tempered over multiple exposures to the heat, the mold is strong. It can help the steel harness the heat, to develop its own strength. So behave like a mold: brave the heat; be firm and steady; and apply the right temperature and pressure.

BRAVE THE HEAT

Not all hot moments are created equal. Sometimes hot moments are unlikely to be productive. In those cases, the heat can be preempted or quenched, when possible. Parents need a way to distinguish between hot moments that are productive, and those that are not.

The distinguishing factor is whether your parenting purpose is being transgressed. If your parenting purpose is at stake, the heat should be braved. For me, they are the times that are potentially harmful to my child's adulthood. For example, an ardent dispute over a toy should not be cut short, but used as an opportunity to develop the concepts of sharing and fairness. Moments like these are prime character-building opportunities; they are opportunities to raise adults.

If your child is begging to leave a bandage on his minor elbow scuff because he is afraid to take it off, then you might decide to alleviate or avoid the heat. If your parenting purpose is not at stake, why not let him wait until tomorrow? Or if he is about to burst with frustration because he is unable to reach a book on a high shelf, what possible reason could there be to not help him?

Hot moments like these are often avoidable because no one knows your child better than you. You will be able to recognize his telltale signs such as whining, irritability, and fidgeting. If a request is made that portends emotional distress, and the potential point of contention is not worth a conflict, then you can comply.

If the child afraid to remove his bandage has an acute wound that you know to be dirty, however, then your purpose will probably tell you to protect him from infection by cleaning the wound. The child will beg to delay the aid until tomorrow. He is afraid to see the wound underneath, to witness blood, or to be left in pain. He wants to avoid the heat. Sidestepping the wound care regimen, and pacifying the child, would certainly be the easiest short-term option for the parent. But infections can be debilitating, and even fatal. The wound must be tended, and the child must cope with his feelings of panic and fear. He must control his impulses to avoid discomfort, and instead exhibit courageous behavior.

If the child unable to reach the book is shouting demands, waging all-inclusive protests, or thrashing indiscriminately, then your purpose may preclude you from immediately handing him the book. Ignoring the outburst and retrieving the book would certainly be the path of least resistance. But making such disrespectful behavior profitable for the child would incentivize him to do it again in the future. For me, that would run counter to my purpose of raising adults. I would deal with the heightened emotions so the child could explore more civilized ways of conveying his needs.

One time, at a gathering, my daughter tried to take a toy away from my son. He held the toy out of reach, and she started crying. I tried to soothe her. I wanted to explain the principles of fairness and not getting everything you want. But another parent had heard the crying and came in to help me by offering cookies. The kids accepted the cookies, the crying stopped, and the toy was forgotten. But nothing was learned from that. Learning to share is hard, especially for a two-year-old. It involves some screaming. Dealing with that is not easy or peaceful. The heat was escaped that day when it should have been braved.

Indeed, the quickest way past such emotional storms is often around them. In many instances, parents accept the bargain of capitulating to the child's demands in order to avoid a protracted impasse. They offer distractions or cede authority for the sake of cooling the child's temper. But immediate relief for the sake of a peaceful kid only diminishes his chances to become a peaceful adult. The most constructive way past emotional storms is not around them, but through them.

Again, you have many demands placed upon you. You will sometimes find yourself without the luxury of being able to see an emotional storm through, even when your parenting purpose is being transgressed. For example, your child may have a breakdown in the middle of an otherwise peaceful airplane flight. You may decide to offer whatever concession is being requested, as the other passengers would not appreciate your handling the situation diligently and patiently. Or you may have a schedule to keep, in which case you may need to forgo any coaching until a more appropriate time. These would be reasonable actions to take. If situations like this nonetheless leave you feeling dismayed because you have lost the opportunity, try to take heart in the fact that your child will probably soon accommodate you with another one.

By braving the heat with your child whenever necessary and possible, you can channel its energy into character development. You can also fortify the relationship between you and your child, demonstrating to him the behaviors he can use to connect with others. The more arduous path, the one that involves enduring the heat, is the one that forges steel.

BE FIRM AND STEADY

Deciding to brave the heat is one thing, but surviving the heat is another. When we decide to brave the heat we are still in the beginning stage, with a child afraid to clean a wound or screaming to be given a book. We can easily envision the end, the child with the wound cleaned having conquered his fear, or with the book in hand having politely asked for it. It is the part between the beginning and the end that we often fail to visualize accurately. We tend to underestimate the middle.

The middle may take longer and involve more twists, turns, delays, and reversals than expected. When we are in the middle, it seems as though the end will not come. We question the decision to brave the heat and contemplate resorting to the shortcuts that we initially rejected. But the end will come and we will survive. When in the middle, staying firm in purpose and steady in your decision is essential.

The child afraid to remove the bandage will know your motives when you verbalize that you love him and will protect him from infection for his future health. He will then understand the unchanging decision that follows from it: the wound must be cleaned. Guided by your purpose, you persuade the frightened child to accept treatment. By listening to your child's concerns, conveying your understanding, and reiterating what must be done and why, you slowly wear down the walls of resistance and fear. You work directly through the source of distress with your child, without acquiescence, distractions, or other disconnected responses. Your child gets the care he needs, and also benefits from the experience of overcoming an obstacle that at first sight seemed insurmountable.

The child unable to reach the book will need time to digest his situation. Surging hormones and wildly firing synapses might direct his behaviors all the while. Allow your emotions to ebb and flow with those of your child for as many cycles as are necessary to get through it, all the while keeping a cool exterior demeanor. Remain firm in the purpose of raising the child to live a life of courteousness. Remain steady in the decision to await a civil request. Shortcuts may make you think you've come to a resolution quickly, but you would find the need to revisit the issue. So let the episode run its course without suppression or premature conclusion.

The mold must remain in place until the steel is cast. Without the sturdiness of the mold, the steel will simply deform under the heat. The mold provides a consistent, secure environment in which the steel may discover its limits and find its form. It remains steady and firm even as the steel pushes back.

Your child, in need of structure and boundaries, may find them both in your firmness and steadiness. He can use the secure environment you provide to develop basic character skills. And the shared experience of finding a path from anguish to calm, your support never wavering throughout the uncertain middle, is a powerful lesson on relationship-building behaviors.

APPLY THE RIGHT TEMPERATURE

It is difficult to remain cool when facing resistance. But if the mold overheats, then the steel will not set. The steel may appear to set while the mold is hot, but, like the child of the authoritarian disapprover who temporarily conforms out of fear, it will run off after the mold is released. The mold needs to be cooler than the steel so it may draw in some of the heat.

Losing your patience undermines your child's confidence. Destructive expressions of anger like yelling, hitting, or throwing frightens him into believing that he is just not good enough. Because something drew such ire from you, he might believe that it must be something about him. He may begin to mistrust his own abilities, or believe his emotions to be invalid. He may feel as though he is undeserving of love. He can become so mentally taxed with questioning himself and his self-worth that he has insufficient cognitive capacity remaining to learn character skills.

Losing your patience also serves to foster resentment. As revenge, the child may intentionally behave in ways that will displease you. And, having learned through your example that aggression is the appropriate tool to use when dealing with others, he directs his aggression squarely at you.

Remain cool in as many hot moments as possible so you can be a model for self-control and for compassion. Your calm demeanor will demonstrate your knowledge that this emotional storm is a temporary state. Your child, confident that he is in chartered territory, may focus his energies on character development and relationship growth. And you get to serve as his trusted coach.

APPLY THE RIGHT PRESSURE

By virtue of being stronger than the steel, the mold is capable of providing firm and steady support under duress. Because of its superior strength, however, it must also be careful not to crush the steel under its power. Overexertion of pressure would compromise the integrity of the steel's structure, much like criticism, humiliation, and mockery crush the spirit of a child, as they simultaneously destroy parent–child relationships.

In *Raising an Emotionally Intelligent Child,* Gottman describes these destructive tactics and their negative effects on a child's self-worth. He relates how some parents express their frustration by mocking their children's comments, laughing at their emotional expressions, labeling them with over-generalized negative descriptions, serving generous portions of harsh censure, or relentlessly peppering them with complaints.[65] He reports that children subjected to such treatment have been shown to have more academic, social, and behavioral problems, as well as higher levels of stress-related hormones and more illnesses.

Because parents using high-pressure tactics can deliver their insults without yelling, they may think their words are harmless. But they would be wrong. Just like the high-temperature parent who erupts in anger, the less explosive high-pressure parent creates conditions where the child expends his energy questioning himself instead of building character skills.

Gottman also discusses the impact on parent–child relationships. He claims that these high-pressure tactics also erode the foundation of trust.[66] Instead of enabling bonds to be built between parent and child, high-pressure tactics brew feelings of bitterness.

The fires of heightened emotions present your greatest opportunities to impact your child's future. You get to steer the impact in a positive direction simply by exercising restraint. You get to seize those opportunities by braving the heat and by remaining firm and steady through to cool-down.

The stakes involved in exercising restraint should not be underestimated. Failures to do so—the hostile actions or snide remarks—are yet another potential impediment to a child becoming who he may, robbing him of some immeasurable part of his potential, and saddling him with some incremental disadvantage that may never be known. When we instead acknowledge that our children are still learning, allow for mistakes, and patiently give them room to grow virtuous behaviors, we help them grow into the adults they can be.

CREATING THE EMOTIONAL ENVIRONMENT

"WHAT'S IN MY MIRROR?" QUESTIONS

Exercising patience is simple, but it is not easy. Children will generously provide you with frustrating circumstances. You will be no stranger to instructions not followed, desires not met, efforts not appreciated, and deadlines not prioritized. Having feelings of anger is often understandable. But lashing out would be a failure to manage that anger.

Lashing out in anger is a sign that you have become imprisoned in your own perspective. Expectations to always be listened to by your child, to always have your schedule prioritized by the child, and to always have messes preempted, do not take others' perspectives into account, and are unrealistic. We lash out when our unrealistic expectations are not met.

In order to remain patient, it helps to consider what the situation might look like from other viewpoints. Much like the first footprint questions from the previous chapter (see pages 123–124), what follows are some questions to help you explore perspectives. Rather than informing how the child might behave, however, the answers to these "What's in my mirror?" questions inform what kind of person you are. A mirror reflects back your own identity—these questions offer different perspectives to help you get a clear picture.

TOOL:
"WHAT'S IN MY MIRROR?" QUESTIONS

Use these questions to explore ways your behavior may be perceived from different perspectives, and how it reflects upon the kind of person you are.

What's in my mirror?
Companies sometimes install large mirrors behind their customer service desks.[67] They do this so that when their staff are visited by irate customers, the customers have a direct view of their own behavior. Angry customers, they have found, are less likely to shout, become aggressive, and exhibit ugly behavior when they can see themselves doing it. Now try to imagine a mirror positioned opposite you as you are about to lose your composure. How would you look? Now go one step further, and imagine it to be a one-way mirror with a camera behind it, recording every moment. If the footage were to be broadcast for all to see—your friends and family, your neighbors and coworkers—how would you look to them? Would you be proud of your management of the situation?

If I saw another parent doing this, what would I think?
Imagine a specific parent you know, one you respect, doing what you are tempted to do. Does the behavior suit your image of that parent? Would it change your image of that parent? Now try it again imagining a parent you don't respect. Does the behavior suit your image of that parent?

If my child could broadcast a message to his friends (and mine) today, what would it say?
What would he say about his own perceptions, motivations, and fears? Will he misrepresent your motives because he

does not understand them? How would you feel reading that tweet (or any other form of mass communication), and knowing that people you respect are also reading it?

If my child is able to remember this day, how will he reflect on it as an adult?

What impact will it have on his behaviors, his abilities, his confidence, his relationships? Will he have any memories of the infraction, or only of your outburst? If he were to write an article about the day's events, what would it say? How would you feel reading that article?

How would I handle this if it were someone else instead of my child?

Imagine the grown-up version of this situation, and someone else (your spouse, a colleague, a friend) is the offender. Would you treat them in a similar way to how you are tempted to treat your child right now? What would it say about you if you did?

How would I like someone to handle a similar situation with me?

Imagine, again, the grown-up version of this situation, but this time you are the offender. How would you like it if your boss or your spouse treated you the way you are about to treat your child? How would you feel about that person afterwards?

Use these perspective questions any time you feel an urge to blow up in anger, to yell, to insult, to coerce, to dismiss, or to disapprove. Pick one that resonates with you. Use it to consider how your contemplated behavior would reflect upon you.

HOT MOMENT LOG

If in the heat of the moment you fail to consider the perspective questions, you can still use them in retrospect to assess what you could have done differently. They can help you evaluate the approach you used, and formulate a plan to manage things differently next time. If you still find yourself losing your temper too often, it is helpful to track the incidents in a log like the one in Table 7 on the following page.

TOOL: HOT MOMENT LOG

Use this template (Table 7) to record the circumstances around emotionally trying interactions. Review the completed log and reflect upon ways these types of situations can be handled differently.

CHILD	DAY	TIME	PARENT EMOTION AND INTENSITY (1–5)	CHILD EMOTION AND INTENSITY (1–5)	SITUATION DETAILS	OUTCOME

TABLE 7. Hot Moment Log Template

What you write will be subjective, and the rankings will be on an arbitrary scale, but that doesn't matter. There are benefits to creating a written record as opposed to confining the events to your memory. Crystallizing your thoughts into written words forces you to ruminate on a description of the events. It allows you to unravel the details, grapple with the context, and process the actual meaning of what happened. Your intellect allows you to conveniently skip these steps when you recall events and draw conclusions in your head, without writing anything down. Downloading your brain onto paper also helps you to concentrate on identifying patterns of behavior and creating workable solutions instead of focusing your brainpower on simply storing the information.

The first time I used the log, I was losing my temper with my son a lot. After making a few entries and evaluating what I recorded, I learned that my anger was getting the best of me at the convergence of two conditions:

1) Pressing time constraints.
2) Unnecessary requests for help.

As an example, I would need to quickly take the kids to school so I could get to work for an early morning meeting, and my son would inexplicably refuse to put his shoes on without help. At four years old, he knew how to put his shoes on just fine. He did not need help. Was he willfully causing delays when he knew I was in a hurry?

With some research, I hypothesized that he was experiencing something called middle child syndrome (even though he wasn't a middle child). He wasn't purposefully delaying me, and he hadn't lost confidence in his abilities to operate independently. He was having an identity crisis.

My daughter was still a baby and getting help with everything. He would look at his sister and feel big and capable. But then he would look at Mom and Dad and feel small and incapable. He was big, but little. He was trying to figure out where he fit in. Maybe he feared he didn't fit in at all anymore.

Perhaps he perceived my stress in these mornings and it played into his insecurity. He needed to be reassured that he wasn't the source of my stress. Being little was his way of drawing that reassurance. So I decided to let him be little when he needed, to help with his shoes in the morning when asked, so he knew that he had a place in the family and was loved no matter what size he was. This must have given him the affirmation he needed, because the unnecessary requests for help stopped within a few days.

Another time I used the log, I learned that the problem was entirely mine. I was needlessly creating hot moments. The pattern that emerged was that I had been lacking compassion when managing multiple demands. For example, I was answering the third pressing question about how a new toy works while trying to use the bathroom, and doing so in an unnecessarily nasty tone.

My lack of patience in a single moment was introducing an air of tension that escalated throughout the day and affected the whole family. When I focused my efforts on reestablishing compassionate behavior, not to mention realistic expectations for life with a toddler and a preschooler, my patience returned. I was able to pleasantly explain that I wouldn't answer questions for a few minutes until I returned to the living room. With that, the familial friction dissipated.

Staying patient in hot moments starts with your mindset. It begins when you view your upset child not as trying to cause trouble, not as enjoying giving you stress, not as wanting to disturb the peace, but as attempting to forge steel. Using your patience, often summoned through consideration of different perspectives, you can let him forge *good* steel.

WE ALL MAKE MISTAKES

This chapter describes my greatest challenge as a parent. When I'm frustrated, exasperated, overtired, or reduced to anger by having to say the same thing ten times, knowing that I need to remain calm isn't always enough to keep me calm. In fact, I somehow manage to consistently find new and creative ways to defy my own advice. I've read enough on the subject of parenting to know that I am not alone in this regard.

So this is a good place to reiterate the point about setting reasonable expectations for yourself. Being patient, composed, and respectful is difficult. While it is good to have an appetite for doing difficult things, just remember to have a matching capacity for self-forgiveness. When you fall short, if you are like me, it will weigh heavy on your heart. But you have to give yourself permission to make things right again. Rather than internally dwelling on your failures or externally defending your actions, you owe it to your family to admit fault and apologize. Once you have done that, you are ready to learn from your mistakes.

You will find that it is not only your child who is forging character during hot moments. As your children mirror your own behavior back on you, you see yourself as you never before have. You learn what you like and dislike about yourself. You start to make your behavior choices much more seriously because they reflect not only on your character, and define not only your path in life, but also those of someone you love more than yourself. You become driven to improve and to reinvent parts of your character. You use your failings to derive strength and become the person you want to be. And all because you have power over and responsibility for, at a level unprecedented in your existence, the course of someone else's life.

The ability to learn from mistakes is one of the hallmarks of the human condition. It is part of the growth that a child needs to become an adult. It is also part of the growth that describes the optimal life experience. And because it is the work of a lifetime, it is never complete. Perhaps the most glorious part about this is that, hard as it may be, you can still learn from mistakes long past. You can reflect on how you raised your children when they were younger, make improvements today, and your children can still improve along with you. There is no statute of limitations on learning. Who you are today is different from who you were yesterday, and your identity continues to develop with each new behavior you assimilate.

Your identity is revealed in your most trying parenting moments. How you treat someone over whom you have total authority goes to the core of your character, right through to the marrow. As said by Abigail Van Buren, "The best index to a person's character is how he treats people who can't do him any good, and how he treats people who can't fight back."[68] What we may not realize is that a distressful episode with our child says more about us than about the child. The kind of parent you are does not simply reflect the kind of person you are. The kind of parent you are *is* the kind of person you are.

KEY POINTS

- Heightened emotions or "hot moments" are important. Your child needs to experience hot moments in order to develop appropriate behaviors for stressful conditions. Those behaviors will facilitate advancement along the well-being cycle.

- Hot moments may be the times when a child forges character, and when parent–child relationships can be strengthened. They may also be the times that spiral out of control and cause emotional damage.

- It is the parent's response that determines whether hot moments are destructive or constructive. The virtues of patience, composure, and respect, when exercised by parents, create the environment for a child to develop appropriate behaviors.

- Welcome and accept hot moments as the natural, normal, and powerful situations that they are.

- Be like the mold that forges the steel: brave the heat; be firm and steady; and apply the right temperature and pressure.

- Use the "What's in my mirror?" questions to help you consider your behaviors from other perspectives, and how they reflect on the kind of person you are.

- Use the hot moment log as a tool for reviewing your behavior in hot moments, and determining what you could do differently.

REFLECTION EXERCISES

What types of circumstances bring out the worst in you?
These are the circumstances for which you find it difficult to
separate your emotions from your behavior. For some people,
it is being ignored. For others, it is being interrupted. Or being
misunderstood. Or being made late for something. Perhaps it is
being inconvenienced by an unnecessary mess. Maybe the general stress from career or social environments carries over into
other aspects of your life. Whatever they are for you, these are
the circumstances most likely to test your resolve to stay true to
your parenting purpose.

_____

_____

_____

What helps you to remain calm in trying circumstances?
Perhaps being aware that you are near the end of your rope is
enough for you to regain control. Perhaps reframing the situation helps. Some reframing techniques were discussed on pages
146–149. Do you need to disengage for a few seconds to maintain
your composure? Some people count to ten before acting.

_____

_____

_____

PART III

Enabling Your Children to Become Their Best Adults

CHAPTER 5

Build Awareness

We are now changing our focus from the development of the parent to that of the child. We have so far discussed how your virtuous behavior as a parent is an access point on your child's well-being cycle, the four-step cycle introduced in Chapter One through which people generate well-being. We will now turn our attention to matter and impact. Matter and impact is another step on a child's well-being cycle, representing a different access point through which parents can transfer momentum.

We have already seen that parents can let their children know that they matter by being responsive (page 52). We have also explored how parents can let their children know they can make an impact through structure. Parental responsiveness is important in the domains of needs, emotions, and interests, while parental structure is important for communicating expectations, contingencies, and observations. We have identified that building awareness—of needs, emotions, interests, rules, contingencies, and the world at large—is a concrete, practical way of being responsive, and structuring the environment. Helping your children to develop these kinds of awareness is therefore one goal for those of you who wish to spur your child's creation of well-being.

In this chapter we will explore five practices for building awareness:

1) Encouraging exploration: encouraging children to discover the world in their own way.
2) Recognizing preferences: acknowledging and accommodating the set of preferences and interests unique to your child.
3) Explaining: communicating in a way suited to your child's preferences and interests.
4) Listening: understanding your child's perspective, taking into consideration your child's way of thinking.
5) Welcoming emotions: identifying and discussing emotions, especially in the throes of hot moments.

Doing all these things consistently will give your child the background to more effectively engage in social situations, and to more adeptly meet challenges. Over time, it will help your child to know herself and what she cares about, so that she is equipped to make her optimal life experience.

By recognizing preferences, listening, and welcoming emotions, you are being responsive to needs, emotions, and interests. By explaining the rules and contingencies, you are communicating expectations that the rules be followed. And by explaining and encouraging exploration of the world at large, you are providing structure and equipping your child with the knowledge to resolve problems.

Building an awareness of one's needs, emotions, interests, expectations, and the world at large does not happen by following a curriculum. And it does not happen quickly. It is an organic process that unfolds over several years, like the slow momentum build of a heavy wheel. It may not be easy, but it is an appropriate approach for parents whose purpose is to raise adults, and for parents who envision their adult children with maximized well-being.

ENCOURAGE EXPLORATION

THROUGH PLAY

A child explores her world through play. She instinctively knows that around corners, under rocks, and within her own imagination are wonderful things waiting to be discovered. As a child manipulates her world for pure recreation, she acquires knowledge across a range of subjects as diverse as the things she encounters.

So make sure your child encounters a diverse range of things that can be used in a variety of different ways. With simple, "open-ended" toys, your child can use her imagination. She can explore. Toys like building blocks (or building logs, building sticks, building magnets, etc.,) stacking and sorting toys, balls, art supplies, and train sets all have limitless possibilities. Likewise, a sandbox, some tools, a wooded area, and riding toys are all things that draw on her knowledge and experience for creative, self-directed play. Playthings like these engage her.

A child learns by playing. She builds mental agility as she sorts toys by colors, numbers, and shapes. She becomes familiar with physical principles like gravity as she pours, rolls, and throws. She learns mechanical principles as she manipulates pulleys, levers, and wheels.

And if her imagination stalls, that's okay too. Boredom is a chance to reflect on recent events, appraise the possibilities, take inventory of concerns, contemplate solutions, plan what's next, and be creative again.

Play is also how a child develops. Hand-eye coordination, gross motor skills, fine motor skills, and muscle strength are all promoted through the physical activity associated with play. As she follows her interests through extended play sessions, your child will build concentration, focus, and memory. She will learn about her unique skills and abilities.

You do not need to keep children in a constant state of engagement. Just make open-ended things available. So put open-ended things in your child's way. Leave a flashlight, a magnifying glass, a retracting tape measure, or some clay where she can reach them, and watch amazing things happen.

THROUGH SOCIALIZING

Make sure your child has opportunities to interact with people in unstructured settings. By sharing her amusement with playmates, she is gaining language proficiency and learning valuable social skills. So go outside without a plan.

Watch your child grapple with social puzzles. How does she find other kids? How does she approach another child with whom she wants to play, who is in a backyard, just out of reach? Or across a street? How does she assimilate herself into a group of children already engrossed in a game? How does she adjust her approach for the audience—is it the same approach for peers as for children slightly older? Is it the same approach for a group of children quietly talking as it is for a different group who are roughhousing? If those children are playing an unfamiliar game, how will she make herself comfortable asking about the rules of play? How does she propose changes to a game or a transition to new activities? What about reintegrating into play after a meal or a restroom break? How should she behave when playing the host, while the play is set at her own home? Does she share her toys and take turns? Does she offer refreshments? Does she ask for help cleaning up afterward? Does she help clean up when she is the guest? How will she handle disagreements? What does she do when implicated in gossip? Or when she is getting left out? When cliques form, and loyalties are inferred from innocent actions? What are the consequences of wronging a friend? Or challenging a rival?

These are puzzles because the right answer is dependent on where you are and with whom you are dealing. The answers are not simple, and need to be learned through trial and error. Even in a simple setting of children peacefully playing, there are layers of complexity under the surface. The children are learning to navigate a web of interdependent desires, decisions, and feelings.

Social interaction at any stage of life is complicated, but involves a fairly constant set of skills. It involves the ability to exhibit behaviors that follow the social rules. A strong foundation of social skills requires lots of practice, and it is best to start early. It is best to start in the home.

AT HOME

Play and interact with your child as the main activity, as the expectation, at home. Have lots of different kinds of games and puzzles available. Playing those games together is great practice in following rules, being fair, turn taking, sharing, strategizing, winning with humility, and losing with grace. Work together on those puzzles to build cooperation, problem-solving skills, and physical dexterity. Have fun roughhousing with your child, like wrestling on the floor or throwing her on the couch. Besides being fun, it helps to master the cycle of building excitement and then calming down.[69] It requires the players to find the right level of energy to exert, gauging the fun being had by the others involved, and detecting whether someone got hurt or is still playing.

However you and your child play, let her lead. Let her explore the fascinating events unfolding all around her. If a walk to the car is derailed by the sounds of a woodpecker, even if time is pressing, sometimes it's okay to spend some time listening to the woodpecker and trying to spot it. Support her creativity as she plays with a toy other than the way it was meant to be played with. Let her bounce a football. Let her break things to see what is inside, how it works, and what the different parts are called. Let some messes get made. Let her figure out what sounds are made when a box of something is shaken or banged upon, or what happens to the stuff inside when the box is overturned. It is tempting to stifle a child to keep things neat and orderly, or to keep a schedule, but doing so often limits the child and creates tension that can fill you with regret. Indulging in such small joys of life, within reasonable limits of course, not only enlightens your child but can also lighten your load.

As you play with your child, observe what she likes and what she does well. Encourage her pursuit of those interests—not your interests or what you think her interests should be. In other words, don't try to get her interested in things; find out what she is interested in and then enable deeper exploration of that.

THROUGH BOOKS

A great way for anyone to explore their interests is through books. Besides exploring immediate interests, reading books opens up topics that would otherwise remain unknown. Have a home rich with books suited to the tastes of your family members and beyond. So strongly do I feel about reading that I submit to you the following five assertions:

1) *Reading is knowledge.* A baby first looking at books comes to know that words are different things than pictures. With time, she observes that the words are arranged from left to right and top to bottom, with some help from punctuation. The words are separated by spaces. They are composed of letters that make sounds.

   Reading expands children's vocabularies much faster than not reading. It shows them new ways to put words together, improving their language skills. Reading introduces children to new subjects, lets them meet new people, visit new cultures, and encounter new situations all without ever leaving the pages of a book. The ability to read puts at their disposal the accumulated knowledge of all human history. Great thinkers and storytellers alike have had their ideas and imaginations reduced to the written word for all to consume.

2) *Reading is power.* It unlocks the world. Instructions for how to do things, directions to get places, and signs that tell you how to stay safe all require reading. Reading improves communication skills, judgment, concentration, critical thinking, and memory. Reading gives children a sense of control. That is why they like to read the same story over and over again. A child predicts what will happen next based on her memory of earlier readings and, as expected, she is correct. Reading also improves understanding of cause and effect, provides practice analyzing logical and illogical scenarios, enhances the ability to predict patterns, and teaches conflict resolution strategies.[70] Reading makes us smarter.

3) *Reading is magic.* It allows you to connect with other people you never met, and never could meet. You can learn from people who are far away and who lived long ago. Carl Sagan likened reading to channeling the author's thoughts, from another time and another place, into your mind.[71]

4) *Reading is fun.* It lets you explore new things, go to other worlds, and become other people through imagination. Trains talk, bears go to school, and sponges live in underwater pineapple houses.

5) *Reading changes lives.* It is nourishment for the mind. It turns you into a different person, someone better than you could have become had you never held a book.

THROUGH PURSUIT OF INTERESTS

Whatever kind of person your child develops into, help her feel accepted and loved. While she discovers the world through reading, playing, and interacting, she can also discover herself. Be sure to support her interests and help them develop into passions.

When my son was three years old, he elected to take a Chinese class held every Saturday near our house. The class was two and a half hours long. I was amazed he could stay focused for that long, and would have expected him to immediately run outside after the classes to play and burn off some pent-up energy. But he didn't. There was a piano in the building, and we usually stayed an extra half hour so that he could play the piano there. He did this every week. Clearly, he was keenly interested in piano. So we got him a toy piano for his fourth birthday. It came with a songbook, which he learned how to use. He taught himself how to play every song in that book. Later that year we were fortunate to receive an old piano as a gift from friends who had just bought themselves a new one. They knew that my son would make good use of it. He did enjoy playing it. When he turned five he started taking formal lessons. I never would have suggested piano as a recreational activity, but he gravitated toward it and so we encouraged his exploration of that interest.

It doesn't really matter what the subject is; the child should be allowed to follow her interests and develop her passions. Whether those interests and passions are career-worthy is irrelevant. There are valuable life skills in any concentrated effort. Even if my son is never destined to be a concert pianist, he is still learning hand-eye coordination, fractions, timing, sounds, and sound waves. He is learning teamwork by playing with others. He is learning patience and conscientiousness when tackling a difficult piece. He is learning to perform in front of a crowd without anxiety. He is learning how to harness his interests and talents in service of his own development. He is learning how to express himself, and most importantly he is learning *about* himself. These are all valuable skills whatever he makes of his future. He is learning these skills because he is exploring his passion, a passion that he is aware of, a passion that he can take with him wherever he decides to go in life.

One time at a friend's party, all the kids adjourned to the toy-filled basement while most of the adults chatted in the kitchen. A group of boys gathered around the air hockey table, clamoring to compete in the next match. One boy, his parents both upstairs, instead gravitated toward the baby dolls, strollers, and dress-up clothes. He selected a mermaid dress and witch hat as his favorites, and put them on. Someone must have reported his unique behavior to his mom, who came down the stairs to see what her son was doing. "Are you still wearing your dress?" she called. He appeared with a smile. She pulled out her camera. He exuberantly extended his arms to show off his costume. She snapped the picture, gave him a hug, and walked back upstairs. With that one small act, she publicly validated his inclination to play with "girly" toys. He wore the dress the rest of the evening, his mother having reinforced his confidence to follow his own path. And by going back upstairs, she allowed him to figure out how to self-advocate. But defending himself was unnecessary because her approval made acceptance of him the expectation.

When a child doesn't feel accepted by her parents, and learns that their parental love is conditional on some preconceived persona, then that child will bear harmful levels of anxiety. Her anxiety will force her to adapt a false self for the purpose of garnering parental acceptance. Over time, she will hone the details of this artificial identity in order to maintain her respectable status in the family system. Sadly, this false self develops at the expense of the true self. The true self will not emerge until later in life, if it hasn't already been forever lost. The child ruled by a false self, limited by internal struggles and coping mechanisms, will not take herself as far in life as she could have.[72]

Consider the example of Gillian Lynne, brilliantly and movingly recounted by British educator Sir Ken Robinson in a TED talk in 2006.[73] Young Gillian, growing up in 1930s England, fidgeted a lot. She could not sit still in school, and was labeled mentally disabled by school officials. On the advice of the school, Gillian's mother took her to see a doctor to diagnose her learning disability and help her find a more appropriate learning environment. The doctor observed Gillian anxiously sit on her hands to control her impulses as they talked, but then contentedly and gracefully move to the music on the radio when the doctor and mother left the room to speak privately. Pointing to Gillian through a window, the doctor said to Mrs. Lynne, "Gillian isn't sick. She's a dancer."

On the doctor's suggestion, continues Robinson, Mrs. Lynne enrolled Gillian in a dance school. Gillian walked into the room that first day of dance class and saw it full of people like her, "people who couldn't sit still," people who thought in terms of motion. Imagine how she felt to discover that she wasn't "wrong," that there was a place where her truest self would be accepted and could grow. More poignant than the fact that Gillian went on to become a world-renowned dancer, choreographing such plays as *Cats* and *The Phantom of the Opera*, is that Gillian discovered herself that day. What a squandering of human potential it would have been, what a tragic deficit in Gillian's personal well-being, if instead of being encouraged to explore herself Gillian was trained to stay still.

As long as a child is exposed to a broad range of subjects, she will discover what it is that makes her tick. She will find her way whether through dance, piano, hockey, robotics, or fashion. So make lots of options available to her. Offer her the world to explore, and as she learns and develops she will cultivate her passion. When she does, keep the doors of exploration open for her. Let her passion be her outlet, her sincere expression of self.

Let her develop the habits of discovering herself, polishing her self-expression, and feeling ownership of the results. Though the subject of her passions may change, she can carry those habits with her into adulthood. A young person who has spent her childhood thoroughly exploring herself and her surroundings, having learned to freely and comfortably express her true identity in context with her environment, will, as an adult, be able to write her own ticket to anywhere.

RECOGNIZE PREFERENCES

ACKNOWLEDGE AND ACCOMMODATE PREFERENCES

When children are aware of their inclinations, they become aware of who they are. The most significant inclinations are the ones thought to be innate and permanent. These are referred to as "preferences." Preferences include whether someone is private or outgoing, methodical or spontaneous, logical or sympathetic, decisive or deliberative, realistic or visionary. These types of preferences, mentioned in Chapter Three (pages 83–84), comprise the temperament part of personality.

Parents provide the environment in which their child's personality takes shape. In addition to helping your child develop character by providing examples, you can help your child discover preferences by recognizing those preferences. Recognizing preferences means acknowledging and identifying them. It also means taking one step further and accommodating them. Accommodating preferences involves allowing for their free expression, seeing the strengths in those preferences, feeding those strengths, and communicating boundaries where those strengths may become disadvantageous. Recognition of preferences, inclusive of acknowledgment and accommodation, is an express affirmation of their validity.

When parents show their children's preferences to be important through recognition, they are being responsive to needs. They are demonstrating that their children's genuine expressions of self are accepted, trusted, respected, and loved. A parent who knows a child's personality traits and makes her feel special because of them, and cares about her because of them—and sometimes in spite of them—lets her know that she matters.

So children must be free to exhibit their preferences so they can make a meaningful contribution to the interpersonal dynamic—an authentic contribution—so that what is being accepted, trusted, respected, and loved is irrefutably themselves.

Not who others want them to be, not who they wish they were, but what they *really* are, the core of their being, their bare selves.

THE MYERS–BRIGGS TYPE INDICATOR

Preferences can be better understood through the works of Katharine Briggs and Isabel Briggs Myers, a mother–daughter team who wrote about these temperamental traits in terms of how people think. According to *Gifts Differing: Understanding Personality Type* by Isabel Briggs Myers with her son Peter B. Myers, a large proportion of people's mental activity falls under the categories of either "perception" or "judgment."[74] The way people view a particular situation is governed by their perception style, and what they want to do about it depends on their style of judgment.

The model described by the authors in *Gifts Differing,* called the Myers–Briggs Type Indicator (MBTI), is well-established among general audiences, but has fallen out of favor in academic circles. Psychologists today more commonly use a model called "the Big Five."[75] The Big Five is a statistically generated list of personality traits, based on the language people use to describe personality. This model offers convenient personality traits to apply to experimental results and to predict behaviors, but does not account for the origins of those traits insofar as whether they are temperament or character.

The MBTI lacks statistical robustness, and is not predictive of behavior. For example, it is not correlated with one's relatedness or competence.[76] As mentioned in Chapter Three, temperament is neither good nor bad; it just *is*. What the MBTI offers is a model for describing what just *is*. It describes the temperament part of personality. It describes how people think. For our purposes, it can be useful simply for understanding how different people might use different thought processes to see from different perspectives. It can be used to help build bridges between parents and children of different temperaments.

The MBTI revolves around four sets of dichotomies involving how perception and judgment are used. This model was originally developed by psychologist Carl Jung, who recorded three dichotomies as empirical observations. Katharine Briggs and Isabel Briggs Myers later adapted his concepts for practical use while adding a fourth dichotomy:

1) *People are either introverts or extraverts.*
Introverts prefer to use their perception and judgment internally, such as on ideas, whereas extraverts are partial to wielding them externally, such as on people.[77] When deciding whether to go to the art museum, an introvert might want to think it through, whereas an extravert might want to talk it over.

2) *People perceive either by sensing or with intuition.*
People who prefer sensing are attuned to the signals coming from reality in order to build upon what is known, whereas those who prefer intuition are absorbed in apprehending the possibilities presented by what is unknown.[78] A sensing person might view a landscape painting by examining its colors and lines, whereas an intuitive person might wonder about the context and meaning behind the image.

3) *People judge either by thinking or by feeling.*
Those who prefer thinking are rational in their judgment, while those who prefer feeling make judgments according to their ideals.[79] A thinking person might consider whether a sculpture of a rider on a horse is true to life, while a feeling person might focus on the sense of nobility it conveys.

4) *People prefer either to perceive or judge the outer world.*
People who prefer to perceive their external environment tend to take in the world as they go through life, while people who prefer to judge their external environment are more apt to live according to some structure.[80] A perceiver may wish to casually browse the exhibits in a museum and go with the flow, while a judger may want to stick to plans and schedules.

Briggs Myers claims that people, from the time they are infants, favor the styles with which they are most comfortable. Children under four or five years old already display their introversion versus extraversion preference and their perceiving versus judging preference. As they grow, their other preferred styles are revealed.

ALLOW FOR FREE EXPRESSION
(INTROVERSION–EXTRAVERSION EXAMPLE)

Consider the introversion–extraversion dichotomy, and how two people occupying opposite sides of that dichotomy approach the world. The introvert derives energy from ideas, and therefore prefers a private environment conducive to quiet reflection. The introvert operates by thinking before acting, and conceives many of her actions in this quiet environment. The introvert slowly ponders new information in solitude, focused on comprehending its theoretical significance. Maintaining privacy in communications with others, the introvert can be hard to know, dealing with fewer people but developing deep relationships with those few.

By contrast, the extravert derives energy from people, and prefers a high activity environment. Surrounded by people, the outgoing extravert communicates freely. The extravert is easy to know and develops many relationships. The extravert processes new information by discussing it with others in a collaborative fashion, focused on comprehending the practical aspects first. The extravert operates by doing, and tries out ideas then thinks over the results.

How might these two different types of people interact? How might they perceive each other's behavior? Without understanding that people have different ways of thinking, the introvert and the extravert may easily misunderstand one another. How easily one might attribute a "poor" behavior choice to a faulty thought process, when in fact it may simply be an alternate behavior choice derived from a different yet equally valid thought process.

Now imagine a parent and child, the former an extravert and the latter an introvert, having just received the child's report card. The marks are lower than expected. The introvert child slips away to a quiet room to ponder the implications of this new information, and is followed by the extravert parent who is already talking about options for improvement. Feeling overwhelmed by the unwelcome interruption to necessary solitary thought, the introvert child rebuffs the extravert parent. Perplexed by the introvert child's apparent covertness despite the necessity for collaboration, the extravert parent's resolve hardens.

The parent meets the child's reserved demeanor with increasingly expressive attempts to communicate. The parent's insistence upon discussion is viewed by the naturally private child as obnoxious. The child becomes perturbed by the behavior of the parent. The child's reluctance to engage is interpreted by the naturally outgoing parent as a sign of being distant. The tone of the parent becomes accusatory.

The extravert parent, frustrated by a lack of progress, faults the child for being idle. The parent can't understand why the child would sit motionless at a time when action is crucial. Likewise, the introvert child, on the defensive, blames the parent's reckless attitude. The child can't understand why critical attempts to reflect on the issues would be thwarted for the sake of springing into mindless action. Distraught by the needless confrontation, the child feels betrayed.

After repeated similar incidents, the child concludes that the parent is intrusive. The parent, on the other hand, sees the child as detached. The parent believes the child to have a problem. Through the inherent credibility of the parent, the child may become convinced that there is indeed something wrong with her.

Although neither party is using a flawed approach to processing the information in the report card, they are each ascribing negative motivations to the behaviors of the other. Why?

Figure 5 below breaks the introversion–extraversion dichotomy into representative sub-dichotomies. Each sub-dichotomy of preferences is illustrated as opposite ends of a continuum. As shown in the first row, people prefer to derive energy along a continuum of ideas versus people. Beneath each continuum are adjectives in colored boxes describing how those preferences manifest themselves. An introvert who prefers to derive energy from ideas may be described as pensive. An extravert who prefers to derive energy from people may be described as sociable. It is possible to take extreme positions within these continua. An introvert may be completely uninterested in people, and be genuinely detached from others. An extravert may be truly uninterested in ideas, and be wholly intrusive upon people trying to think. However, occupying the extremes is rare.

TOOL: MYERS-BRIGGS DICHOTOMY CHARTS

Use the following charts (Figures 5–8) to help you to understand your child and yourself, and to find ways to communicate better.

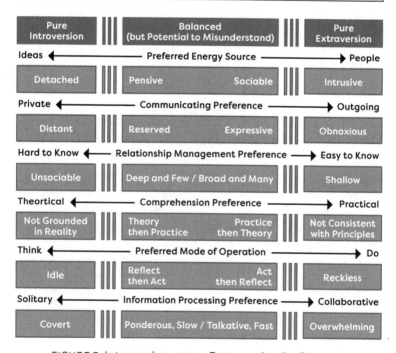

FIGURE 5. Introversion versus Extraversion Preferences

Ideas or people, as with the opposites in any other MBTI preference, are not meant to be mutually exclusive. People focus on their preference and then counterbalance it with some degree of the opposite. The common introvert and the common extravert are each concerned with both ideas and people, but in different ratios. The introvert who prefers ideas knows that she must have people with whom to share her ideas. The extravert who prefers people knows that she must have some ideas to share with those people. Thus, the preference and its opposite are complementary. They must be balanced.

You can use Figure 5 to assess the preferences of your child, yourself, and others. Simply consider which words best describe someone. Are those words predominantly on the left or the right side of the chart? Keep in mind that although the MBTI describes thought preferences in an insightfully formulated set of opposites, people do not necessarily conform to either-or categories. It is possible for someone to be in the middle of a continuum, or to switch between left and right depending on the circumstances.

Those who have one preference are easily misunderstood by those with the opposite preference. A people-centered extravert may be unable to comprehend an idea-centered introvert's tempered sociability, and perceive the introvert to be unbalanced, to be totally unconcerned with people. The extravert may wrongly label the introvert as being detached. Conversely, an introvert may wrongly label an extravert as intrusive.

The introvert child and the extravert parent from the example have mischaracterized each other in just this way. The parent, using an extravert's frame of reference, assumes that a person either likes to be around people or is detached. The child, using an introvert's frame of reference, assumes that a person either likes to germinate ideas or else they intrude upon the ideas of others. The parent perceives a dichotomy of pro-people versus anti-people, while the child perceives a dichotomy of pro-ideas versus anti-ideas. Neither parent nor child recognizes that the real dichotomy is ideas versus people.

The parent and child were framing their thoughts on different axes. Not only were they misreading each other with regard to preferred energy source, but they also failed to connect on preferred communication styles, preferred mode of operation, and preferred information processing mode. Unless they can find some common reference points, they will continue to talk past one another, their words never meeting in the middle. They are doomed to miscommunicate unless they find a way to understand each other's perspective.

Consider how well you see your child's perspective. Which words from Figure 5 best describe him or her? Is it those words that are in the "balanced" portion of Figure 5, or at the extremes? If you find yourself choosing words at the extremes, you and your child may be opposite types. This is where MBTI is most useful: for identifying ways you may be misunderstanding someone, and for finding ways to see their perspective.

If you perceive your child to be detached, and you are an extravert, consider that you may be misunderstanding her. Tell her that you notice she enjoys thinking quietly, and wait for her to confirm. Then share with her that you like to think by talking things over, and explain that both ways are okay. Your child learns that you are a social extravert, and you learn that she is a pensive introvert. So give her the freedom to exercise her preference for ideas over people. Give her the opportunity to be pensive.

Discuss with her what she really needs. You may find that your warm home, a crowded hub of bustling activity, a haven for extraverts, is providing her with daily torment. She may view it all as an intrusion into her personal space, a continual interruption to her precious train of thought. She may cherish the people in the house, yet need some time away from them. She may need a quiet place to unwind, a room with a door, where she can go to think after school, before bedtime, or when surprising report cards are received. Such a room would drain energy from an extravert much like the high level of people activity in your home drains her energy. But this room will be her energy source, her place to go to refuel. She will use it to decompress, to reflect, and to create.

An extravert parent may be inclined to protest that nurturing a child's introversion like this will dull her ability for extraversion, that indulging her love for ideas will reduce her capacity to enjoy people. After all, if she is spending her time being pensive, she is necessarily doing so at the expense of being sociable. And knowing how to be sociable is a necessary skill. It often seems as if the world is made for extraverts. Should not extra energy be expended coaching the child in extraversion behaviors? *Gifts Differing* offers the guidance that children will naturally learn to behave counter to their preferences as circumstances dictate, provided their parents' acceptance of their true preferences has been established.[81]

Consider the case of an introvert parent and an extravert child. The parent may need to make extra efforts to meet people outside of the home, to attend events, to facilitate the joining of teams, and to host gatherings. This may put the parent out of a comfort zone, but it will be nutritive for the child's development. The main effect of these measures will not be to dampen the child's ability to think, but to facilitate her ability to socialize.

Granting a child unrestricted freedom to her preference, rather than limiting her, will prime her readiness to call upon its opposite when necessary. Rather than clinging to her preference in an effort to defend her autonomy, she will feel free to venture into the opposite territory of her own volition. Allowing free expression of her preferences is one way of recognizing them.

Borne of a simple conversation about a preference, the child in our original example's whole situation will have changed. She will have gained insight into how her mind works, with validation from her parents that her preference, while unique within her home, is okay. She will now have a place to practice what she was born to do: think about ideas. She will have a whole new outlook with which to go about the business of being herself.

SEE THE STRENGTHS
(SENSING-INTUITION EXAMPLE)

Similarly, consider the sensing–intuition dichotomy, and how two people occupying opposite sides of that dichotomy perceive the world—see Figure 6 below. A sensing person, focused on the actualities, observes the concrete details of something new, methodically discerning the workings of the component parts until the relevant facts have become familiar. Realistic in nature, the senser is interested in what something was meant to do and discovers how to use it effectively. The senser fills any knowledge gaps by inquiring about additional data.

An intuitive person, on the other hand, likes to observe the abstract elements of something new, becoming familiar with the big picture aspects of how it fits within a broader context. Knowledge gaps are filled by inquiring within, using insight. The intuitive person discovers visionary ways to use it, looking for what *else* it can do. Different methods of using something new are tested in a spontaneous fashion.

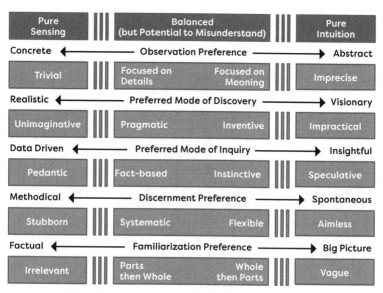

FIGURE 6. Sensing versus Intuition Preferences

As with the introversion–extraversion dichotomy, the potential exists for misunderstanding. Imagine a sensing parent and intuitive child examining a new board game, readying themselves for play. The parent, having some experience with the game, wants to convey the known facts. Following a tried-and-true system, the sensing parent reviews each rule one after the other while pointing out the corresponding part on the game board. But the intuitive child is uninterested in such routine. Following the known path is the way of the senser, but the intuitive child prefers to blaze a trail. She is already manipulating the game pieces around the board to familiarize herself with the whole of the game layout. "Let's just play!" she says. The parent, whose attempt to teach has just been thwarted, is irritated.

Using her flexibility to mentally leap between aspects of the game as her instinct calls for it, the intuitive child has identified patterns in the game's design. She now understands how its parts work together and has a general sense of how the game works. She wants to start the game and deduce the finer points of the rules as gameplay proceeds. She may then devise alternate variations on the game and find unconventional ways to use the game's components, much to the chagrin of the parent.

How disconcerting for that methodical, data-driven, fact-oriented parent to watch the child speculate about rules that are within arm's reach, and do so in such an aimless fashion if only to gain a vague notion for what the game is supposed to be about. The sensing parent, whose mind cannot be put at ease until the actualities are covered, ends up pleading with the child to "Just follow the directions!"

But the child is not satisfied slogging through the mundane content of the instructions, and is disheartened by the stubbornness with which the parent implores her to do so. She does not want to find herself embroiled in some pedantic discussion about the particulars of a rule that is irrelevant anyway until the overall meaning of the game has been uncovered.

The intuitive child does want to play the game, but she also wants to decode the thoughts of the game maker. To understand why the game has been made as it has, she must exercise her insightfulness, spontaneity, and big-picture thinking. She is not content to gradually accumulate details; she must instead dive into the possibilities presented by what is in front of her.

In all probability, the intuitive child will develop abilities both to master details and to uncover possibilities. As an adult, she will be able to follow the path or blaze a trail as needed. But it is impossible to do both simultaneously; she must choose one or the other for each situation. Because her tendencies point to blazing trails, she will naturally practice doing so more often and more earnestly. Given the opportunities to focus on its development as a child, she may grow to excel at trailblazing as an adult. But if she is instead forced to gap-fill her attention to detail, for which she will go through the motions only to please her parents, her development will be less dramatic. She will improve marginally at path following, and will do so at the expense of trailblazing. She may be unexceptional at both, and have a rather bland mix of perceiving skills with which to enter adulthood.

Too often parents focus on what their children don't do well. They want to address perceived shortcomings, and spend their energy pushing their children into practicing things for which the child has neither interest nor talent. What they fail to recognize is that those perceived shortcomings are usually the flip side of a strength. A child who often overlooks details, such as which items were on the grocery list, might be very intent on understanding abstract concepts, such as how a credit card transfers money from you to the grocery store. A child who is easily unsettled by abrupt changes in plans might be able to stay focused on a task, such as building a model spaceship, until it is completed. Rather than bemoaning the different approach of the child, such as the weakness in following the path, the parent could encourage the corollary trailblazing strength. As expounded upon by Tom Rath in *Strengthsfinder 2.0*, growing one's potential is not an exercise in smothering out the bad, but in breathing more life into the good.[82]

The child's trailblazing nature shouldn't be stifled; it is part of who she is. She could be made aware of it. She could be recognized for it. How refreshing it would be for her to hear, rather than an admonition of how speculative, aimless, or vague she is, recognition of her preference to use instinct, to remain flexible, or to look at the big picture.

Imagine that the instructions for the board game are unclear. They indicate that gameplay proceeds after the first player reaches the goal, but the exact rules of engagement are not stated. Does the player at the goal continue to draw cards? Are that player's assets at risk? If another player draws a card that sends all players back one space, does that player become removed from the goal? To come to answers, one cannot reference the rules; they are incomplete.

Many people find themselves stymied when the prescribed pathways are unknown, but not the trailblazing child. She thrives in such conditions, using her gifts to seize the moment. In the board game example, someone is needed to conceive of the available options for gameplay and then to channel the game maker to determine the best option. The parent, verbalizing that this is the child's strengths, can look to the child for suggestions. What a grand testament to that child's worth, to have her natural talents recognized by her parent and requested to be exercised for their mutual benefit.

This is also a prime opportunity for the parent and child to use their opposite preferences to complement one another. The child can help the parent see the possibilities when the relevant facts are unavailable, and identify the best one, because she knows why the game's rules are made as they are. She blazes a trail because she is practiced at envisioning the future. The parent has learned from the past, and knows how the game's rules are made to fit together. The parent can help the child avert disaster by sharing experience and common knowledge of that which could imperil the trail about to be blazed. Recognizing and appreciating their differences, they can communicate more effectively and work better as a team.

Simply by seeing the strengths in the child's preferences, the parent is recognizing those preferences. The result is that instead of pointing to faults, the parent is now pointing the child in directions where her preferences can be utilized as strengths; where she can use her natural gifts to be engaged, build confidence, and be fulfilled.

FEED THE STRENGTHS
(THINKING–FEELING EXAMPLE)

To be clear, a preference is not automatically a talent. But because a child prefers to spend her time and mental energy thinking in a certain way, she is likely to develop an aptitude for that way. For example, a child who prefers to resolve issues using logic is likely to develop an aptitude for rationality.

A child who prefers to resolve issues using logic is using thinking judgment. The thinking child searches for the truth when reaching conclusions, and states those conclusions in terms of the objective evidence. She criticizes inconsistencies in opposing arguments in order to persuade, and ultimately seeks fairness when reaching agreements.

The feeling child, by comparison, is sympathetic to others when resolving issues. She will look to her values when reaching conclusions, and states those conclusions in terms of those same values. The feeling child is complimentary of opposing positions when attempting to persuade, and ultimately seeks consensus when reaching agreements.

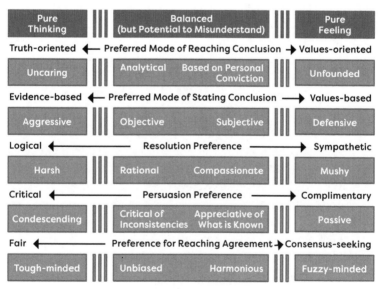

FIGURE 7. Thinking versus Feeling Preferences

Perhaps you have identified your child as being rational and logical. Tell her that you have noticed that she is the type of person[v] who likes to analyze information to find the truth. Once she has verified your observation, you will know that you have a thinking child.

So give her the chance to be rational, but don't stop there. Help her develop her ability to reason. Feed her strengths. Present some options and find out what she really loves to do with her gift of rationality. Expose her to mazes, anagrams, riddles, and codes. Discuss cause and effect. Talk about ways a book might end. Examine baseball statistics. In time, you may find that what your child loves most are data and facts, cold and hard.

So give her access to data so that she may spend her time teasing out its secrets. Have things like thermometers, yardsticks, calculators, and graph paper around the house. She can use these tools to generate data and facts about whatever interests her, and then swim in her talent for using the data. She can measure all sorts of things. She might decide to measure the dining table dimensions and try to figure out how it got through the door, or measure the hourly temperature and try to explain the variation. Unswayed by values, unmotivated by agendas, not offended by scrutiny, her data can then be probed, prodded, and tested until she is satisfied that the truth has been revealed and her curiosity has been satisfied.

A feeling child can also be given opportunities to develop her capacities. You can discuss your values with her, and ask her about her values. Some of the questions from the reflection exercises in Chapter 3 can even be used (see pages 127–129). You can play board games that incorporate negotiation, such as those that involve trading properties. You can play games involving cooperation, such as those where everybody wins against the game only when all their pieces advance to the finish line before gameplay ends. You can enlist her help in finding solutions to real disagreements.

---

[v] According to John Gottman in *Raising an Emotionally Intelligent Child*, such statements help a child build a sense of self.

Feeding the strengths in a child's preferences is another way for the parent to recognize those preferences. Because the child is inherently driven to use those preferences to her advantage, a parent need only make available the tools with which the child may turn her preferences into strengths. The parent thus enables the child to learn to use her gifts to their full capacities.

COMMUNICATE BOUNDARIES (JUDGING-PERCEIVING EXAMPLE)

Each MBTI type comes with gifts, and each type comes with challenges. While developing the gifts to their full potential, one needs to be careful not to ignore the challenges. Consider the judging–perceiving dichotomy. It is tempting for a perceiving type, who just missed an appointment because she indulged a distraction, to use her knowledge of her MBTI type to excuse her unreliability. "That's okay," she may think, "as a perceiver I am naturally unorganized, but I make up for it with my other qualities." In the same way, a judging type might excuse her inability to change a decision based on important new information, or defend her dictatorial style when dealing with others. But the challenges inherent in any preference are never to be construed as a free pass for poor behavior. Challenges are meant to be overcome.

Help your child overcome challenges in her type by communicating boundaries where exercising her preferences may become disadvantageous. It is possible to communicate boundaries around a child's preferences while still recognizing, while still acknowledging and accommodating, and still allowing for free expression of those preferences. This is done by identifying the times when a child is relying too heavily on one preference and must learn to call upon its opposite. These are the times when she exercises her preference to her own detriment or to the detriment of others. At those times, the safe zones within the boundaries where the child may exercise her preference unfettered may simultaneously be identified. We will keep with the judging–perceiving dichotomy to illustrate this further.

A judging person seeks closure, gathering just enough information to make a decision and then executing it decisively. Judgers organize things in a tidy manner, and formally manage their tasks. They structure their life, opting for a productive lifestyle, and attempt to instill the same level of order when directing others. A judging person wants to organize the world.

A perceiving person wants to adapt to the world. A perceiving person is open-ended, preferring to gather information in a continuous stream and then deliberating extensively before making a decision. Perceivers take a relaxed approach to organizing things, and manage their tasks in the same informal manner. They experience life, as opposed to structuring their life, and stay receptive to all it has to offer. They carry over the same level of freedom when directing others.

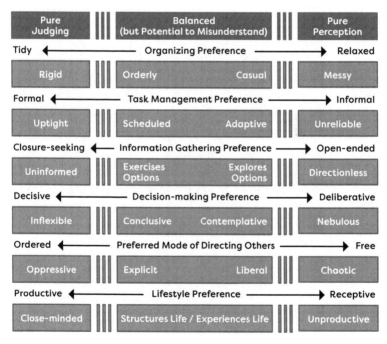

FIGURE 8. Judging versus Perceiving Preferences

It is entirely possible that your child may actually be exercising one preference when its opposite would be more appropriate. Suppose she has a strong preference for perceiving. How can she be coached to judge when needed? Start by recognizing her perceiving style.

Perhaps she dawdles in the morning. Make her aware that her informal approach, while acceptable, can be disruptive to the morning schedules of others. Then tell her that to accommodate the inevitable distractions, you need her to wake earlier so that she can get ready according to her preference while everyone else gets ready according to theirs. In this way, she can retain her informal approach, but it will not make her unreliable. Of course, there are times when building in a time buffer is not possible, and punctuality must be observed. In between back-to-back appointments is one example of when there is no room for informalities. A boundary needs to be drawn here. Acknowledge that it is uncomfortable for her to do so, but that she must learn to structure life in those circumstances. She is free to do it her way every morning, but then there are other times when she must observe a schedule.

The same child will probably enjoy exploring options. Not content with outdoor playtime experiences being confined to a yard and sidewalk, she may feel driven to explore the possibilities of playtime in the street. Like with the morning routine example, her preference can be recognized, some boundaries can be applied to it, and safe zones can be communicated. Recognize such a child's preference to explore options by taking her into the street when there are no cars around, so she can satisfy her curiosity about being in the street. Then communicate boundaries by explaining the danger of cars, and that she may only go in the street when accompanied by you. Other times, she must exercise her options to play only in safe zones of the yard, the sidewalk, or the driveway. Having already experienced the street with a watchful parent, she will not need to run and see for herself what being in the street is like.

In the same way, a judging child may prefer to adhere to plans. She may protest any deviation from those plans. For example, an anticipated outing to the beach might be cancelled on account of rain. This child might benefit from a discussion about how unexpected events are a part of life. She also may be shown how to make contingency plans, for example, by brainstorming ways in which plans may be disrupted, and making alternate arrangements in advance for such eventualities.

RECOGNIZE YOUR CHILD'S PREFERENCES

How preferences manifest in one's personality is complicated. It is dependent upon environmental factors, influenced by behavioral choices, and refined over time. Some preferences are readily observable, while others are less evident. Additionally, one's preferences do not simply sum together; they interact in complex ways. Discerning someone's preferences is not always as easy as in the limited examples given here, nor is recognizing preferences always as straightforward.

It is not necessary to become an MBTI expert in order to be an effective parent. However, it helps tremendously to simply be aware of the different preferences people may have. Appreciating that your child may think in different ways than you do is the first step to finding ways to parent and to communicate more effectively. For the most part, common sense is all that is needed to adjust your parenting approach to match your child's needs.

Acknowledge and accommodate your child's preferences. Allow for free expression of preferences like the extravert parent giving the introvert child a space of her own. See the strengths in her preferences, like the sensing parent calling upon the intuitive child to interpret the rules of the game. Help feed the strengths in her preferences, like the parent supplying the thinking child with tools for thinking. Communicate boundaries around preferences, like the parent who explores the street with the perceiving child, but forbids street play at other times.

Try to allow your child to develop her preferences within her comfort zone, so that she has a secure base from which to develop her preference opposites when necessary. As an adult, she will be able to draw upon these opposites as the situation calls for it. In *Gifts Differing*, the following guidance for parents is given:[83]

- Allow introverts time to themselves.
- Give extraverts access to people.
- Don't tie intuitives to only what is known.
- Allow sensing children to learn by doing and by getting involved.
- Provide thinkers with your rationale, and let them give you theirs.
- Give feeling types an amicable environment.
- Allow judging types to make decisions.
- Allow perceptives to figure things out.

Of course, all eight pieces of advice apply to everybody to some degree. The key is recognizing what blend of these is right for your child. There is no "one right way" to parent. But there is a right way for each child.

There is no simple methodical way to get to know your child. It happens by spending lots of time together. You become aware of your child's preferences during the "get-tos," the times when you get to do things like change diapers, feed meals, brush little teeth, give baths, and have meandering discussions.

As you learn your child's preferences, you get to recognize them. You get to adjust your parenting style to be more compatible with your child's thinking styles. Because you so readily embrace your child's innate tendencies, she will know that she matters. She will be able to approach others with the same attitude of acceptance, and be primed to enjoy a lifetime of relationships, an enduring sense of relatedness, and well-being.

She will also be positioned to learn how to use her strengths to work toward her potential. Through self-acceptance and self-understanding, she will be able to use her talents to build capabilities. She will be able to develop an enduring sense of competence, and enjoy a lifetime of well-being.

EXPLAIN

THE BRAINS OF CHILDREN

Children have brains that are twice as active as adult brains.[84] In the article "Kids' Brain Power," Steve Nadia makes an analogy between using that mental energy and consuming food. Children truly *hunger* for information to digest. By the time they are two years old, children will have made roughly 1,000 trillion neural connections. Some of those connections are the scaffolding for further brain development. The connections that are repeatedly used become stronger, like footprints in the snow becoming the set paths.

By the time the child has become an adult, roughly half of those connections, having gone unused, will have been lost.[85] Children pursue knowledge with such zest and urgency, as if they know that idle connections will be shed. Children crave knowledge. They yearn for those connections to be stimulated, to be kept alive by electrical impulses. So feed your child's intellect, arouse her mind. Present her with a "banquet"[86] of information to satiate her cognitive appetite, to use the food terms adopted by Nadia. Let life be a "feast"[87] of knowledge for her.

A child experiences all kinds of wonderful new things. Using her five senses, she takes in the world around her. As she interacts with the world, she experiences the consequences of her actions. Within herself, she finds thoughts and feelings. Help her apply words to all these experiences. Explain them all to her starting from infancy, and continue to do so as she grows.

KEEP TALKING

At home, you can explain to a child, even one in her infancy, that the ticking sound is coming from the clock. Help her zero in on it by moving her closer to the clock to make the sound louder, and farther away to make it fainter again. Describe the different parts of the clock using shapes and colors, and how people use the clock to get to places on time. She will absorb plenty from your communication despite being too young to fully understand the subject matter, and she will come to understand sooner than you might expect.

Take a walk outside and listen to the birds singing. Point to the birds in the trees. Spend some time contemplating wings, feathers, and the patterns that the bird is wearing. Then switch focus and help her tune in to the leaves rustling in the trees. Feel the rough bark, and tell her what it does for the tree. Let her experience the same breeze that rustles the leaves cooling her skin and blowing back her hair. Notice the feeling of the ground against the feet. Is it soft grass, hard cement, mushy mud, or smooth sand? Smell the flowers. Which fragrance does she find more pleasant, the daffodils or the tulips?

Back indoors, experience and describe the textures of walls, furniture, toys, and foods. Some are soft, some are hard. Some are fuzzy, woolly, smooth, rough, prickly, sharp, bumpy, or gooey. Look for colors and patterns all around. There are solids, stripes, polka dots, pastels, brights, and more. During bath time, enjoy the shampoo fragrance. Does it smell anything like the flowers outside? Smell a candle and then light it. Does it smell the same when it is burning, or different? Describe the foods you are eating. Berries are sweet, lemons are sour, soy sauce is salty, curry is spicy, and olives are bitter.

Take a look in the mirror when she tastes that bitter olive. Describe the face she makes, and that she is making the face because she feels something called disgust. Use the mirror to help her learn to recognize other emotions like happy, sad, and angry. Have fun mimicking her facial expressions, sounds, and actions. Attuning with her emotional state, even as part of a game, helps her to make sense of her feelings while demonstrating that you are paying attention to her. Then reverse the game and have her mimic your expressions. This is good practice for her to attune to others. Even though the game is fun, it is okay to tell your child about its other purpose, and how understanding how other people might feel will help her to be a good friend.

Explain what you are doing and why, even when your child is too young to have a conversation with you, and even when you think she is not yet ready to understand. A trip to the grocery store, for example, can inspire discussion about many things: the different types of food that are there, how they are classified, how the store is organized, why some foods are kept chilled, how certain foods are selected by you to go in the cart, the different prices of items, the anatomy of the financial transaction at the register, the route to take back home, and more. The different foods can be spelled, counted, categorized, or worked into a rhyming game. Anything and everything can be explained. Your child will learn a lot from being communicated to, and from hearing all those words strung together, even if she doesn't yet understand how credit cards work.

Explain what is going to happen next. Convey the sequence of events and how long they will take using words like "before," "after," "last month," "next Tuesday," "in ten minutes," and "now." This helps her develop a concept of time, which she needs in order to successfully predict when transitions between events will come. She can then take some control over those transitions and start learning how to manage her time.

If you are taking her to the grocery store tomorrow, tell her that you are taking her to the grocery store tomorrow. It gives her a chance to experience anticipation, and to figure out how far away tomorrow is. And when you are about to leave the grocery store, explain to her that the next step is the checkout line and you expect to be out of the store in ten minutes. She will develop a sense for how far away ten minutes is. This also helps her mentally prepare for the transition and to bring her activities to closure. Maybe she was counting on seeing the watermelon display one more time, and now she can request a quick ride through the produce aisle before shopping time ends. If she needs to have her nose wiped while in the produce aisle, explain to her that you are going to wipe her nose now. She may prefer to do it herself, and will have a better time communicating that to you when she knows your plans.

All of the explaining you do benefits your child in many ways:

- It builds her awareness of different subjects.
- It advances her communication skills.
- It provides a platform for parent–child bonding.
- It prompts her to search for new ways to connect neurons and organize her brain activity.

Your explanations are beneficial not just for small children, but for children of all ages. After all, learning is never completed, but is the work of a lifetime. The topics should, of course, change to match the child's advancing intellect. As the child ages, the explanations will become more of a conversation than a monologue. Some explanations will pique her curiosity, and some will not garner much of a response. That's okay—learning happens best when it is driven by interest. An interested learner not only absorbs explanations, but also follows up by asking questions.

ENTERTAIN QUESTIONS

If you can entertain your child's (sometimes seemingly endless!) questions, it is priming her to think. And thinking happens in questions. Your child will conjure many different types of questions in her quest to feed her brain.

The website criticalthinking.org enumerates the different purposes for many types of questions. A child may ask questions to:

- uncover reasons;
- disentangle details;
- verify knowledge;
- authenticate what seems obvious;
- foresee consequences;
- confirm facts;
- test theories;
- consider other perspectives;
- classify information;

- search for disparities;
- resolve the finer points; and
- corroborate conclusions.[88]

By the time your child learns to talk, she will ask enough questions to make up for her nonverbal stage. Indulge her. Make curiosity profitable for her. As you provide answers, you will learn about her interests as she figures them out for herself. The information in your answers provides your child with a foundation of *what* to think, but the process of formulating questions is teaching her *how* to think. Your answers, by rewarding her questions, encourage more questioning. Your answers encourage more thinking.

In the book *A Brief History of Time*, Stephen Hawking relays an oft-repeated story of a scientist discussing planetary motion with an old woman. Discarding the scientist's claim that the spherical earth revolved around the sun, the old woman asserted that the flat earth rested upon the back of a giant turtle. Naturally, the scientist pressed for an explanation of how the turtle was supported. Anticipating the scientist's follow-up questions, she rebuffed his entire line of reasoning on the grounds that it was "turtles all the way down."[89]

It is an amusing anecdote, if it ever really happened, but it also carries a lesson. Perhaps, at one time, the prevailing theory among a group of people was that the earth was resting on the back of a giant turtle. Understood to be true, taken for granted, until someone stepped back, examined what they were taught and questioned the assumption of truth, questioned the accuracy, and formulated the question, "What is the turtle resting on?" The answer may have come back as another turtle, and who knows for how long that was accepted until the question was asked again, "What is that turtle resting on?" Now it has become a question of implication, a question of logic. One can imagine just how many turtles, figuratively, it took to get to the galactic model.

Answers that end the line of questioning, like "turtles all the way down," end the thinking. Real understanding, real engagement, real critical thinking comes when the answers lead to more questions. Entire fields of study, such as cosmology, are nothing more than questions derived from the previous answer. Answers that generate more questions become a glorious fountain of thought and knowledge. Perhaps all of science, with all its different limbs and branches, millions of practitioners, trillions of research dollars, breathtaking advances, and surprising discoveries, owes its forgotten genesis to a curious child's first question.

A toddler's questions may seem like infinite regression, continually asking what the previous turtle is standing on. Consider the following exchange between my three-year-old son and me:

Son:	"Why are you reading?"
Me:	"Because I like to read."
Son:	"Why?"
Me:	"Because I like to learn new things."
Son:	"Why?"
Me:	"So I can know more."
Son:	"Why?"
Me:	"So I can do more things."
Son:	"Why?"
Me:	"So I can be better at my job."
Son:	"Why?"
Me:	"So I can better provide for my family."
Son:	"Why?"
Me:	"Because I love my family."
Son:	"Oh."

The "turtling" could have been quelled with a tersely delivered "just because" or "because I said so." But that would not have been very satisfying for either of us. It would have done nothing to nurture more questioning, to encourage more forays into critical thinking, to grow the wondrous ability of how to think.

By turtling down deep enough, you really get to the root of the matter. You expose the real reasons, and find out what is truly important. Imagine how my son felt when he learned my underlying motives, that what was really important to me was him.

Tired parents are easily worn out by a child's turtling, especially if they suspect its purpose is not to satisfy genuine curiosity but to hold the parent's attention. Either way, there are some good ways to break the monotony and stimulate thinking. If the child is repeatedly asking a one-word question such as "Why?," try asking "Why what?" so the child has to consider what she really wants to know and then articulate the question. Or consider that her vocabulary may not permit her to ask the way she wants. A "why" question may really be a "how" or a "what" question, or it may even be an open-ended "tell me more." Help your child find the right question before giving an answer. You could also reflect a question right back, as in "Why do you think candy is not for breakfast?" Or answer the question directly, but create a dialogue by asking a question of your own. "No candy for breakfast because you need to start your day with healthy food. Which foods in this kitchen do you think are healthy?"

EXPLAIN THE RULES

It is especially easy to get worn down by turtling when you are directing the day's activities. It would be nicer not to have your instructions questioned. Prompt compliance from your child may be more convenient for you, but it is not very enlightening for your child. It is more instructive for you to explain your directions, expectations, and rules.

Explaining the rules is something a parent should do whether the child prompts an explanation or not. In fact, a child will be more apt to follow the rules when she understands the reasons. "Drinks kept at the table's edge are easily knocked over, please adjust" is more likely to elicit the proper response than a terse "Move your cup to the other side of your plate."

A child should not be required to display blind obedience; it is not a very useful trait for her to carry into adulthood. As a human being, she deserves to know the reasons for the rules she is expected to follow. And if you cannot explain the underlying reason for the rule, the bottom turtle, then maybe it is not a very good rule.

The underlying reason for many rules is "because I love you." "No candy for breakfast because I don't want you to grow up to be an undernourished, chronically sick person with holes in her teeth. I want you to be healthy and strong because I love you. You can have fruit and cereal instead. The answer is no to candy because I love you." Your child will find rules easier to accept when she trusts you and knows you love her and have her best interests at heart.

Note the placement of "I love you," and how the other words lead up to it. This arrangement is helpful not only because it positions "I love you" as the bottom turtle, but also because it helps to prevent you from saying "I love you, but no candy for breakfast." Words like "but," as described by Adele Faber in *How to Talk So Kids Will Listen and Listen So Kids Will Talk*, work like erasers.[90] They wipe out the words that came before them. A child only registers what comes after the "but," and the heart of the message—the "I love you" part—is lost. When your wording does not work against you to sabotage your message, explanations become a bit simpler to deliver.

Such explanations, however, can still be complicated for a small child. Unless you allow time for the child to process the meaning, she may feel as if she is being hit with a wall of words. Keep the messages brief, and pause periodically so the child has time to absorb the message. "No candy for breakfast because I don't want you to grow up to be an unhealthy person with holes in her teeth." *Pause.* "I want you to be healthy and strong because I love you." *Pause.* "You can have fruit and cereal instead." *Pause.* "The answer is no to candy because I love you."

Another way to say no is to offer other perspectives. In addition to planting the seeds of empathy, exploring other perspectives is also a good explanatory device. "It is okay to feel dissatisfied with something, but it is not okay to deal with your disappointment by screaming at us. If Mom or I screamed about wanting candy for breakfast, you can say the same thing to us, that it's not okay. You can tell us that candy is not breakfast food, and that we can have fruit and cereal." The fairness of all this, once comprehended, can have a calming effect.

Here is another perspective: "You can have fruit and cereal. When you grow up and become the parent, you can decide to feed your family whatever you want for breakfast." This reframes the discussion and makes it about the child and the fascinating idea that she will not always be the same, that she will grow up and become the grown up. This can spark her imagination. She is not forever beholden to your rules. She will grow up and become the rule-maker.

So show her how to be a good rule-maker. Explain your rules. And show her how to be a good explainer. Make sure your words hold value. Mean what you say and say what you mean.

I once saw a six-year-old child ask his father to tie his shoes for him. The father scowled and said, "Why should I? You know how to tie your own shoes." And then he bent down and tied his shoes. This man's words were meaningless. If that was a representative interaction for them, then he was teaching his child not to listen to what he says because his words have no bearing on anything.

Another time, we were at a park and the only other people there were a woman and her two children. She told her kids that if they got in the car without fuss, then they would go to another park. Her kids quickly and happily got into the car. I didn't know those people, but I seriously doubt they left the park in which they were already playing to go to a different park. I believe she was just trying to make leaving the park easier. Again, this woman made her words meaningless. She may have a difficult time being heard because, in time, her children may come to disbelieve her explanations of rules, consequences, and everything else.

If you expect your child to tie her own shoes, then, after you teach her to tie her own shoes, explain that you will no longer tie them for her. And then do not tie them for her. If you tell your child that if she gets in the car quickly then there will be time to go somewhere fun, then you had better take her somewhere fun after she complies. Or simply tell her that it is time to get in the car and go home.

Make your words mean something. When you claim that you will do something, whether it is pleasing to your child or not, then make sure that you do that thing. When your child comes to expect that you say what you mean and mean what you say, she will be ready to listen to all the wonderful things you have to explain to her.

LISTEN

LISTEN TO UNDERSTAND

Making your words mean something is necessary but not sufficient. In order for your child to listen to you, you must also show her how to listen. You must therefore listen to her.

This is critical because you are best positioned to help your child understand herself. But to help your child understand herself, you must first understand your child. The only way to understand your child is to listen to her.

Listening is not simply hearing her words, but finding out what she means when she says them. In the book *The 7 Habits of Highly Effective People*, Stephen R. Covey calls it "empathic listening."[91] For empathic listening, you must be completely present in the moment; not thinking about what you want to say, or what else you want to do right now, or what you will do once you get your child to see your side of things; not judging, solving, or internally disagreeing; not interrupting or finishing her sentences; not reading something on your phone, but listening. Being fully engaged and listening not just to her words, but to their pitch, their tone, and their rhythm; to the body language accompanying the words. When you are attentive to your child's whole person as she tries to communicate to you, and you truly try to understand her, then you are really listening.

A child who is not listened to feels invisible. She feels unimportant, frustrated, and resentful. She feels as if she doesn't matter. And she has little reason to listen to whoever is making her feel that way.

ELICIT INFORMATION

Just be there to listen. This may sound passive, but it is not. You may actively elicit more information by simply using listening words. As suggested by Faber and Mazlish in *How to Talk So Kids Will Listen and Listen So Kids Will Talk*, "yes," "I see," and the like are good ways to let your child know that you hear her and want to know more.[92]

Use questions to elicit information. An illustration is provided by my two-year-old daughter, who was eating dinner and asked for more cabbage. We pointed out that she still had cabbage on her plate. She insisted on more cabbage. It didn't make sense to give her more before she finished what she already had, we stated. She was adamant, she had to have more. She looked at her cabbage with disgust, yet asked for more of it. We finally started asking some investigative questions, and learned that she liked the soft, thin cabbage leaves but not the crisper, thicker ones. "Oh, so you are the type of person who likes soft cabbage," we said. She beamed.

She was happy to get the kind of cabbage she wanted, but not as happy as she was to be understood. We could have written off this kind of behavior—asking for more of what one already has—as irrational. But then we would not have been listening. We would not have been registering the look of disgust, and following up with questions. If all we had heard was "more cabbage!," we would have failed to hear the real message of "Don't you know who I am? I am the kind of person who likes soft, thin cabbage. Don't you understand me?" A child cannot always tell you the intricate details. They don't know how. You have to elicit the right information before you can act upon it.

One might argue that the favoritism of one type of food over another type of food doesn't qualify as a need, and therefore doesn't deserve to be responded to. But such superficial preferences still deserve recognition. No matter how trivial an inclination may seem, it is part of someone and deserves acknowledgment. Parents can make a child feel understood simply by acknowledging a proclivity for one thing over another, even if they opt not to accommodate the request.

Whether a taste for thin cabbage over thick cabbage, a more pivotal trait such as a penchant for fashion over air hockey, or an even weightier preference such as introversion over extraversion, all inclinations deserve some form of recognition. And your child may not explicitly volunteer information about all these inclinations. You have to take the time and effort to know your child. You have to observe, interpret, question, and listen.

Ask questions about her day: what she did, who she sat with, what she learned, what made her feel bad, and what made her feel good. Ask what she was thinking about when she made that painting of a forest, and how she learned to draw fish like that. Ask what it felt like to earn that gold star at school. Intersperse such questions in normal conversation, so they are an organic part of the dialogue, not rapid-fire interrogation. Sometimes your child can't or won't answer these questions, and that's okay. She will know that there is someone there to listen to her whenever she chooses to share information.

Listen especially when your child is scared, confused, or doing the wrong thing. Applying your own interpretations, assessments, and solutions in hot moments without regard for your child's perspective can be like pouring gasoline on a fire. It is easy to assume what might be behind her behaviors, but those assumptions might be wrong. Listen, and believe what you are told. If a child knows her words are taken at face value, she will feel listened to, and she will feel a responsibility to speak the truth.

BE LISTENED TO

I have heard parents complain that their child does not listen to them, no matter how much they explain, persuade, or even yell. I often wonder, "Have you tried listening to her?" Being listened to and understood makes people feel validated, confident, and important. Being listened to and feeling understood makes people feel that they matter. And it shows them how to listen. It teaches them how to understand you back. It makes them *want* to understand you back.

When a parent takes the time to really listen to their child and to understand her, that parent learns how to communicate effectively with that child. A parent who perceives their child's feelings, who knows her preferences and respects her opinions, begins to understand the child. When a parent understands their child, he can begin to help that child discover herself, for example, verbalizing that she is the type of child who likes some quiet time to color. He can begin to relay meaningful information, and do so in a way that the child will find meaningful.

In order to be responsive to your child's emotions, needs, and interests, you need to know first and foremost what those emotions, needs, and interests are. So build your own awareness as a prerequisite to building your child's awareness. As a parent, you must listen.

WELCOME EMOTIONS

IN HOT MOMENTS

It is possible to welcome emotions by listening to, accepting, and explaining your child's emotional episodes. Doing so builds your child's awareness of emotions. It demonstrates general responsiveness to emotions. And it conveys to your child the sense that she matters.

Listening empathically is always important, but it is especially important during an emotional episode. Dr. Harvey Karp offers some good advice in this regard. Crouch down so that you are both at the same level. This is a sign of respectful listening. Make eye contact to show that you are listening intently. Make physical contact, like a hand on her shoulder, to convey concern. Use the "fast food rule" to assure effective listening.

The fast food rule states that before you offer any suggestions, you should reflect your child's words back to her.[93] It is like what happens at a fast food restaurant: before anything else can happen, the restaurant worker repeats your order back to you to confirm a mutual understanding. Repeat your child's "order" using not only words, but also compassionate tones indicating your under-standing of her state. Attuning to your child's emotional state is an effective form of empathic listening.

When my daughter was almost two years old, she bumped her head and would not stop crying. It seemed as though she was in a great deal of pain. I wanted to tell her I knew how much that hurt, but decided to let her tell the story from her perspective before attempting to attune to her state of mind. She was crying too hard to talk, so I crouched down and asked her if she was in pain. She shook her head. Then I asked if she was scared. She nodded. I mirrored her affirmation back to her in a hug, repeating that she was scared. I get scared sometimes too, I added, and, after examining her head, reported that it was fine and would soon return to feeling normal. She stopped crying right away. She needed attunement and understanding, which I would have been unable to give if I simply assumed she was hurt, if I hadn't listened to her, if I hadn't reflected her communication to me back to her using compassionate tones.

Speaking in compassionate tones, in addition to being a valu-able listening technique, implies acceptance of your child's plight. Your acceptance—your willingness to endure emotional suffering alongside your child—serves to legitimize her emotional state. With your acceptance, your child is likely to follow your lead and accept her own emotional state. She will believe her own feelings.

Imagine how my interaction with my daughter would have gone if I had refused to accept her feelings. Imagine what would have happened if I had judged her fear to be unwarranted and demanded quiet. Or if I had protested her assessment of her feel-ings, insisting she was hurt, not scared. According to Gottman, in any of these scenarios a child may not only disbelieve her feelings but come to distrust her very self as well, for which her self-esteem will surely suffer.[94]

When my son came to me screaming and crying that his sister, with whom he was in an argument over spilled fish food, had kicked him in the stomach, I questioned how the girl, who was much smaller than him, could have done any real damage. I then sent him away to solve the problem himself. Of course, he wasn't there to have me alleviate his physical pain, but to attune to his emotional pain. I should have known better because, ironically, I was in the middle of writing this section in this chapter at the time. But I didn't listen to his emotional outpouring, I didn't accept his emotional state, and I certainly didn't help him build awareness. In essence, I told him that he shouldn't feel hurt and that I wouldn't be by his side as he worked toward a resolution with his sister.

I made the situation worse, and he let me know it. He just wanted to tell me what happened and get a hug, he reported, but—still using his words—I didn't care about him. I made him feel like he didn't matter. As a result, he left in a rage to reengage with his sister while she retreated behind the locked door of her room. It took a long time for them to work this out, and things got worse before they got better. Later that morning after tempers finally cooled, we rehashed the encounter and I owned up to my poor handling of the situation. Hugs were shared but they felt empty at that point. I carried the guilt from that incident with me for the rest of the day. I did the only thing I could, and committed to doing better in the future.

Without parental acceptance of emotions, children have trouble accepting their own emotions. Without self-acceptance, they have more difficulty working their way through emotional storms. And this makes it difficult to focus on the source of the distress and seek a resolution, which is a skill they will need to call upon their entire lives.

EMOTIONS VERSUS BEHAVIOR

It is important to note that acceptance of emotions is not to be confused with acceptance of behaviors. Behaviors do arise from emotions, but that does not mean they should be treated the same. Emotions should be accepted unconditionally; not so with accompanying behaviors. With emotions and behaviors mentally compartmentalized, it becomes possible to limit behaviors without relinquishing your acceptance of emotions.

In the incident with my son, I could have easily accepted his feelings. Perhaps he was shocked by the uncharacteristic physical assault from his sister, for which I could have expressed an equal measure of shock. I could also have insisted upon a talking voice, as screaming at Dad is not okay. I could have then reminded both children that violence is unacceptable. Rather than issuing a wholesale rejection of emotions and behavior, I could have rejected some behaviors while accepting the emotions.

IDENTIFY EMOTIONS

Once you have accepted your child's emotions, you are ready to explain them to her. This involves identifying and describing the emotions. Identifying emotions is of prime importance in building emotional awareness. It can be very comforting for a distressed child to know that what she is experiencing can be reduced to a name. After all, if there is a term commonly understood to convey what she is experiencing, then what she is experiencing must be normal. Knowing that a name exists for the way she is feeling allows her to let go of the notion that she is falling apart. Being able to then describe what she is experiencing represents an even greater measure of control, in that she can use descriptions in the future to define her feelings according to her own estimations.

You can equip yourself to identify emotions by developing a vocabulary of emotions. There are several models of emotional classification, but exploring them all is beyond the scope of this book. Table 8 provides words representing three layers of an emotional hierarchy, as described by relationship and emotion researcher Phillip Shaver, et al.[95]

The Shaver table is organized in a way conducive to progressive learning. The terms listed as primary emotions, being the most common as well as the simplest, are perhaps the most relatable to children. For example, the concept of sadness is easily grasped by most children. The secondary terms are subsets of the primary terms. Secondary terms offer more specific descriptions that are variations on the primary terms, and then likewise for the tertiary terms. For example, the secondary term *disappointment* describes a certain kind of sadness associated with expectations not being met. The tertiary term *dismay* offers still richer detail, connoting disillusionment and the lowering of future expectations. As they grow, children can be familiarized with more and more of the secondary terms, and finally the tertiary terms.

TOOL: EMOTION TABLE

Use Table 8 to mentally organize descriptive words to make them readily explainable to your children. This table should help you to build your emotional vocabulary so that you can identify emotions with your child.

Primary Emotions	Secondary Emotions	Tertiary Emotions
Love	Affection	Adoration, Love, Fondness, Liking, Attraction, Caring, Tenderness, Compassion, Sentimentality
	Lust	Arousal, Desire, Passion, Infatuation
	Longing	Longing
Joy	Cheerfulness	Amusement, Bliss, Gaiety, Glee, Jolliness, Joviality, Joy, Delight, Enjoyment, Gladness, Happiness, Jubilation, Elation, Satisfaction, Ecstasy, Euphoria
	Zest	Enthusiasm, Zeal, Excitement, Thrill, Exhilaration
	Contentment	Pleasure
	Pride	Triumph
	Optimism	Eagerness, Hope
	Enthrallment	Rapture
	Relief	Relief
Surprise	Surprise	Amazement, Astonishment

Primary Emotions	Secondary Emotions	Tertiary Emotions
Anger	Irritation	Aggravation, Agitation, Annoyance, Grouchiness, Grumpiness
	Exasperation	Frustration
	Rage	Outrage, Fury, Wrath, Hostility, Ferocity, Bitterness, Hate, Loathing, Scorn, Spite, Vengefulness, Dislike, Resentment
	Disgust	Revulsion, Contempt
	Envy	Jealousy
	Torment	Torment
Sadness	Suffering	Agony, Hurt, Anguish
	Sadness	Depression, Despair, Hopelessness, Gloom, Glumness, Unhappiness, Grief, Sorrow, Woe, Misery, Melancholy
	Disappointment	Dismay, Displeasure
	Shame	Guilt, Regret, Remorse
	Neglect	Alienation, Isolation, Loneliness, Rejection, Homesickness, Defeat, Dejection, Insecurity, Embarrassment, Humiliation, Insult
	Sympathy	Pity
Fear	Horror	Alarm, Shock, Fear, Fright, Terror, Panic, Hysteria, Mortification
	Nervousness	Anxiety, Tenderness, Uneasiness, Apprehension, Worry, Distress, Dread

TABLE 8. **Emotions**

DESCRIBE EMOTIONS

After identifying your child's emotions, you can describe the indicators that accompany those emotions. Those indicators are behavioral impulses, facial expressions, and physiological changes.[96] Table 9 summarizes all three types of emotional indicators for all of Shaver's primary emotions. Disgust, one of the six emotions considered by facial expression expert Paul Ekman to be universal[97] but not recognized as primary by Shaver, has also been included. In addition to these descriptions, Table 9 also includes translations (as inspired by the works of children's book author Cornelia Spelman) potentially useful for very small children.

> ### TOOL: EMOTION DESCRIPTIONS TABLE
>
> Use Table 9 to help you apply words to the different manifestations of emotions.

EMOTION	BEHAVIORAL IMPULSES	FACIAL EXPRESSIONS	PHYSIOLOGICAL CHANGES	TRANSLATIONS FOR SMALL CHILDREN[98]
Love	Approach, caress, hug, nurture[99]	Very subtle, not well-documented	Warmness in the chest[100]	Feeling warm and fuzzy
Joy	Laugh, continue as is	Wrinkles formed around eyes, cheeks raised, lips turned upward[101]	Moderate increase in heart rate[102]	Feeling light and easy
Surprise	Rapidly shift attention[103]	Eyebrows raised, eyes widened, mouth opened[104]	Muscles tense, especially in neck[105]	Feeling dizzy and stiff
Anger	Immediate protective action, stare at target,[106] ball fists, strike something	Eyebrows pulled inward and downward,[107] lips tightened,[108] jaw clenched[109]	Increased breathing rate, faster heart rate, flush face, blood flow to limbs and extremities, tense muscles, focused attention,[110] burst of energy,[110] perspiration	Feeling big and fiery
Sadness	Hunch over, move slowly, withdraw, cry[111]	Inner corners of eyelids raised, eyelids loosened, lip corners pulled downward[112]	Muscles relaxed	Feeling slow and weak
Fear	Fight, flight, or freeze	Eyebrows arched, eyes widened, mouth stretched[113]	Increased breathing rate, faster heart rate, blushing, tense muscles, sweating, goosebumps, butterflies in stomach[114]	Feeling small and shivery
Disgust[115]	Withdraw from or discard object of disgust, shudder	Eyebrows narrowed, nose wrinkled, upper lip curled, tongue possibly extended	Lower heart rate	Feeling yucky and sick

TABLE 9. Descriptions of Emotions

Describing emotions during hot moments is hard work. By the time your child begins to calm down, your energy may be spent. However, while it is tempting to disengage from describing emotions after a meltdown has peaked, there is a lot of value in walking your child all the way through the emotional arc. In fact, the descent back to baseline emotional intensity provides a good opportunity to calmly discuss topics that were impossible to broach in the throes of the hot moment.

Consider a toddler having a tantrum. As her feelings rapidly intensify at the onset of the tantrum, it becomes too late to head off the meltdown. Her receptivity to coaching sharply diminishes, with any attempts to communicate only overwhelming her further. Perhaps some rudimentary emotional identification, partial emotional descriptions, and behavioral limit setting is all that will be possible. "Oh my goodness, you must feel angry. Your face is all red and you're thrashing about. No throwing, though."

There comes a point in most tantrums where a predominantly angry feeling transitions to a predominantly sad feeling.[116] When your child's anger finally starts to wane, you may feel like shutting down your efforts so you can have a break. But this is the point at which her receptivity to coaching returns. After the anger has run its course, the time is ripe for listening, describing, and limit setting. You may need to elicit information. Consider the following phrases:

- "Why did you do that?"
- "You were feeling big and fiery, weren't you?"
- "Were you angry, very angry, or very, very angry? Oh, then you were furious."
- "I'll bet your heart was beating very fast. Does it seem like it's slowing down now?"
- "Your eyebrows were pulled down when you were angry, but now they are raised up. Are you feeling sad now?"
- "Different people do different things to calm down. Let's try breathing in and out together. No? Okay, let's try counting to ten. Would a hug help you feel better? How about coloring? Reading?"

- "What do you think would help next time you start to feel angry?"
- "Some things are okay to do when feeling angry, other things are not. Let's talk about what those things are."

It is okay if this turns out to be more of a monologue than a conversation. Try to keep it short—there is no need to cram all of the information from Tables 8 or 9 into a single conversation. You'll have lots of opportunities to cover bits at a time.

Having these types of conversations with your child helps her to take the mystery out of intense emotions. No longer needing to rely on a hyperactive imagination, the child instead uses her growing library of descriptions to make sense of her emotional experiences. And with her growing body of experience she may begin to recognize the behavioral, expressive, and physiological changes signaling the onset, peak, and decline of the hot moment. She will come to know that hot moments follow a predictable pattern. She will learn to gauge the intensity of emotions. She will learn the best soothing techniques for her. With her growing knowledge comes growing power. Instead of being managed by her emotions, the emotionally aware child gradually learns to manage her emotions.

THE EMOTIONS OF OTHERS

As she builds awareness of her own emotions, your child will be able to apply her knowledge to the emotional experiences of others. She will realize that the emotional experiences of other people can be identified using the same words that she has learned to name her own emotions. It will also dawn on her that the emotions that others experience conform to the same descriptions.

Awareness of self and awareness of others go hand in hand. Make the attainment of both types of awareness as natural for your child as possible. Regularly describe others' feelings, including your own, to encourage others-awareness.

Imagine again the conversation with the tantrum-struck toddler, with talking points drawn from the list of phrases already provided. This time, instead of an exclusively toddler-centric dialogue, the discussion is peppered with some items oriented toward other people:

- "Did you notice how scared that little boy became when you started throwing things? His eyes became as big as saucers and he ran away."
- "I'm glad you are starting to calm down. I felt worried you might hurt yourself or someone else."
- "I felt irritated when you screamed at me as I tried to comfort you. I'm still sweating."
- "Taking a short walk helps me to cool down. Would you like to come along with me?"

Speaking openly about emotions like this accomplishes several things:

- It demonstrates that emotions are normal, and that they are safe to share with those you trust.
- It emphasizes that others have emotional experiences.
- It highlights the fact that the child's behavior has an effect on the emotions of others.

Understanding this last point is a key for developing empathy. In *Emotional Intelligence*, Daniel Goleman reported on research showing that children exhibit greater empathy when they are given clear explanations of how their misconduct affects the emotional states of others.[117]

Empathy may emerge alongside others-awareness, but recognize that it goes one step further. In addition to comprehending the emotional experiences of others, empathy includes sharing in those emotional experiences. In order to increase the likelihood that your child's awareness of others' emotions blossoms into empathy, you can show your child ways to assuage someone in distress by example, another practice recommended by Goleman.[118]

In the case of the toddler having a tantrum, this advice is best heeded by first tending to any children victimized by the out-of-control child. A child in the vicinity of the meltdown's onset may become frightened by the ensuing projectiles. Comforting the frightened child as the first order of business provides an opportunity for the offending child to see firsthand the consequences of her misbehavior, which can then be expounded upon with her after the tantrum subsides. It also ensures that the misbehaving child is not rewarded with immediate attention.

Determining where to first focus your awareness-building among multiple children is tricky when you were not there to witness any wrongdoing, or when more than one party is in the wrong. Fortunately, circumstances sometimes allow for more than one child to be effectively addressed at a time. When my four-year-old son noticed that his one-year-old sister was using up his new stickers, for which he was not asked permission, he became alarmed. He ran up to her, screaming, and ripped the stickers from her hands. She retaliated by swiping them back and running away. He howled in frustration, appealing to me for support. She kept her distance, safeguarding the stickers.

Keeping her within earshot, I tried to explain her perspective to my son while also acknowledging his perspective. She may not have considered that these playthings, of all the playthings in the home among which she generally had free access, were not available to her. Given the single-use nature of stickers, his feelings of panic were understandable. But from her perspective, she was playing quietly when he, a larger person, ran up to her while yelling and whisked away her plaything.

How would he feel if someone did that to him? Scared? Confused? That is probably how she felt. He needed to provide her with context. We discussed how he could approach her by explaining that those were his stickers, that he wanted to use them himself, and that he felt it was unfair for her to stick them all. He could also get her sticker book and offer that to her as an appropriate alternative. None of this was necessary to do, however, because my daughter had been listening and simply offered him his sticker book in return for hers.

Being aware of the perspectives of others, inclusive of their emotions and how one's behaviors affect those emotions, is central to relationships. The behaviors of each party in a relationship are in large part responses to the way the counterparty makes them feel. Each volley in the emotional dynamic is like a fiber of the shared relational bond.

Building awareness of the opposite perspective in a social exchange therefore need not be confined to hot moments and matters of wrongdoing. Every opportunity can be taken, including routine interactions. Prompt a child contemplating whether to share a toy to consider what it would be like to have toys shared or not shared with her. She may come to appreciate the sacrifices and joys others experience when sharing with her. Give a child about to have her hair brushed the opportunity to brush the hair of one of her dolls. She may learn that brushing hair isn't just something done to her, it is something done for her. Show a child who just poured milk using poor technique what her technique looks like by using it yourself and asking for improvement advice. She may see her errors in a different light, through the eyes of the one doing the coaching, and take some ownership of their correction.

A child aware of the perspectives of others will be more adept at making positive contributions to the emotional climate. She can decide when and how to grant acceptance, trust, respect, and love to her relationship partners based on how they make her feel. And she will experience her relationship partners responding with acceptance, trust, respect, and love. Because she is aware of her preferences, interests, and general circumstances, she will understand that what is being accepted, trusted, respected, and loved comes from her, and is uniquely hers. Only when she has built a solid platform of awareness will she be able to participate in relationships with authenticity, and truly connect with others.

KEY POINTS

- Building children's awareness of their emotions, interests, and needs, as well as introducing some coping strategies, lets them know that they matter. It demonstrates involvement and responsiveness to needs, emotions, and interests.
- Building children's awareness of expectations, consequences, their general condition, and the world at large helps them to make an impact. It demonstrates expectations to follow rules and provides structure conducive to solving problems.
- Encourage exploration. Play. Socialize. Read. Let your child pursue her interests.
- Recognize preferences. Allow for their free expression. See the strengths. Feed those strengths. Communicate boundaries.
- Explain lots of things—preferences, interests, emotions, rules, facts about everything. Answer questions.
- Listen. With empathy. Elicit information.
- Welcome the free emergence of emotions. Identify them. Describe them. Speculate about the feelings of others.

REFLECTION EXERCISES

Which preferences are the key contributors to your personality? Which preferences are the key contributors to the personalities of each of your family members?
Feel free to go beyond Myers–Briggs preferences for these questions, if it is helpful to do so.

_____

_____

_____

How do disparate preferences create tension between your family members? What opportunities are there to reduce the tension due to disparate preferences? What opportunities are there to create mutual benefits between family members by combining complementary preferences?

_____

_____

_____

How can you best utilize your preferences to make a difference? Can you utilize your preferences to support your parenting purpose, vision, and goals?

_____

_____

_____

CHAPTER 6

Give Decisions

G iving decisions to children is perhaps the most potent tool available to parents for setting and enforcing rules and expectations. This is because giving decisions can be used to match the incentives between parent and child with regard to rules and expectations. Giving decisions is also a powerful way for parents to access their children's well-being cycles. It allows you to simultaneously be responsive, provide structure, and support autonomy. It lets your children know that they matter, while also helping them believe that they can make an impact.

It does so in tiny increments over countless repetitions. Each given decision transfers a small amount of momentum to a child's well-being cycle. Over time, it shapes the person the child is to become.

Giving decisions is an appropriate goal for parents whose purpose is to raise adults. By the time they are grown, children who know how to make decisions will be able to live to their full potential. They will be able to decide how to meet the changing circumstances of life. They will be able to decide how to continually balance their competence pursuits with their relatedness pursuits. They will be able to live lives of resonance.

THE NATURE OF GIVING DECISIONS

Successfully giving decisions to children involves a balance of responsiveness and structure; an interplay of parental warmth, involvement, and benevolence, with parental guidance and supervision. Responsiveness is exercised by considering the child's personality, and giving an appropriate level of autonomy. Structure is provided by giving an equal dose of responsibility.

RESPONSIVENESS IS GIVING AUTONOMY

Responsiveness comes into play when setting rules and expectations. For example, rules and expectations may be devised so as to take a child's needs and emotions into account. Better yet, rules and expectations may be set in a way that empowers the child to accommodate his own needs and emotions. This is done by setting rules and expectations in terms as general as possible without diluting the spirit of the requirements. For example, a child wishing to unwind after the day at school can be given a chance to do so, and be expected to find an alternate suitable time to do his homework. In another example, a child wanting access to library books can be given his own account, and be expected to personally manage his dealings with the library. Setting broadly defined rules and expectations in this way grants the child a measure of autonomy.

Autonomy involves being instrumental in the events of one's life. It encompasses the sense that life is not a series of things happening to you, but a progression of things that you make happen. This is important because if a child is ever to learn how to live a life of resonance, a life lived by developing according to personally sanctioned pursuits and relationships, he must become versed in exercising autonomy.

Deci and Ryan, discussing autonomy as the third primary need recognized by self-determination theory in the *Handbook of Self-Determination Research*, describe autonomy as having one's actions arise from within. Autonomous action can be contrasted with actions of external origin, such as obedience to another's explicit instructions, or even deference to another's implicit wishes. However, Deci and Ryan allow that autonomy may still be exercised while submitting to the direction of others, provided the action is aligned with your own intentions and beliefs, and reflective of your individuality.[119]

A wide berth provides room for a child to find congruence, to determine for himself how to align your rules with his own preferences, interests, and abilities. However, parents need to be careful not to be hyper-responsive: a child's every whim should not be satisfied by overgeneralized rules and expectations. The rules and expectations need to be just broad enough so that the child is not forced to compromise the core of his self in order to comply. Parents need only see *that* the child learns to comply within a broadly defined structure, while the child has agency over *how*.

For example, a child with a borrowed library book is expected to return the book in the same condition in which it was loaned. The challenge for parents then is to refrain from giving exacting and unyielding instruction as to how to do that. It is difficult not to micromanage a small child who lacks the experience to do things as adeptly as you would. The parent may be tempted to stipulate that the book may only be read in the presence of the parent so that the parent can continuously monitor the child's handling of the library book and ensure that every page is turned with care. The parent may be tempted to require that the book be stored on a designated shelf when not in use, and then intercede when the book is left on a wet sink to personally transfer it to the dry shelf. But as long as the child is not purposefully mistreating the book, most interventions should be unnecessary. The parent could simply convey to the child that he is expected to return the book in the same condition in which he received it, and grant the child agency over how to do that.

Exercising his agency within such broadly defined structures is the child's training for negotiating constraints throughout his lifetime. A child who can find his own way within the constraints of his parents' rules and expectations will be able to apply similar methods even when his parents are not there. He will be able to work within the constraints of social, societal, and cultural forces to develop behaviors according to his preferences, interests, values, and abilities. He will ultimately be able to take the conflicting constraints thrust upon him by life, including the everyday random events, and weave his unique skills and capacities into a coherent and transcendent life purpose. The autonomous child can learn to forge integrity and purpose in a world that is messy, dynamic, and noisy.

PROVIDING STRUCTURE IS GIVING RESPONSIBILITY

But autonomy is not without cost. It is not a free license to operate in pursuit of whatever suits one's fancy. For autonomy to facilitate well-being, it must be counterbalanced. The natural trade-off for autonomy is responsibility. Responsibility entails fully experiencing the effects of one's autonomous action. And this is where structure comes into play.

Because the autonomous child has wider boundaries in which to operate, he has more room to maneuver. Therefore there is necessarily more opportunity for him to make mistakes, to stretch boundaries, and to run afoul of rules and expectations. The structure-providing parent allows consequences to play out unimpeded, but sees that the child is made to deal with any negative repercussions (which incidentally may include curtailment of autonomy). This affords the child a measure of responsibility.

Responsibility is living out one's choices. This is important because if a child is ever to learn how to live a life of resonance, a life of attunement between relatedness and competence within the context of his individual purpose, he must become accustomed to experiencing misalignment of relatedness and competence as a result of his own choices, and finding his own ways to adjust course and realign. He must perceive the connection between his actions and their outcomes. He must become accustomed to taking responsibility.

Assigning responsibility to children is a means for parents to ensure their beliefs, values, and principles are observed. However, parents need to guard against being hyper-structured: their every whim should not be satisfied by overly expansive rules and expectations. The rules and expectations need only cover enough areas so that the parents do not compromise their integrity. Parents convey the rules, expectations, and consequences, while the child is required to live them.

Recall the child with a borrowed library book who is expected to return the book in the same condition in which it was loaned. The child might fail to meet that expectation. In that case, the challenge for the parent is to withhold paternalistic protections. The temptation to reimburse the library for a damaged book on the child's behalf is high. But a child who has lost or damaged something with which he was entrusted is responsible for its recovery, repair, or replacement. It can be difficult not to mitigate any negative consequences the child has made for himself, and to instead demand responsibility. Personally rectifying his carelessness with the library is a valuable lesson for the child, one that incentivizes him to, of his own volition, turn every page with care and keep books on a dry shelf.

COMBINING AUTONOMY AND RESPONSIBILITY

Giving decisions truly represents a dual challenge for parents. The first challenge is giving autonomy, which requires formulating effective rules that account for a child's individuality and agency. It would certainly be easier to have your instructions be unquestioningly followed than it is to watch a child labor through something that, for adults, is simple or obvious. The second challenge is giving responsibility, which requires allowing consequences to play out naturally. It would certainly be easier to fix a child's mistakes than it is to have life grind to a halt while he bears the responsibility of doing it himself, perhaps clumsily so. The impulses to restrict autonomy and to absolve responsibility are strong. But if you want to do what is best for your adult child, you must do things that are hard. You must resist those impulses, and offer autonomy and responsibility.

For children, autonomy and responsibility may each feel like a mixed blessing. Autonomy means they can enjoy the freedom of finding their own way, but it also means that they cannot rely on comprehensive instructions from others. They must experience the struggle of finding their way when the path is unclear. Responsibility means they get to experience firsthand the joy of trying something that works, but they also have to feel the sting of attempting something that doesn't. They must fully own their feats and missteps alike, taking credit when earned and shouldering blame when deserved. Children must be able to draw in the full experiences of their autonomy and responsibility, good and bad, in the unpredictable world.

MATTER AND IMPACT

The importance of decisions for our self-esteem is recognized by Nathaniel Branden. Branden's model of self-esteem has the core elements of worthiness and competence. Branden describes decisions about behaviors as calculated expressions of our worthiness.[120] How we arrive at such decisions, according to Branden, is perceived as a reflection of our competence.[121]

The elements of worthiness and competence are practically synonymous with the concepts of matter and impact. Giving decisions is simultaneously a parent's testament that a child matters and is capable of making an impact. Those early matter and impact signals are a crucial part of building the self-esteem that will blossom into well-being.

Gottman also states that giving decisions is a means to helping children grow their self-esteem.[122] From Gottman's viewpoint, a child's request represents a decision the child has made but does not yet have the ability to implement. Noting that preschoolers have been observed to make three requests per minute, he acknowledges that giving many decisions, even small ones, can be taxing—but insists that doing so will be worthwhile. He gives such examples as arranging a meal's presentation for a girl who likes to keep her foods separate, buying a girl's preferred kind of dessert from the grocery store, leaving a lamp on for a boy afraid of the dark, and leaving the TV on for a boy who wants one more appearance from his favorite character.[123]

Gottman also intimates that giving decisions is an affirmation that the child's desires—and by extension the child himself—matter, and further that, by carrying out those decisions to produce outcomes, the child has made an impact.

GIVE LOTS OF PRACTICE

DECISIONS ARE PERVASIVE

It has been estimated that people make 35,000 decisions every day. Although this number is widely reported online, the source is elusive so it may be nothing more than Internet myth. Credible research has revealed that we make more than 200 decisions daily on the topic of food alone.[124] So thousands of daily decisions are plausible, and tens of thousands are certainly possible. Ten thousand daily decisions translate into 625 decisions for each of the 16 waking hours, or 10 decisions every minute. That's a decision every 6 seconds. Whatever the actual number is, suffice it to say that we are continually making decisions that affect our lives.

Some decisions are of minor consequence, such as whether to wake up or hit the snooze button, how much toothpaste to use, or which radio station to listen to. Some decisions are of moderate consequence. Among them: whether to stop at the gas station on a given day, determining which items a project will require, and considering who needs to be copied on an email. Others decisions are of grand consequence, such as whose company to keep, to what endeavors one should apply the most time, and when is the right time to have a child.

Nobody reaches the optimal decision every time, but it is easy to appreciate that adults who know how to make good decisions, especially in situations for which making good decisions is vitally important, can lead happy, fulfilling lives. Yet a lot of adults fail to make good decisions. Adults lacking effective decision-making skills can be expected to lead very troubling lives.

The stakes are too high to leave a child unprepared for the thousands of daily decisions they will have to make. We spend practically every moment of our entire lives making decisions, and the earlier we learn the skill the more time we will have to develop it. The skill of decision-making should be instilled in children while they are young so that it may grow with their growth. A child should be continually gaining experience with decisions, always making decisions that are as big as he is.

DECISION-MAKING IS COMPLEX

Making decisions can be a fairly big task to begin with. In fact, it is too big a task to consciously learn. Decision-making techniques are best learned by doing. As an illustration of the complexity of making decisions, consider the following.

Before reaching a decision, one first needs to recognize that a decision is needed. And then come the three main components to decision-making:

1) Situation: the situation must be assessed.
2) Course of action: courses of action must be surveyed.
3) Outcome: the outcome must be evaluated according to preconceived criteria.

Only then is the decision implemented and its consequences experienced. These steps are represented as a progression in Figure 9 below.

FIGURE 9. Basic Decision-making Steps

This multi-step process is actually simplistic. These steps can be expanded into interdependent sub-steps:

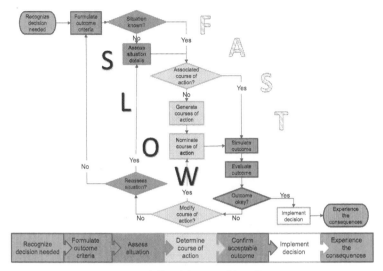

FIGURE 10. A Decision-making Process

Different pathways through the sub-steps are associated with different types of decision-making, classified as fast or slow.[125] Different methods of performing those sub-steps are associated with various kinds of shortcuts, heuristics and biases,[126] habits, and modes of intuition.[127] The possible permutations on the elements of the full decision process are incomprehensibly diverse.

One can't be expected to consciously navigate all these possibilities. The steps are taken as second nature, the result of years of practice making decisions and experiencing the consequences. More practice garners more familiarity with the various options, which brings more proficiency.

DECISION-MAKING REQUIRES PRACTICE

It is not through explicit teaching that a child develops decision-making methods, becomes adept at choosing from among them, and learns to apply them effectively. The only way to do this is through practice. Making decisions is like using language in that respect.

It has been estimated that people speak about 16,000 words per day.[128] That is on the same order as the number of daily decisions. We are continually using words in ways that affect our lives. The nuances of something as pervasive as language are too mentally taxing to learn explicitly. Like decisions, much of language is learned implicitly, and performed on the subconscious level. We learn how to use words—nouns, verbs, adjectives, and all of the other parts of speech—not by being drilled in the definitions of each word, nor by word classifications and grammar rules, but by being immersed in language usage and using it to interact. In fact, a study conducted by Betty Hart and Todd Risley[129] showed that three-year-olds whose parents provided language-rich environments had vocabularies that were twice as expansive as their language-deprived counterparts.

A child may not be able to define every word he uses nor be able to discuss past participles and noun–verb agreement, but he will be able to use language just the same. He may invent words and put them together using clumsy sentence structure, but he will be able to convey information. With enough exposure and practice, he will co-opt proper words into his vocabulary and learn how to assemble them in grammatically correct patterns.

It is easier, at least in the moment, to keep a child in silence than it is to accept all his questions and comments. Perhaps this is why some parents do just that, restricting dialogue with their children for their own convenience. But a child needs to hear and use words in order to learn language, a critical thing to master for a satisfactory life, a life replete with 16,000 words every day.

Similarly, a child needs to master decision-making for a satisfactory life, a life awash in as many as tens of thousands of decisions every day. It would be easier for parents to keep their children away from decisions as surely as it would be easier to silence a child. And perhaps for that reason, some parents do just that, restricting their children's autonomy for their own temporary convenience. I contend that decision-deprived children are forced to meet life from a deficit similar in magnitude to that of their language-deprived counterparts. Decisions are just as pervasive as language, and should garner equal recognition. No child should be kept a stranger to the decision process, nor be conditioned to feel intimidated upon recognition that a decision is required.

A child does not need technical lessons in the particulars of decision-making. Instead, a child needs autonomy in the form of lots of practice making decisions about what activities to engage in, how to do routine tasks, and with whom to play. He will need to make decisions using different methods, and at times doing so ineptly and producing negative consequences, in order to eventually become an effective decision maker.

ALLOW CONSEQUENCES TO FOLLOW

FROM DECISION TO CONSEQUENCES

A decision set loose into the world does not always return instant feedback in the form of consequences. As discussed in my previous book, *The Optimal Life Experience*, the ultimate consequences of a decision are often revealed with the passage of time. This is partly because we are each a part of a vast and complex interdependent network. Decisions can have implications for people within the decision maker's sphere of influence. As the decision maker's social ties assimilate a piece of his decision into their own pursuits and carry it forward, it propagates through to their spheres of influence.

The passage from decision to consequences may therefore be not only lengthy but also complicated. A decision may domino along tortuous paths before finally tumbling back into the lap of the decider as consequences. Decisions to behave unvirtuously are especially disposed to delivering consequences via complicated pathways.

Children, whose interpersonal networks are less extensive than those of adults, make decisions that deliver consequences via a much more direct route. The path is shorter, and so is the gestation period. These smaller scoped decisions make it easier to discern the patterns that connect consequences back to decisions. With enough practice, a child comes to learn that certain types of decisions—those made to control impulses, delay gratification, exercise empathy, and apply self-recognition—tend to return favorable outcomes.

Note the parallel between the decision-making steps and the well-being cycle (see Figure 11 below). Recognition that one is entrusted to make a decision that will produce consequences simultaneously reinforces the beliefs that one matters and can make an impact. The courses of action linked to favorable outcomes by the practiced decision maker are those conforming to emotional intelligence. Implementation of the decision equates to virtuous behavior, the consequences of which are consistent with the building of relationships and capabilities. The decision maker then feeds those consequences back into his thought process the next time he is called upon to make a decision. Through practice, good decisions are increasingly made that engender favorable outcomes.

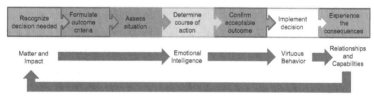

FIGURE 11. Decision-making Steps and the Well-being Cycle

Through the same practice, a child comes to learn that the countertype of decisions— those made to behave unvirtuously— tend to return unfavorable outcomes. Examples might include throwing a ball in the house, hiding candy under a pillow, or using a playmate's toy without asking. The practiced decider may not be able to predict *what* the negative consequences of unvirtuous decisions will be, but he will be able to predict *that* negative consequences will be. His wisdom comes not solely from a childhood of making perfect decisions yielding good consequences, but also from his experience with bad decisions yielding unfavorable consequences.

MANUFACTURED CONSEQUENCES

In order to learn how to make good decisions, the entire decision process needs to be traversed. Experiencing the consequences is the final step in the decision process. Parents often let children get tantalizingly close to the conclusion of the process, but then interfere at this last step. When they perceive good decisions to have been implemented, they offer rewards, praise, and even bribes in their eagerness for a repeat performance. A child sharing his toys might receive a gold star on a chart, or be commended for a "good job." When they perceive poor decisions to have been implemented, perhaps lacking in patience, they disrupt the feedback of natural consequences by inserting manufactured consequences such as punishments, scolding, and time-outs. A child hoarding his toys might be admonished for being "selfish," or sent off to stand in a corner. We can refer to such rewards or punishments as "manufactured consequences."

Chapter Two discussed how parents often distort reality by fabricating signals of matter and impact, by sending these manufactured positive signals that overpower the real negative signals coming from a child's relationship and capability failures. Manufacturing consequences is a similar practice, but instead of trying to protect the child from reality the parents are trying to teach the child more proficiently than reality. They are sending manufactured signals that overpower the real signals coming from a child's decision-making successes and failures. The parent is distorting reality a different way, but it is a distortion nonetheless and bound to be an inefficient teaching method for that reason. It breaks apart the consequences from the decision, burying the lesson that one is begotten by the other.

When consequences are manufactured by parents, the child's decisions come back to him dressed in his parents' clothes. The lesson that actually gets learned is that the source of the consequences are his parents. The child adjusts his behavior according to his parents' controls, but not necessarily in the way intended.

Imagine a child blaming his sibling for a lamp that he broke. The parents could first provide emotional support to the falsely accused child. They could discuss the offending child's motivations and feelings with him while explaining the effect on his sibling, and then work out a plan to remediate the broken lamp. But instead, let's imagine the offending child is scolded for lying, and sent to his room as punishment. His parents instruct him to think about the lies that he told while he is there. The child stews over his confinement. His anger, which he directs at his parents, brews. He builds resolve to not let them catch him lying again. He begins to prepare even more elaborate stories. He uses the mirror to practice delivering them more convincingly. As retaliation for his punishment, he concocts unflattering stories about his parents to share with his friends.

The child responds to negative manufactured consequences by applying his capacities to its source: his parents. The child contrives more sophisticated techniques for his questionable decisions to escape his parents' notice. Or he adopts a revenge mindset to balance the scales with his parents.[130] Or he construes his problems to be insoluble, resigning himself to the capriciousness of his parents' consequences.

Similarly, the child responds to positive manufactured consequences by applying his capacities to its source: his parents. The child contrives more sophisticated techniques for his good decisions to be noticed by his parents. Or he fixates solely on the manufactured consequences, striving for praise and rewards through sanctioned behaviors when the parents are present, and abandoning the same behaviors when the parents are absent.[131] Or he develops an attitude of apathy, having no zest for the kinds of activities that produce the real rewards of relatedness and competence.[132]

NATURAL CONSEQUENCES

When consequences are allowed to flow naturally, decisions come back to the child in his own likeness. A child sharing his toys makes his playtime with friends more fun. A child hoarding his toys creates a less enjoyable social atmosphere. The lesson learned is that the child himself is inextricably linked to the consequences. The child can respond to these natural consequences and apply his capacities to its source: himself. The child can devise more sophisticated techniques for his decision-making. He can pursue relatedness and competence rewards for their own sake. He can construe his successes to be his own doing, and may yearn for more of the same. He can construe his self-created problems to be soluble, and be driven to find self-created solutions.

Because natural consequences implicate oneself, there is no escaping them. Their inescapability is what makes natural consequences the most powerful educators. A wise teacher has the patience to let natural consequences take their course so a child may focus his energies on their true maker, that which he is most capable of affecting—himself.

There was a television show called *The Wonder Years*, which focused on the formative events in the life of young Kevin Arnold. One episode[133] focused on a rash of cheating in Mr. Collins's algebra class. A group of three students had acquired the teacher's edition of the textbook from which quizzes were drawn, and had transcribed the answers to be referenced during the quiz.

Because the class was graded on a curve, the cheaters weren't only inflating their own grades, they were deflating everyone else's grade. Kevin secured a private audience with Mr. Collins and tried to clue him in to the scheme without implicating specific classmates. Mr. Collins, seemingly oblivious, cryptically noted that the solution always lies within the problem.

Believing himself to be in an unfair situation that would not be addressed by the authority figure, Kevin decided to rectify the inequity himself by joining the group of cheaters. But he was not prepared for the consequences. Mr. Collins was keenly aware of the dishonest activities, and was allowing the natural consequences to run their course.

The immediate consequence for Kevin was that he was transferred to the advanced algebra class whose material was more suited to his apparent mathematical prowess. There he struggled mightily with his algebra homework without access to teacher notes. He struggled equally with his conscience as his friends and family celebrated his improvements and his girlfriend suggested he tutor her in math. Only after he approached Mr. Collins to admit his indiscretion was he allowed back in the regular classroom.

By then, the original band of cheaters, after acing quiz after quiz, had taken the unit test. The unit test was not from the book as they expected, and they wound up failing. The unit test accounted for half of the final grade. With their failure, the grading curve again shifted, this time back in favor of students who were doing honest work.

Both Kevin and the other cheaters were on the path to failure. Kevin redeemed himself through eventual honesty. His honesty was not a reaction to any punishment, but stemmed from being enlightened to his self-made consequences. By blaming himself and approaching the teacher to confess, Kevin did more than just resolve his problem. He made himself into the kind of person who does not cheat.

Mr. Collins could have cut short the whole adventure in chicanery. In fact, he would have been perfectly justified failing the boys, filling them with shame, assigning them detention, and carrying on with class. This would have been an example of manufactured consequences.

Instead Mr. Collins had the wisdom to let them take their chosen path to its natural conclusion, where they could see that they had led themselves to their own failure, one that they could not blame on a vindictive teacher or an unfair system. There were no apparent interventions. They did not receive a failing grade on the test as a penalty; they received a failing grade because their chosen method of taking the test was woefully inadequate.

They did initially blame Mr. Collins and resort to some infighting, but in the end, as long as they were accustomed to looking inward as a result of natural consequences, they would have had to change something about themselves. Cheating was a method they would have been unlikely to repeat, as their best efforts to cheat were unfettered by authority and still brought them to a place of no comfort. They could not improve upon their efforts by trying again with greater stealth so as not to get caught. They could not plot revenge, for no one interfered that they could paint as an antagonist. The only sensible thing left was for them to focus their attention inward. This solution lied within the problem.

NATURAL VERSUS MANUFACTURED CONSEQUENCES

The appeal to parents of manufactured consequences is understandable. Natural consequences are irregularly paced, not always commensurate, and of variable effectiveness. They are messy, dynamic, and noisy. By contrast, manufactured consequences are measured, controlled, and swift.

And they are real possibilities in the world. Traffic tickets, fines, and prison sentences are all examples of manufactured consequences that are vital for regulating an adult society. A judge will not wait for one's conscious to slowly but surely wear a perpetrator down until he changes his ways. The judge is there to ensure manufactured consequences are applied with measure, under control, and swiftly. A potential criminal must decide whether the deed is worth risking the manufactured consequences.

But weighing the risks of crime are not the kinds of decisions for which I am trying to prepare my children. More important than considerations of getting caught are considerations of the underlying reasons for a given behavior. An honest person decides to take the honest path not because he fears that the dishonest path will hurt him, but because he believes in the honest path, he has grown to love the honest path, and he has made the honest path part of who he is. If the prospect of facing prison time turns out to be the only thing separating my children from decisions to commit unspeakable acts, then I will consider myself to have failed as a parent.

Conversely, if my children pursue unsavory courses of action merely to comply with a patently unjust rule or norm, then I will also consider myself to have failed as a parent. Social controls should be complied with only as they align with one's beliefs and values, and allow one to maintain a sense of integrity. That way, an unjust rule, an unethical supervisor, a wrongheaded peer can be contradicted. For the child who knows why he adopts the right behaviors, opposing such controls when they are unjust can be done with as much conviction as supporting them when they are just.

The patterns of behavior that a child weaves into his character are partially a product of the environment. They incorporate the feedback of a universe that is messy, dynamic, and noisy. The underlying reasons for a virtuous person's honesty were learned in an environment whose consequences were irregularly paced, not always commensurate, and not always effective. As a child, the virtuous person must have experienced a great number of successes and failures in such chaotic conditions to become the kind of person he is.

The well-earned successes must all be allowed to play out naturally in the unpredictable world, and so must the hard-to-swallow failures. Letting your child succeed is the easy part. Failures, on the other hand, offer greater temptations for parental intervention. This is unfortunate because I believe the failures to be better teachers than the successes. In order to succeed as a parent, I therefore need to let my children fail while they are small. I need to let small acts of dishonesty naturally come to light, and allow unfair treatment to play out between siblings. It is the only way they can learn to succeed as adults.

FIT THE DECISION TYPE TO YOUR CHILD'S DEVELOPMENT LEVEL

We are now ready to discuss the different types of decisions that are typically given to children, with examples of how to apply them. I consider there to be two main classes of decisions: easy and hard. Easy decisions are those that lack a meaningful trade-off, while hard decisions balance autonomy with responsibility. As a child's development level grows, easy decisions should grow into hard decisions. We will only briefly cover the easy decisions and then dedicate the remainder of the chapter to three types of hard decisions. Because these hard decision types vary in complexity level, you can more easily choose one that fits your child's development level.

Recall John Gottman's examples with the girl who didn't want her foods to touch, the boy who wanted to see his favorite character on the TV one more time, the girl who with a specific dessert preference, and the boy afraid of the dark. Each of these types of requests—a preference for one thing over another that has been expressed to a caregiver—represents a decision. Parental compliance with such requests is consistent with the definition of responsiveness. Granting such requests whenever it is reasonable to do so (and *only* when it is reasonable to do so) confirms to the child that he matters. The main consequence of granting these requests is the child having affected his condition by making his preferences known. It is the child making an impact.

The importance of giving easy decisions, especially for very small children, cannot be underestimated. I contend that the parent should not only respond to these appeals by giving easy decisions when reasonable, but that giving easy decisions should be done proactively as well. The choice of which pair of shoes to wear, whether to have an apple or pear for a snack, whether to first brush teeth or get dressed should all be presented to the child when circumstances permit.

These decisions are easy for the child because the consequences are strictly positive. The child gets to have something they want, or chooses between things that they like. The consequences do not counterbalance the autonomy. That is what makes these decisions easy for the child.

However, giving easy decisions is not easy for the parent—remember that, on average, these decisions manifest themselves in three requests per minute for a preschooler. These requests are generally made of the parent because the child lacks the abilities to fulfill them for himself. The daughter who didn't want her foods to touch was not developmentally ready to prepare her own dinner plate. The son who wanted to see his favorite character didn't know how to work the television controls. The daughter who preferred a certain dessert did not contribute to the family's grocery shopping activities. The son who wanted the lamp on was unable to reach the switch. Granting these requests confers a degree of autonomy that a small child is generally denied. But the negative consequences of the child's autonomy—the effort needed to make the choice a reality, and any associated responsibilities—are subsidized by the parent, at least temporarily.

The subsidies are gradually removed as the child becomes more self-reliant. He then gets to satisfy his own preferences according to his abilities, the decisions to do so each being a concomitant acceptance of the corresponding responsibilities. The daughter gets to prepare her own plate, bearing the burden of carefully quarantining meats from vegetables. The son gets the freedom to operate the television, and is expected to survey other viewers before making his preferred adjustments. The daughter gets to make cookie recommendations while she helps with the grocery shopping, performing such tasks as pushing the cart, retrieving items, and crossing entries off the list. The son gets to turn on lamp switches to suit his own needs, and is required to turn them back off when no longer in use. As the child slowly grows, his decisions make commensurate transitions from the easy type to the hard type.

A child is able to make these transitions when he is accustomed to performing up to his abilities. When he has been receiving signals of matter and impact for his endeavors all along, a child does not resent the costs of his newfound autonomy. Instead of resisting the transfer of negative consequences to him from his parents, he is likely to welcome it. He *wants* more independence; he *wants* additional opportunities to grow his competences; he *wants* greater responsibilities. Embodying a readiness for these things is consistent with the kind of person he believes himself to be.

Children do not simply grow into hard decisions. Hard decisions are often given out of necessity. When important principles are at stake, when boundaries are overstepped, when one's behavior impacts others unfavorably, hard decisions must be given.

I classify hard decisions into three different categories: **coupled choice**, **limited choice**, and **open choice**. The degrees of autonomy and responsibility increase across these three respective decision categories. As autonomy and responsibility increase, the predictability of consequences decreases (see Table 10 on the following page).

DECISION TYPE	DESCRIPTION	RANGE OF AUTONOMY	LEVEL OF RESPONSIBILITY	PREDICTABILITY OF CONSEQUENCES	EXAMPLE
Coupled Choice	Choose this or that / (Choose this and that)	Low	Low	High	Eat carefully or clean the floor (Eat your way and clean the floor)
Limited Choice	Choose from among these	Medium	Medium	Medium	Family-style dining (Self-serve from shared dishes)
Open Choice	Choose within this structure	High	High	Low	Serve as meal manager (Administer all the meal's activities from start to finish)

Table 10. Hard Decisions

A coupled choice is one where two opposing options are offered. It is not the two options that are coupled, however. It is the autonomy and the responsibility that are coupled. The situation, the courses of action, and the outcomes are all explained to the child faced with a coupled choice.

A limited choice is one where a menu of options is offered. This allows a bit more autonomy than does a coupled choice. It also adds a bit more complexity than a coupled choice. There is a greater potential for unforeseen consequences. With a limited choice, the child is made to understand the situation and the possible courses of action, but must apply more of his own effort to develop a sense of the likely outcomes.

An open choice is one where the options themselves are not given, only the basic structure in which the decision is to take place. This offers the greatest degree of autonomy but also the greatest degree of uncertainty. The situation is explained to the child, but he must ascertain the courses of action and the outcomes for himself.

Depending on your child's development level, the nature of the situation, the complexity involved, and other constraints, such as the need for urgency or accuracy, one of these three decision types will usually conform to the specific need. I have found that considering these three simple types of decisions greatly simplifies the formulation of decisions to be presented to the child. And this really is the only reason to have a classification scheme at all: it helps to turn ambiguous family situations into "color inside the lines" exercises.

GIVE "COUPLED CHOICE" DECISIONS

Coupled choices can be thought of as "this or that" propositions, but I do not like to present them that way. Gottman's example daughter can be told to either segregate the entrée portions herself or take the peas and potatoes as they are given to her. The son can be told to either operate the television himself or watch whatever is selected by those who do operate the television. The other daughter can be told to either help do the grocery shopping or accept the food that is brought home. The other son can be told to either operate the hall light or be in the dark. But these sound less like statements of empowerment and more like outright dismissals.

To tell a child to "either do this or be stuck with that" is to present the child with a predicament. While an accurate representation of the decision which lies before the child, it does not offer much in the way of inspiration. The child must choose between two negatives, either to accept a burden or to be neglected. I prefer to reframe the choice in a more evenhanded manner. Rather than using "this or that," I like to use a "this and that" construction that couples the autonomy with the responsibility. Enjoy this autonomy *and* perform that responsibility, or vice versa. To tell a child to do this and get that presents the child not with a predicament but with an opportunity.

TECHNIQUE: COUPLED CHOICES

Present your child with some autonomy, and then couple it with some responsibility.

Fix your own plate *and* have dinner your way. Actualize your television preferences *and* consider the other viewers. Help with the grocery shopping *and* make some selections. Turn the hall light on when you need it *and* turn it off when you don't.

The "this and that" construction does not present an explicit dilemma like the "this or that" construction does. The situation is just as simple, the outcomes are just as clear, and the decision between the courses of action is the same—but arrived at differently. Instead of being led directly to a fork in the road by a forceful hand, the child takes himself there at his discretion.

Before continuing with "this and that" examples, it should first be made clear that there are situations where "this or that" is appropriate. When deciding how to apportion limited resources such as time or money, the choices are often naturally evenhanded. With only ten minutes left before bedtime, a parent and child can either do a puzzle or read a book. If they decide to do the puzzle, there will be no time left to read the book, and vice versa. With only one dollar, either this toy or that toy can be purchased, but not both. A decision to buy one toy is necessarily a decision not to buy the other toy. There may be more than two choices for how to spend time or money in theory, but in practice the decision often boils down to two favored options. Such decisions are unambiguously dilemmas, and would not benefit much from being recast as "this and that" decisions.

EXAMPLES

When my six-year-old son wanted to enter a tae kwon do tournament, I was reluctant to consent. It represented a nontrivial commitment of time and finances. The tournament was a full-day event, and required the payment of an entry fee and various other associated costs. I surmised that he wanted the prestige of competing in a tournament, he wanted the trophies, and he wanted the glory of competing in the big convention center downtown. But there is more to a tournament than simply getting things. It is a competition and requires preparation. Tournaments should be entered to satisfy a drive to compete, a drive that is matched by the will to train hard. In fact, we did not participate in the first two tournaments for which he was eligible.

For the third tournament, my son (now seven years old) again asked to participate. I wanted him to either train hard or skip the tournament again. But I didn't offer an either/or proposition. I told him that he needed to commit to three weekly lessons for the month leading up to the tournament instead of his usual two, and I would commit the resources to participate. Train hard *and* register for the tournament. He did, and I did.

We struggled with another "this or that" proposition in our home for a long time before translating it into a successful "this and that" construction. I calculated that the children were told at least one thousand times—that is, at least once a day for three years—to eat over their plates. Yet they still leaned back to eat their food and got crumbs all over the floor. So the mantra became "Eat over your plate or clean the floor." They continued to lean back as they ate their food every day, and then vacuumed the crumbs when they finished. They chose from the options provided, but not the way we had hoped. So we finally removed the conditional: "Eat your way *and* clean the floor." Maintaining a clean floor beneath their table settings became the children's responsibility regardless of how they ate, and how they ate was left for them to determine without pressure from Mom and Dad. With this structure, without the will of Mom and Dad being imposed through suggestion, they finally did the sensible thing and started to eat over their plates of their own accord. There were days when they didn't need to vacuum at all because there were no crumbs to clean. And Mom and Dad could finally eat without struggling to contain our frustration.

An uncooperative toddler can try the patience of the most even-tempered of parents. Consider the behaviors in the following scenarios. You are ready to leave the house for an appointment, and as you reach for your child's coat he emphatically declares, "No coat!" You are enjoying dinner at home later, and your child realizes, "Oh, spilling milk gets your attention? Then I think I'll keep doing it." You have just drawn a bath for your child after dinner, but he protests, "No bath now. Play instead!"

The next twenty minutes in each of these scenarios are sure to be difficult. But some of the best times to give **coupled choice decisions** are when your child is being uncooperative and the alternatives presented are difficult. Giving decisions is possibly best done in hot moments, while life is happening, raw and unplanned and under stress.

That is quite less convenient for you, the busy parent. But if you think of these situations as lifelong teaching opportunities instead of twenty-minute inconveniences, they can be some of the most satisfying aspects of parenting. They are great moments to teach children about making decisions.

Imagine the following responses. "It's your choice to wear a coat or not. It is cold outside." Or, "If you choose to spill your milk, there won't be anything for you to drink. I won't be pouring another cup." And finally, "The bathwater is ready. The longer you wait, the colder it will get. You decide when to start."

The power of the "this and that" construction, delivered clearly and calmly, is evident here. Bundle yourself up however you wish *and* experience the weather. Apportion your milk as you like *and* regulate your thirst. Pick a suitable bath time *and* abide the water temperature. Each "this and that" pair couples autonomy with responsibility.

CONSEQUENCES

Each pair also embodies natural consequences. A child who recognizes his need for warmth will wear a coat and naturally feel warm; a child not using self-recognition will reject the coat and naturally feel cold. A child who can control his impulse to spill milk will naturally have enough to drink; a child not controlling impulses will spill his milk and naturally feel thirsty. A child who can delay his gratification will play later and naturally have a comfortable bath now; a child seeking immediate gratification will play now and naturally feel uncomfortable in a cool bath later. Just as it is unnecessary to encourage good decisions with positive manufactured consequences, it is unnecessary to discourage bad decisions with negative manufactured consequences. The child's actions will produce their own consequences, positive and negative.

Discovering one's self-begotten negative consequences is a personal experience. It is important for the child to meet his creations free from intrusions. Resist the urges to say "good job" as he climbs in a warm bath; to give treats in exchange for not spilling milk; to grant special privileges when he dresses for the weather; to give gold stars for cleaning up crumbs; and to offer monetary incentives for good performance in the tae kwon do competition. Resist the urges to say "I told you so"; to chastise his decision to immerse himself in uncomfortable bathwater; to mock his empty cup as he bewails his thirst; to shame him for shivering without a coat; to ground him for his messiness after he drudges over his crumbs; and to put him in time-out after he expresses regret for deciding not to commit to extra training, thereby missing the tae kwon do tournament. Tempting as it may be to praise the child who has made a good decision and to lecture the child who has made a bad decision, doing so often just scrambles the signals from reality. It implies that you deserve credit for consequences that the child himself created.

Let the natural consequences speak for you. Let the child's comfort, quenched thirst, warmth, leisure, and feelings of satisfaction give the praise. Let his discomfort, thirst, shivering, drudgery, and feelings of regret conduct the lectures. These natural consequences will speak to the child in a clearer voice than you can. They will speak in the child's own voice.

COMMUNICATION

This is not to say you need to be unresponsive to your child's decisions and behaviors. The following three types of response can be used to accompany the natural consequences:

1) Your feelings (about expectations or behaviors).
2) Objective commentary (about behaviors, reasons, or consequences).
3) The child's feelings (empathic discussions about the struggle or success).

These types of responses are useful for communicating with the good decision maker and the bad decision maker alike. There is value in giving a well-placed expression of appreciation for the child who promptly climbs in the bath, offering some objective commentary about how the child moved his cup to the far side of his plate to avoid spillage, and engaging in an empathic discussion about how he feels to be wearing a coat. "I'm glad we are doing bath time now, because we finally get to relax afterward. The water would have gotten cold before too long. Is it comfortable now?" Conversely, there is value in expressing disappointment that bath time is later than your expectations, offering some objective commentary about the price of milk and the need to conserve food, and engaging in some empathic discussion about how the shivering child feels without a coat. "I wish you didn't have to be thirsty. It takes a lot of hard work to be able to pay for groceries. We could get our money's worth out of that milk if we drank it all."

The child who makes a good decision may develop the notion that he has earned something special. My son once asked me at a party whether good behavior will earn him cake. "Logan's dad said he can have cake if Logan [not his real name] plays nice with the smaller kids. Me too?" I reminded my son that I don't do punishments or rewards, and asked him whether he wanted to start getting punishments and rewards. He didn't. I then told him that he was going to have cake because this was a party, and that I expected him to be good to the smaller kids anyway because that is what a good person would do, and I expected him to make himself into a good person. I found opportunities throughout the evening to make observations on his ability to share and take turns with the smaller children, to comment that I saw how he helped a fallen child get back up, and to ask him about how much fun he had playing with the smaller children.

In the case of the child who makes a bad decision, there will be more than enough opportunities to express feelings, offer objective commentary, and engage in empathic discussion about the child's feelings. The child may wail when he dips a toe into the cool bathwater, refusing to go further. He may scream that he is dying of thirst without a milk refill. He may balk at walking the full distance to a destination without his coat. He may cry about having to clean the crumbs for a long time before he actually picks up the vacuum cleaner. He may beg to go to the tournament before, during, and after every tae kwon do lesson leading up to the competition date. Demanding that your child grapple with his self-created consequences can be an excruciatingly drawn-out experience. But when done so supportively instead of adversarially, with discussion of feelings and objective comments on what the child is going through, it is doable. Through his struggles, a child may need to hear, "I feel cold just looking at you shiver without a coat. If we jog together, we will get there faster. Plus, the movement will help warm you up," or "It must be hard to hear the other children talk about the tournament. How often do you think they are training? If you want, we can ask when the next tournament will be."

Let the child forge his own steel, for no one can do it for him. Support the child emotionally as he struggles, but do not over-involve yourself. Stick to expressions of feelings, objective commentary, and empathic discussion while your child follows his decisions to their natural conclusions.

In another example, a child may want the freedom to choose his own snack to bring to school. You can allow the child to choose his own snack within healthy limits, and also demand that he be responsible for remembering to bring it with him. Because this snack is the product of his own autonomy and responsibility, he will enjoy it all the more. But if he forgets the snack, his omission will naturally lead to afternoon hunger. When you drop him off at school, he may beg you to go back home to retrieve his snack. Be supportive of his plight, expressing concern over the forgotten snack, commenting on how the snack was left on the counter instead of being put in the book bag, and discussing the child's feelings of regret. Also be steadfast in your refusal to comply with his request.[vi] Let the forgetful child skip his snack. Let his hunger

---

[vi] I need to qualify this statement. If it is essentially costless to get the child's snack for him, and if it is not a common occurrence, then it would seem vindictive not to do it. I am not recommending you model vindictive behavior. By all means, get the easily retrievable snack and, if possible, have the child come along when you do it. For most parents, however, retrieving the snack will make them late for work, miss an appointment, or throw off their schedule for the whole day. It is to these parents that the recommendation applies.

be his reminder for next time. It will speak to him as he leaves the home for school.

RAISE ADULTS NOT KIDS

The inconvenience of such situations is often compounded by their surreal mundanity. How can a forgotten snack derail your whole morning? How can a few crumbs on the floor justify a lengthy meltdown that stretches your evening so much later than anticipated? How can a few ounces of milk demand so much of your attention? Many of these things might seem unworthy of the creative energy required. A busy parent may feel justified just getting it done, whether by force, or through yelling, or with the help of a sticker chart. But these seemingly mundane things are important enough to be top priorities. The snack, the milk, and the crumbs are not just things that happen in between life's real events; they *are* life's real events. The interactions between you and your child during the small things are interactions that matter. That is where life happens. Shortcuts are not good enough.

Endure the inconveniences of bad decisions along with your child. Brave the judgmental eyes of other parents as your child shivers without a coat or goes to school snackless. Wait as long as it takes for him to get into the bathtub. Teach your small child how to operate the vacuum cleaner even though it would be faster to do it yourself. In the long run, those inconveniences won't matter. In fifteen years, whether your child caught another cold as a toddler, or didn't have a snack one day in school, or anguished over a few crumbs will be irrelevant. But whether he can make good decisions will be extremely relevant.

Will your child always make the right decision? No, and that's okay. Making bad decisions is a pretty good way to learn how to make good decisions. The bad decisions are best made under your loving supervision and when the stakes are low. Don't wait until the teen years to allow your child to start making decisions, when mood-altering substances, cars, and dating are introduced. Think of the consequences of poor decision-making at that age.

They are life altering—involving health, safety, and wellness. It will be too late to make safe mistakes. By contrast, a cold bath as a toddler while you endure some whining is small stuff, and should be embraced as a learning experience.

Let the bad decisions run their course so you can have the satisfaction of watching your child make good decisions later. It is a good parenting decision to delay gratification and take some inconvenience now for something better later. And that's the best example you can set for your child.

GIVE "LIMITED CHOICE" DECISIONS

Limited choices offer more variety than the "this and that" construction of coupled choices. Instead of considering only "this and that," the child must contemplate "all of these." There are a greater number of possibilities for courses of action attached to a given situation. This necessarily means greater possibilities for outcomes. Limited choices offer more autonomy and less predictability.

TECHNIQUE: LIMITED CHOICES

Present your child with a menu of options from which to choose.

Limited choices may grow naturally out of coupled choices. Consider the child who makes her own dinner plate so that the foods don't touch. As she grows, she will be able to take more responsibility for her meals than simply arranging meats and vegetables to her liking. She will be ready for family-style dining.

FOOD EXAMPLE

Family-style dining entails putting all the food on the table in large serving bowls, and allowing family members to help themselves. The selections, serving sizes, number of helpings, and arrangement on the plate are all up to each individual eater. The picky eater may decide to keep meats and vegetables separate by having one first, then the other. Another eater may skip the vegetables entirely and have only potatoes and meat loaf. Maybe two helpings of potatoes. Or extra helpings of bread for a meat loaf sandwich. It is up to each eater to decide how to fill his plate using the variety of options before him.

This autonomy over one's meal represents a responsibility to oneself. Failure to fulfill that responsibility will result in negative consequences. An eater who decides not to balance food types— for example, all vegetables and no meat or vice versa—may get indigestion. An eater with poor portion control may have an achy stomach from overeating.

An eater who overestimates his appetite will have to deal with the surplus. In our home, family-style dining always included the "take all you want but eat all you take" contingency. This meant that unfinished meals were to be stored in the refrigerator and consumed at the next meal. So an overzealous self-server will have to watch the rest of the family eat a freshly cooked meal the next day while he finishes yesterday's leftovers.

In addition to responsibility to oneself, family-style dining also entails responsibilities to others. The entire family is serving themselves out of the same serving bowls using the same serving spoons. Each family member is entitled to their turn at getting a fair share using clean utensils. Each family member therefore is responsible for passing dishes and taking turns, exercising restraint, and using sanitary serving practices. Failure to meet these responsibilities will frustrate fellow diners, leave an unfavorable perception of the transgressor, and may result in curtailment of family-style dining privileges.

MONEY EXAMPLE

Limited choices are not only useful for meals, but may also be applied to snacks. As healthful as parents try to make snacks, children are masters at creating opportunities to eat junk food. Working in their favor is an almost inexplicable inflow of candy, at least into homes like ours. Although we never bought candy, it seemed to materialize out of thin air. The children would receive bags of candy whenever schoolmates celebrated a birthday, they would be gifted candy at holiday gatherings, and they would even be given candy at restaurants. And for Halloween, they would score well over a hundred pieces of candy from trick-or-treating. The result was that each child had their own personal hoard of candy. In order to reduce the quantity of candy, we instituted a voluntary candy buyback program.

The candy buyback program was nothing more than a standing offer of $0.25 for any package of candy. It was a limited choice in that it only applied to each child's stash of candy. The offer did not apply to any other food in the house, to toys, or to works of art. The children could only earn money through the buyback program by deciding to sell from their stores of candy. The children could decide to sell all of their candy, they could decide to sell some of their candy, or they could decide to sell none of their candy. They could sell their least favorite pieces, they could sell the smallest pieces, or they could sell random pieces. They could sell candy on Halloween night, or the day after, or in the middle of July. They could sell however they decided within the limitation that the candy come from their own stores.

TECHNIQUE: CANDY BUYBACK PROGRAM

Maintain a standing offer to purchase candy as a way for your child to learn how to make calculated choices.

The consequences of their decisions could be either good or bad. The immediate consequences were invariably good, because they would not make the exchange unless they valued the money more than the candy. Negative consequences would only appear later if the child came to regret the exchange. A child who has no candy to eat while his sibling enjoys a sucker may lament his decision to sell too much candy. Conversely, a penniless child watching his sibling buy something at the toy store may lament his decision to eat all his candy. The sibling buying a toy may do so hastily, and come to bemoan his impulsive purchase. But because I take the candy to work and share it with colleagues, my candy purchases are irreversible. The child has to live with the consequences he created.

A child who first starts earning his own money will want to buy a toy. Planning a special shopping trip can be done according to another limited choice. A child with $15, for example, can be given a choice of three stores. He can buy a toy at the dollar store, at the discount store, or at the regular toy store.

The difference between these stores lies in the prices and quality of toys. A very cheap toy that will probably break soon can be purchased at the dollar store. A moderately cheap toy that is somewhat more robust can be purchased at the discount store. A regularly priced toy that is well built can be purchased at the regular toy store.

Any of these choices involve a trade-off, and will have both good and bad consequences. The dollar store toy is likely to offer limited enjoyment, but will leave the child with $14 in his bank. The discount store toy is likely to offer more enjoyment, but may leave the child with only $10 in his bank. The regular toy store toy is likely to be the most enjoyable, but will probably leave the child with little or no leftover money. These consequences can be explained to the child in advance, but to fully understand the trade-offs involved he will need experience making choices and living the outcomes for himself.

Once inside any one of these stores, the child finds grander choices before him. But those choices are still limited. They are limited by availability, price, and preferences. The child in the dollar store has the entire store from which to choose. The child inside the discount store may also have the entire store to choose from, or may need to be guided to the aisles that are appropriate for him and his budget. The child in the regular toy store will have greater restrictions placed on his options, and will need to learn how to read price tags before he can independently make a purchasing decision.

These choices may not sound very limited, but there are inherent restrictions. The toys in the dollar store and in the discount store are competing for the child's attention against the toys that he imagined to be available. He may imagine an aisle full of mechanical dinosaurs, or dream of finding the same electric scooter there that his neighbor has, or think that the bouncy house that he saw in a commercial will be available there. But he is limited to the toys actually in the store. The child in the regular toy store will get to meet mechanical dinosaurs, electric scooters, and bouncy houses "in the flesh." But he is limited to the money in his pocket. He has to walk past those toys and not buy them.

The limitations inherent in a shopping trip may be inconvenient and exasperating for the child and parent alike. The child holding money in a toy store may whine, cry, and resist. The parent may have to explain, reason, and persist. It may not be the fun educational lesson that was planned, but it will be an important educational lesson nonetheless. Whether he decides to leave the store empty-handed or decides to turn his money over to the cashier with excited hands in exchange for a new toy, the child will learn something.

There are also things to be learned when shopping for someone else. A child can be taken to the store to shop for a friend's birthday gift. Similar to when he is shopping for himself, he will be limited by a certain price range and by the availability in the store. He will also be limited by his friend's preferences.

He needs to demonstrate some level of others-awareness in order to decide on a proper gift. If he is able to put himself in the shoes of his friend, to exercise some degree of empathy, he will choose a gift that the friend appreciates and enjoys. If he instead chooses a gift according to his own preferences, his offering may be met with some disappointment.

He also needs to demonstrate some self-restraint. Buying a gift for someone else means not buying something for himself. If the child decides to shop for his friend undistracted, to exercise some degree of impulse control, the outcome will be an efficient shopping trip. If he decides to bargain and beg for a toy of his own as well, the outcome will be a rough time.

TIME AND OTHERS EXAMPLE

Like money, time may be subject to limited choice decisions. Scheduling a program of activities is an example. Depending on the timeframes involved, activities can be scheduled using a calendar, a clock, or a simple scrap of paper. These types of decisions are of the limited choice variety because the defined activities and timeframes (the situation) can only be given so many arrangements. The objective is to create an arrangement (the course of action) that produces a good outcome.

An example of an activity needing to be scheduled in our home was one-on-one days. These were days that were dedicated to one-on-one parent–child interactions. One of the children went to day care as usual on these days, while the other one would spend time with me. For my son, they were called Father–Son Days and for my daughter they were called Daddy–Daughter Days.

I would use my vacation time from work to schedule one-on-one days. I would do this once or twice mid-year, and again at the end of the year when I was required to use or lose my remaining vacation days. We would also have one-on-one days whenever the children required doctor or dentist visits. Because I had to miss some work to take them to their appointments anyway, I often took the opportunity to take the entire day off.

TECHNIQUE: ONE-ON-ONE DAYS

Set aside a special day for just you and your child. Allow the child to have some input deciding how to spend the day.

One-on-one days usually consisted of one or two special activities such as roller skating, fishing, bowling, or going to a movie. These special activities were interspersed among routine items including meals, snacks, and rest. When the children were younger, I would choose and order the activities myself. As they got older, I would let them propose activities and do the scheduling.

For a while, we used a drawing of a clock, with squares corresponding to each hour (see Figure 12 below). The activities were written on sticky notes, which were adhered to the paper beside the clock. The child was to apply each sticky note to the square corresponding to the time chosen for the activity.

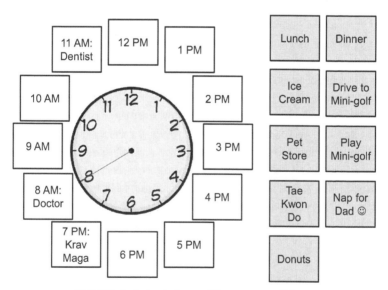

FIGURE 12. Scheduling a "One-on-one" Day

Some activities were already assigned. If the children had an appointment, such as a doctor or dentist visit, then the squares for those corresponding hours would be prepopulated. If I had an appointment, such as a Krav Maga self-defense class, then the square for the corresponding hour would also be prepopulated. In Figure 12, three hours are prepopulated for just those activities. This leaves nine hours yet to be assigned.

Figure 12 is a recreation of an actual scheduling activity to be performed by the children. It does not, however, represent a true one-on-one day. On this day, when the children were seven and four years old, my daughter had a doctor appointment and they both had dentist appointments. So there were actually three of us doing the day's activities, which the two children had to work together to schedule. Figure 13 below is a recreation of their actual scheduling decisions:

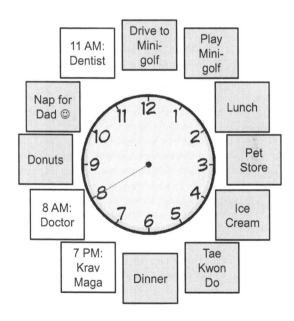

FIGURE 13. A Scheduled "One-on-one" Day

The children decided to have breakfast at the donut shop immediately following the doctor appointment that started the day. They made this decision partly because they couldn't wait to have donuts. The donut shop was right by their school. It was within reach on a daily basis, yet we very rarely went there. Going there was a real treat for them. They also made the decision to start their day at the donut shop partly because they had the self-awareness to recognize that they would be hungry for breakfast by 9:00.

They decided to let me have a nap at 10:00. This was a good item to include in the day, not only because I like to take naps, but because it was also a good exercise in others-awareness. There was time to schedule the nap in the early afternoon, but we would not have been at home. I would have had to sleep in the car, and the children recognized that I would not be very comfortable doing so. They opted to schedule the nap in the late morning, after the doctor appointment when we would be close to home. They had to consider whether this was too early for me, but rightly decided that it would work. I wake up very early, so have no trouble napping in the late morning—especially after a big breakfast. Plus, it gave them the opportunity to play quiet board games, something they enjoyed doing in the mornings.

Following their 11:00 dentist appointments, the children decided to drive to the mini-golf course at 12:00. There were mini-golf courses closer to our home, but this day was in the middle of winter. We needed to play at an indoor mini-golf course, and those were harder to find. The course we went to was about a half hour away, so we were able to begin playing before the scheduled time of 1:00. Keeping this cushion in the schedule was necessary to allow time for the drive back home, which was not indicated in the schedule because the hour allocated to drive there was intended to cover the round trip.

But the combination of mini-golf and lunch took longer than expected, and we lost our drive-time cushion. We were finishing lunch and it was approaching 3:00. We needed to find some way to make up the time.

The children decided to improvise a rearrangement of the schedule. They ordered ice cream immediately after lunch, in the same restaurant. This saved us the time of transferring locations, and we regained our cushion. The children finished their ice cream at around 3:00.

There was a pet store nearby, and the children were eager to pick out what were to be their first pets: goldfish. But goldfish do not survive long in the plastic bag typically provided by pet stores. Because we did not want to risk making a long drive home with goldfish in the car, the decision was made to drive to a pet store near home.

We arrived at the pet store before the scheduled time of 4:00. This allowed enough time for several limited choice decisions. The children picked out fishbowls, plastic plants, and decorative gravel, all from the low-price sections. They then made the most important decisions of the trip, and picked out their new pets from the aquarium. When we arrived home the children helped the new pets, Goldie and Snowflake, get settled in their habitats.

We then left for tae kwon do and arrived in time for the 5:00 class. The class was forty-five minutes, which allowed time to drive back home for a 6:00 dinner. Dinner was essentially the end of the day. Following dinner, I left alone for my Krav Maga class.

One-on-one days (and when there were three of us, one-on-one-on-one days) were highly anticipated events. The fun that we had was magnified by the fact that these days were not very frequent. I believe that the enjoyment was magnified even further by the control the children were given over the day's activities. They were given the power to realize their personal inclinations through the decisions that they made. This made them feel like they mattered.

The decisions gave them a sense of ownership in the day's activities. They weren't simply being carted around to donut shops, medical offices, golf courses, restaurants, and pet stores so that they could enjoy the spoils therefrom. They played real roles in the planning process. They also took an active part in determining how the day was carried out in real time. They made an impact.

The children got to enjoy a measure of autonomy, and as a result assumed a level of responsibility. They got to choose how best to enjoy their donuts, mini-golf, and ice cream, and also felt a responsibility to make sure that I enjoyed my nap—proactively taking pains to get home on time and then tiptoe quietly as I slept. They got to make decisions about the schedule, and also bore the responsibility of keeping the day on schedule—willingly sacrificing a trip to a specialty ice cream parlor in favor of a simpler substitute in order to do so. They got to take home affordable pets and accessories of their own choosing, and because of this readily bore the responsibilities of caring for them—regularly feeding the fish and cleaning the items without prompting.

UNIVERSALITY

Dad's naps, altered schedules, ice cream, and affordable pets are recurring themes in this chapter. Not the items themselves, but the categories to which they belong: other people, time, food, and exchange (i.e. money). These four items appeared in the section on coupled choices, they appeared in this section on limited choices, and they will appear in the next section on open choices.

The reason for the centrality of these four themes is that they are universal. No matter who you are, no matter where you live, and no matter what epoch you live in, you will need to make decisions about others, time, food, and exchanges. The constraints presented within these categories transcend all human differences.

This book is intended to remain relevant over generations and across cultures. I have always been writing this first and foremost for my children. But I have also always hoped that some version of this writing would make its way to their children, and their children's children, and so on. So I have decided to work from universal concepts. As you read this, you may be in a place far away, reading in a language that is strange to me, in a time that I cannot fathom. I may not know exactly who "you" are, yet this book was written for you.

As you read this, regardless of your life circumstances, you will need to allocate limited resources such as time and money between yourself and others. Doing so will require the use of self-recognition and empathy alike to balance what you value with what others value. Doing so will require you to find complementary apportionments, like an hour suited to both those who value morning board games and those who value naps. Doing so will also require delayed gratification and impulse control alike to deny yourself something now to get something better later without overindulging, like waiting to buy a goldfish so that it makes it home alive, and appreciating modest pet accessories. The difficult decisions involved—to behave with compassion or indifference, patience or impatience, and temperance or gluttony—makes the difference between a life of relatedness and competence and a life devoid of meaning. These difficult decisions, over time, make the difference between a life of well-being and a life of ill-being.

GIVE "OPEN CHOICE" DECISIONS

Open choices offer even more variety than limited choices. There are so many available courses of action, in fact, that they defy itemization. The child offered an open choice can be made to understand the situation, but must work out the courses of action and the outcomes for himself. Open choices offer the highest level of autonomy and the lowest degree of predictability.

TECHNIQUE: OPEN CHOICES

Present your child with a structured situation, within which the child has free rein to operate. Be sure to present open choices only when your child is developmentally ready.

FOOD EXAMPLE

A child ready for open choices need not be given a spread of prepared dishes from which to assemble a meal. He can be allowed access to a kitchen in which to prepare a meal. The ingredients are many and the combinations thereof are virtually limitless.

Preparing a meal may not require any exceptional culinary skill. A child making his breakfast may do no more than wash a piece of fruit, pour a bowl of cereal, and add milk. Or he may crave scrambled eggs. If he doesn't know how to make scrambled eggs, he will ask for them. He can then be instructed how to break an egg, how to scramble the broken egg using a fork, and how to use the microwave oven to cook the scrambled egg. He can then be left to resume managing his breakfast.

My children were allowed to alternate holding the formal title of Breakfast Manager. A Breakfast Manager was often needed on the weekends, when the children were ready for breakfast at an earlier hour than Mom and Dad. The Breakfast Manager was responsible for supervising all activities related to breakfast. Those responsibilities were to be filled according to three criteria: healthy breakfast, clean kitchen, and clean children.

There was a lot of room for autonomy within these three constraints. A healthy breakfast meant that foods like cake and cookies were off-limits, but the children generally had free rein to make responsible food choices. A clean kitchen meant that the kitchen needed to be just as clean after breakfast as it was before breakfast. The kitchen could be made as messy as it needed to be in order to prepare breakfasts, as long as the children took the responsibility to clean it up afterward. Clean children meant simply that hands and faces were to be washed after eating breakfast. Making breakfast might make for messy children, and that was okay as long as the messy children met the responsibility of reverting themselves back to clean children when finished.

There was also a lot of room for unintended consequences within these three constraints. The child might find himself eating something he doesn't actually like because he did not know that apple juice does not complement cereal very well. He might find himself cleaning the vacuum cleaner because he wanted cheese on his bagel, and did not know that partially melted cheese shreds could not be vacuumed. He might find himself administering first aid because he wanted to eat an orange, and did not cut away from himself as he sliced open the peel.

There was also a lot of room for unintended consequences outside of the constraints. A child might find himself spending a lot of time cleaning sticky cabinet handles and doorknobs because he neglected to wash his hands after breakfast, and didn't realize just how many things he handles in the course of his day. He might find his Breakfast Manager privileges suspended because he indulged in some candy for breakfast, and didn't anticipate his parents would notice the fresh candy wrappers in the garbage. He might find himself doing all the work because he tried to delegate an unfair share of the breakfast tasks to his sibling, who became uncooperative as a result.

The children were generally trusted to perform their duties as Breakfast Manager, but good performance was occasionally verified through post-breakfast audits. Corrective instructions were given for minor infractions such as sticky hands, to be carried out at once. Major infractions such as breakfast candy resulted in suspension of the privilege to serve as the Breakfast Manager.

Playful titles like Breakfast Manager are not necessary for open choice arrangements to be effective, nor are embellished descriptors of actions such as "supervise" and "audit." But for us, they added some levity to otherwise routine tasks. At the same time, they served as a tacit reminder that, for the children, such tasks are not so routine.

TIME EXAMPLE

Open choices do not necessarily need to be formally given, or even made explicit. Sometimes the child can be left to discover an open choice for himself. A child with time on his hands may ask what he should do, and can be reminded that he is in charge of himself. He will find himself in an open choice situation, for which he must work out the courses of action and outcome.

Getting children ready in the morning can be a struggle for parents who need to ensure the children get to school on time, or that the parents get to work on time. This may change when the child realizes that the faster he gets ready, the more time he has for other things. The options for how to spend the extra time are virtually limitless.

A child with an extra ten minutes in the morning is limited only by his imagination. He can decide to write a story, read a book, play a game, do a puzzle, watch some television, or finish that last bit of homework that should have been completed last night. Such a child will learn to get ready quickly in the mornings because he values the open choice associated with that hard-earned block of time. Such a child will also readily accept the associated responsibilities.

My son often decided to use his free time playing a video game that he purchased using the proceeds from 110 pieces of candy. Associated with this choice was the responsibility to turn the game off when it was time to leave for school. The consequences of the decision to play were that he got to enjoy the game, and also had to stop playing, often before the game was over, even in a critical part of the game.

My daughter sometimes decided to join her brother in the game, but usually opted to spend her free time making her own breakfast to take to school. She did this so that she could choose her own breakfast instead of having to eat whatever I would have given her. Associated with this choice were the responsibilities to have a healthy breakfast, to keep the kitchen clean, and to keep herself clean. The consequences of her decision to make her own breakfast were that she got to eat exactly what she wanted, and forwent other fun activities in order to do so.

MONEY AND OTHERS EXAMPLE

Like managing time, the handling of money also offers virtually limitless possibilities. In fact, the handling of money can involve open choices in three different areas: earning, storing, and spending money.

Earning money can be made an open choice by presenting a child with a simple situation: you, the parent, are willing to pay the child a fair price for valued services. This is different from a typical pay-for-chores arrangement where the child is given chores and prices. The situation described has more of an entrepreneurial slant, in that the services to be performed and the prices to be paid are not specified. Rather, they are left to the child's discovery and negotiation skills. The child must himself decide upon a course of action that delivers his anticipated outcome.

In order to earn money under this entrepreneurial arrangement, the child must have a keen sense of awareness. He must first be mindful of the work that needs to be done. He must also be mindful of the baseline expectations. Further, he must be attuned to his parents' needs well enough to understand what they value.

The entrepreneurial arrangement was first presented to my children when my six-year-old son expressed a desire for income streams beyond that from trading candy. He immediately began proposing offers to set the table, clean his room, and brush his teeth well every morning. These services were all things that needed to be done, and were certainly valued by the parents, but were not beyond baseline expectations. These offers were all rejected on the grounds that they were expected to be done anyway as part of contributing to the family and taking care of oneself.

Next came an offer to take out the garbage every week. Taking out the garbage was my job, and therefore satisfied the criteria of being beyond the baseline expectations of the children. And it certainly needed to be done. But it wasn't valued by me. Taking out the garbage was not onerous enough for me to be willing to outsource it. So this offer, too, was rejected.

There must have been twenty rejections before an offer was accepted. At some point during this string of rejections, my son began to realize that instead of thinking about the work he *wanted* to do, he needed to be thinking about the work I *didn't want* to do. He needed to consider the value of his services to others. He needed to see the world from the perspective of someone else.

What he knew about me was that I hated to vacuum the floors. Vacuuming the floors was my job, and one that I was constantly reminded needed to be done. From my perspective, vacuuming the floors was an onerous job. So when my son offered to vacuum the floors for five dollars, it was worthy of consideration. A price of three dollars was agreed upon, and vacuuming the floors became his job. Whenever he wanted to earn three dollars, he would ask me if it was time to vacuum yet. If the floors went unvacuumed for too long, I would give him the chance to do it, or lose the opportunity for the couple of weeks after I did it myself.

This course of action carried both bad and good unexpected consequences. From this arrangement, my son found himself repairing a hole in the wall. He didn't realize how heavy the vacuum cleaner was, and dropped it while taking it down the stairs. From this arrangement, my son also found himself making extra money. The house sometimes needed to be vacuumed before the arrival of guests, whether that time was convenient for him or not. He learned that he was justified renegotiating in these situations, and charged a special event price of five dollars.

We were both better off from having decided to exchange money for vacuuming. My son was happier vacuuming the floors and earning the money than he would have been had he spent his time any other way without getting paid. It was harder work than he expected, and he often subcontracted parts of the job to his sister for one or two dollars. She, too, was happier with the money than she would have been had she not spent her time cleaning floors. For my part, I was happier without the money than I would have been had I spent my time cleaning the floors and holding onto the money.

There were far more rejections than agreements, but eventually similar arrangements were worked out. The children collected small rocks from the yard for five dollars per bucket.

They swept the garage for two dollars. Such courses of action, each one a voluntary exchange first proposed by the children, always had mutually beneficial outcomes.

Storing this hard-earned money could be made into another open choice. The simple situation that could be presented to the child is that you, the parent, are willing to function as an interest-paying bank. The child can then decide to make deposits and withdrawals at any time and in any amount he wishes. He can divide his money between his bank account and cash holdings in any proportion he wishes. If the child decides upon effective courses of action, he will experience good outcomes characterized by maximized utility from his money.

The idea of a parent functioning as a bank was detailed in David Owen's book, *The First National Bank of Dad: The Best Way to Teach Kids About Money.*[134] One of Owen's key insights is that the interest rates typically given by real banks (2–3 percent annually for savings accounts at the time the book was written) is meaningless to children. At that rate of interest, a child having ten dollars would need to wait an entire year to earn twenty or thirty cents in interest. If the child is five years old, then he is waiting 20 percent of his life for a sum of money that isn't enough to buy anything worthwhile. This level of interest offers no reasonable incentive for a child to delay gratification and save money.

By opening their own bank, parents get to control the rate of interest. Owen gave his children an interest rate of 5 percent per month. This rate offers a reasonable incentive for children not to spend their money. The child with ten dollars deposited in the bank can earn fifty cents at the end of the month as long as he keeps his money in the bank. That is a real difference, in a time horizon that a child can comprehend. As the child grows and his earning potential grows commensurately, the interest rate can be gradually adjusted down. When I opened "Bank of Dad" accounts for my children, I used Owen's interest rate of 5 percent per month.

Also, like David Owen, I supplied the children with monthly bank statements. The bank statements provided the children with objective records of their decisions and consequences (see Figure 14 below).

The Bank of Dad			
Account Holder	"Son" Vondruska		
Account Number	1		
Account Summary			
Monthly Statement	Oct-15		
Balance	$ 0.33		
Monthly Interest Rate	5%		
Monthly Activity Summary			
Beginning Balance	$ 0.30		
Deposits	$ 13.00		
Withdrawals	$ 12.99		
Subtotal	$ 0.31		
Interest	$ 0.02		
Ending Balance	$ 0.33		
Monthly Activity Details			
Date	Activity	Amount	Notes
9/6/15	Deposit	$5.00	Air show souvenir money
9/7/15	Withdrawal	$3.49	Yugioh cards from Amazon
9/20/15	Deposit	$5.00	Rock bucket
9/24/15	Deposit	$3.00	Vacuuming
9/24/15	Withdrawal	$1.00	Subcontracted some vacuuming to "Daughter"
9/25/15	Withdrawal	$8.50	Book fair

FIGURE 14. Bank of Dad Statement

Figure 14 shows a high activity month with lots of spending. My son only earned two cents in interest this month. I did not need to deride him for not saving, or offer any kind of reminder at all. His bank statement did the speaking for me. By the same token, I did not need to congratulate him for earning five dollars by forgoing a souvenir at the air show.

This was another of Owen's practices. Most parents will buy a souvenir for their child to commemorate an event, or buy something for their children at the gift shop when they go somewhere special, or provide some money for the child to take on a field trip. What Owen did was not only provide the money directly to the child so that he could make his own purchase decisions, but remind him that if he opted not to spend it, he could deposit it into the Bank of Dad where it would earn interest. Under this arrangement, he found, the child made much wiser purchase decisions.

Using money to make purchases is another open choice. The simple situation for the child is that he can use his money to make purchases as he wishes. The only restrictions are that the family rules must be observed. The child cannot use his own money to buy dangerous ninja throwing stars or bags of candy, in our case. Aside from that, it is the child's money to spend wisely or foolishly. As long as family rules are heeded, the Bank of Dad cannot refuse a withdrawal.

The child is then responsible for all purchases. If he regrets a purchase, if he overspends and cannot buy something that he wants even more than what he just bought, or if he mistreats a purchased toy and wants his money back once the toy is broken, he is out of luck. He must live with his consequences. In many cases, the child is happy to live with his consequences. He appreciates his toys more when he sacrificed his own money to buy them, and takes better care of them because he understands the trade-offs they represent.

As the owner of his purchases, the child is empowered to play with them as he wishes. His treatment of his toys is an open choice. He can play nicely with them. He can break them. He can trade them. He can hoard them. He can share them.

He is responsible for living with the consequences of his treatment of his toys. He can savor his toys through proper treatment. He can squander them through mistreatment. He can put others first and use the toys to build relational bonds through sharing. He can put the toys first and build relational barriers through hoarding. There are any number of outcomes, intentional and otherwise, that can result from his decisions.

PROVIDE BALANCE

It is the combination of autonomy and responsibility that will ultimately motivate a child to make good decisions. Giving autonomy alone will not suffice; that is permissiveness, and it is too soft to be effective. Lax parenting simply does not motivate a child toward good decisions, if it motivates at all. Giving responsibility alone will not suffice either; that is authoritarianism, and it is too hard to be effective. Parenting through fear and control definitely motivates, but often toward the wrong type of decision.

The right balance must be kept. I have known permissive parents to compensate for their excessive allowance of autonomy with bouts of overprotectiveness. But overprotectiveness does not contribute to a sense of responsibility, only a sense of insecurity. I have known authoritarian parents to compensate for their excessive assignment of responsibility with lavish gifts. But lavish gifts do not contribute to a sense of autonomy, only a sense of entitlement. Excessive autonomy cannot be balanced by overprotectiveness, and excessive responsibility cannot be balanced with excessive rewards.

It is autonomy and responsibility that must be balanced. They complete each other, and there are no substitutes. Together they motivate a child to make good decisions about toys, other people, money, time, food, and countless other things, countless times a day.

Because decisions permeate life, autonomy and responsibility must permeate childhood. They need not be offered sparingly on special occasions. They need not be given with fanfare as part of grand productions. They are part of the fabric of life, to be exercised in small doses thousands of times a day.

In the end, what sets a child's direction is not exorbitant outings and special treats. It is not grand adventures, expensive vacations, or elaborate birthday parties. Nor is it over-involvement in life's milestones or obsession with a child's endeavors.

What sets a child's direction is the small things, the unremarkable things, the common occurrences. It is a crying child given comfort after being shunned by a playmate for not sharing. It is a frustrated parent coolly explaining that his child has exhausted his funds and cannot purchase that toy in the store. It is a child dissatisfied with his breakfast cereal shown where to find a bowl and eggs, instructed how to use his hands to mix and cook, until the breakfast that was once only a thought sits before him, an actual bowl of steaming, self-prepared scrambled eggs. These are the things that matter. These are the things that enable children to turn themselves into the men and women they can become.

KEY POINTS

- To give decisions is a way to exercise responsiveness, provide structure, and be autonomy-supportive.
- Giving decisions to children grants them autonomy and responsibility. When well-balanced, this lets children know that they matter and that they can make an impact.
- Because decision-making is complex and pervasive, children need lots of practice.
- Let natural consequences follow so that children understand that virtuous behavior will be gratifying. Let them also understand that unvirtuous behavior will be exposed somehow, that they will have to live with the consequences, and that those consequences will often be unpredictable.
- Depending on the child's development level and the circumstances, give coupled choice decisions, limited choice decisions, or open choice decisions.

REFLECTION EXERCISES

Are you more comfortable granting autonomy or giving responsibility?

If you like to let people do things their own way and at their own pace, and excel at dealing with uncertainty, then you are probably very comfortable granting autonomy, and perhaps uncomfortable giving responsibility. If you are driven to stay abreast of what others are doing, tend to offer advice on how to do it, and like being in charge of schedules, then you are probably very comfortable giving responsibility, and perhaps uncomfortable granting autonomy.

_____

_____

_____

Brainstorm some ways you can grow out of your comfort zone.

If you are uncomfortable giving responsibility, for example, perhaps you could insist that shared areas in the home, such as the kitchen, be kept organized. If you are uncomfortable granting autonomy, perhaps you could allow some clutter in designated private areas, such as in a child's room.

_____

_____

_____

CHAPTER 7

Solve Problems Together

S olving problems together is the final goal in my parenting philosophy. It uses the matter and impact access point on a child's well-being cycle. Solving problems together advances a child through the cycle in many of the same ways as building awareness and giving decisions. In fact, problem-solving requires both awareness and decision-making abilities. Awareness is required to understand a problem. Decision-making abilities are then used to determine what to do about it.

Problem-solving and decision-making have a lot in common. They both involve figuring out the proper course of action in a given situation to produce a good outcome. The difference is that for problem-solving, the situation necessarily involves a problem. Decision-making may entail figuring out what to eat, how to treat others, or how to spend time or money. In problem-solving, those considerations may still apply, but instead of being born of opportunity they are born of adversity.

In a universe that is messy, dynamic, and noisy, adversity will always arise. Problems continually surface that threaten to misalign our relatedness and competence drives. We need the ability to solve problems in order to maintain resonance of relatedness and competence. The seeds for that ability are sown in childhood.

Solving problems together with your children requires so much of you. It requires you to:

- maintain responsiveness to her needs, emotions, and interests in real time, even as complications arise;
- remain steadfast in your expectation that your child contributes to the resolution of problems;
- set an example for how to solve problems;
- remain cool as complications compound;
- encourage exploration, recognize preferences, explain, listen, and welcome emotions;
- give decisions and allow the consequences to play out; and
- be creative.

Solving problems together requires the best of you.

Every time you so apply yourself over the course of your child's childhood, you are raising an adult. Whenever you help her deal with an uncomfortable seat belt, you are making a small but finite contribution to the person she is to become. With every resolved disagreement over a snack, you are transferring just a bit of momentum to her well-being cycle.

You are building your child's awareness of herself. You are helping her to believe in herself. Those beliefs will stir her to behave in ways that build relationships and capabilities, which in turn reconfirm her beliefs. As she grows, she draws herself toward bigger challenges and more complex relations. She solves problems along the way, turning adversity into opportunity. She decides which challenges and people are the best fits for her distinctive, purposefully created self. Because of the small things you did every day, every seat belt and every snack, she is motivated from within to continually become her best self, for purposes beyond herself, and to foster closeness with other people who are enriched by that best self. She lives a life of resonance.

UNDERSTAND THE PERSON BEFORE THE PROBLEM

Many problems can be solved either together with your child or by your child alone. A lost sock, a building block tower that keeps falling down, and an action figure that won't seem to fit in its helicopter are examples of such problems. Depending on your child's developmental level, she may need help, she may just need some coaching, or she may be able to handle these problems on her own.

But some problems are impossible to solve alone. Disagreements, incompatible motivations, and misunderstandings are examples of such problems. These are problems between people, and must be solved between people. The same basic problem-solving concepts which apply to solving problems together also apply to solving problems alone. The difference is that the former can only be solved through an agreement between people. These are the types of problems featured in this chapter.

Solving problems begins with awareness. That includes awareness of the problem itself, and awareness of the person or people involved. Awareness of the problem is secondary to awareness of the person. Problems between people start with people.

Problems between people are often emotionally charged, especially when one of those people is a child. In Chapter Four, we discussed how emotions need to be managed before behaviors. The same concept applies here. People need to be understood before the problem is understood.

Problem-solving is addressed in many of the references used for this book. Three problem-solving approaches culled from my favorite references are described in Table 11: John Gottman's approach; Adele Faber and Elaine Mazlish's approach; and the Augusta Lewis Troup Middle School's approach as related by Daniel Goleman.

Source	Technique	Key Elements
John Gottman	Emotion Coaching[135]	Once you recognize the child's emotional state, you can commit to using it as a springboard to strengthen the parent-child bond, and to offer guidance. Discuss your child's emotional state, getting her point of view. Identify the specific emotion. Consider what should and shouldn't be done to find a solution.
Adele Faber and Elaine Mazlish	Problem-Solving[136]	Discuss the emotions and perspectives of both parent and child. List solutions that may work for both parent and child. Prioritize the list, and pick the best one to implement.
Augusta Lewis Troup Middle School in New Haven, as related by Daniel Goleman	"Stoplight"[137]	Red: Stop and reflect on your behavior Yellow: Identify what's wrong, how it makes you feel, what you would like to happen next, ways to make it happen, and potential outcomes Green: Implement your top idea

TABLE 11. **Problem-solving Techniques**

There are three noteworthy similarities among these techniques:

1) People are addressed before solutions are considered.
2) Problem-solving entails generating solutions.
3) Investigations of the reasons for the problem are omitted.

With regard to the third similarity, I feel it is important to make explicit: a problem cannot be solved optimally unless it is understood. So, I offer a generalized problem-solving technique that incorporates this step:

1) Build awareness of the people.
2) Build awareness to understand the problem.
3) Decide upon a solution.

In our home, building awareness of the people often started with the traffic light. The traffic light was inspired by the stoplight described by Goleman. A traffic light seemed fitting because the three steps could be mapped to the three lights, the colors of which offered a strong visual reminder. My adapted traffic light, designed for smaller children, had simpler steps (see Figure 15 below).

FIGURE 15. Adapted Traffic Light

The traffic light starts with a red light, at which point the problem is stated. This is a brief statement such as "You keep telling me I have to wear my seat belt." It signifies recognition of the need to do something.

Next is the yellow light, at which point feelings are declared. Again, a simple statement, such as "It makes me feel mad," is sufficient.

Finally, there is the green light. The green light is an opportunity to discuss outcome criteria. Here, a child might say, "I don't want to wear it."

TECHNIQUE: TRAFFIC LIGHT

Use these three questions to build awareness of the people involved when dealing with a problem: What's wrong? How do I feel? What now?

The prerequisite for the traffic light is that it is delivered in a talking voice. It is used to simply initiate a calm problem-solving discussion. It is a springboard for emotional discussion and understanding. The parent who is presented with a calm appeal according to the traffic light can respond in kind.

The parent may begin by listening intently. "You are mad because I want you to wear a seat belt," the parent might say. "It can be frustrating when someone disagrees with you."

The parent might continue by eliciting more information. "Why don't you want to wear your seat belt?" The parent might learn that the child feels uncomfortable wearing the seat belt. If this child is known to have a sensing perceptive preference, then this would be understandable. "You are very sensitive to straps. I learned that when you wouldn't wear your blue dress because of the belt," the parent might offer.

The parent can then deliver traffic light statements of his own: "We can't drive until everybody in the car is wearing a seat belt. I'm surprised we have to talk about this now because we've used our seat belts so many times before. I need you to find a way to be okay wearing it."

If the child has no questions, the parent can further explain his reasoning. The seat belts are there to keep everyone safe. The child needs to wear a seat belt because she is loved, and he wants to keep her safe.

The child is mad and doesn't want to wear her seat belt because it is uncomfortable. The parent is surprised and insists that the child wear her seat belt because it is the safe thing to do. A decision is needed, but the child and parent have different desired outcomes. This is the problem. With the people having made themselves understood, the problem can be now tackled.

UNDERSTAND THE WHY

Once the people are understood, the problem becomes pure decision-making, as described in Chapter Six. The child has already recognized that a decision is needed and has formulated outcome criteria. The parent has formulated different outcome criteria. Now the two target outcomes need to be reconciled through situation assessment, course of action determination, and outcome evaluation, before implementing the decision and experiencing the consequences. Situation assessment is the second step of my generalized problem-solving technique, with everything thereafter being the third step (see Figure 16 below).

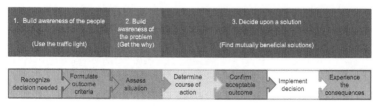

FIGURE 16. Generalized Problem-solving Technique

Situation assessment for problem-solving, as opposed to regular decision-making, has only one added component. When making decisions about an opportunity, situation assessment involves understanding the "what." When making decisions about a problem, situation assessment involves also understanding the "why."

Awareness of the problem may begin to be built while building awareness of the people. In the seat belt example, some of the why was uncovered through the traffic light. The child did not want to wear the seat belt because it made her uncomfortable, and the parent required the seat belt to be worn because it was safe.

But both reasons warrant digging a little deeper. Why wasn't the seat belt uncomfortable yesterday? Why is today different? The parent might find out that the child is wearing a thicker coat today than yesterday. With the thicker coat, the child feels more constricted by the seat belt. And why does the seat belt make anything safer? The parent can show the child some videos of crash test dummies smashing through windshields without their seat belts, and give a rudimentary physics lesson. Both the parent and child can affirm that they understand each other's reasons.

From here, the child may be coaxed to reformulate her outcome criteria as "be more comfortable wearing a seat belt." The potential courses of action are many. She may decide to take her coat off while in the car, and then put it back on at the destination. She may need to have her belt settings loosened. She may decide to put the seat belt on herself so she can adjust the straps to their most comfortable position. She may not even mind the discomfort now that she is aware of the dangers of not using her seat belt, and just wear it—and this was the actual decision made by my daughter in this situation.

Perhaps understanding the why of seat belts was enough to persuade her to buckle up. Or perhaps having her why understood was all she really needed. I have found that when time is taken to go through the first two steps of understanding the people and the problem, the third step of deciding upon a solution often happens effortlessly.

Understanding the why can change the game for parents and children alike. It opens up courses of action that would otherwise not have been considered. Consider the reluctant bather from the previous chapter who was offered the coupled choice of choosing his bath time and experiencing the water temperature. The parent asking this child why he doesn't want to get in the bathtub might find that he is afraid of sea monsters coming up from the drain.

In addition to offering the coupled choice, the parent could take several other courses of action while awaiting the child's decision. The parent might use something to plug the drain. The parent might ask what size sea monsters are, and then suggest that the child explore what size toys will fit through the drain. The parent might spray monster repellant in the tub.[vii] All the while, the parent can do his thinking out loud, considering how monsters might get through the drain and how to stop them, generating possible solutions, considering the plausible ones, and rejecting the implausible ones. For his creative efforts, the parent may find the child sitting in the bathtub sooner than he first expected.

Solving problems together means that both parent and child need to contribute to understanding the problem and coming up with solutions. This requires a level of trust and an atmosphere of mutual respect. Without trust, the counterparties would not subject themselves to the vulnerability of disclosing the true emotions which lie behind the problem. Without respect, they would not risk rejection by offering solutions. A trusting, respectful atmosphere allows for the open communication and cooperation necessary for the parent and child to both take an active role in solving problems and reaching target outcomes.

Children can be just as creative in reaching a target outcome as their parents, or perhaps more so, when they understand the why. And coming up with their own solutions gives them a sense of ownership over the solutions. This is why Faber and Mazlish suggest writing down all possible solutions—be they good or bad, novel or customary, serious or silly. The parent and child

---

[vii] "Monster spray" might be colored water or even a simple magic spell. I always made clear to my children that monster spray was just pretend but that was what was needed because so were the monsters—imaginary spray repels imaginary monsters.

can later take turns crossing off the implausible ideas, but first crystallizing the child's ideas in writing gives those ideas an air of legitimacy. Contriving a legitimate solution and being recognized for it provides a real incentive for making the solutions work.

Parenting author and lecturer Alfie Kohn related a story about how his four-year-old daughter devised a creative course of action and made it work.[138] The problem was a typical one: the child was taking too long to get ready in the morning. After stating the problem, Alfie made an effort to understand the person. He asked his daughter what he sounded like when trying to motivate her in the morning. She performed an imitation. This was different from using the traffic light, but a good way to make a connection and understand another perspective. He then asked her what she thought she could do to get ready on time. She thought about the problem, and observed that getting dressed took the longest. She understood the why of the problem, that she was often late because getting dressed takes so long. She then suggested something that a parent would not have—going to sleep in the clothes that she was to wear the following day. That is exactly what she did, and it worked. Alfie did not poke holes in her solution because it was imperfect or because it was not a suitable solution for an adult. It was okay for a four-year-old. So he let her try it, and it worked.

She solved their problem. She only needed to shift her responsibility of getting dressed from the morning to the previous evening, and possibly endure some wrinkly clothes. Alfie did not object to her solution, being wise enough to understand that the consequence of wrinkly clothes for a child is irrelevant to the kind of adult she is to become. But the control over her own life and the ability to solve problems for herself is certainly something she could build upon and take into adulthood.

FIND MUTUALLY BENEFICIAL SOLUTIONS

Sometimes problems between people are solved by one person moving their target outcome to align with the other person's target outcome, like the child accepting that she must wear her seat belt. Other times, both parties move their target outcomes into alignment. An example would be a give-and-take resulting in a later bedtime for a child ready for the responsibility—not as late as she wanted but later than her parent had wanted. But the best kind of solution is the kind that aligns the target outcomes while preserving the positions of both parties.

Mutually beneficial solutions are possible when both parties understand each other, and understand the reasons for each other's target outcomes. The more time they each spend exploring the other person's viewpoint, the more likely they will arrive upon a mutually beneficial solution. As suggested in *Gifts Differing*, two people must first combine their perspectives on a problem—regarding what is, what may be, and what might result—in order to see the full picture and arrive at a satisfactory solution.[139]

A standoff over the appropriate attire for a family holiday gathering is one example. While the parent may demand that a new dress be worn, the child might insist on a ripped T-shirt. With the family running later and tensions running higher with each passing minute, this situation has the potential to devolve into a shouting match.

Some inquiry may reveal a mutually beneficial solution. Following the traffic light discussion, the parent can convey the formality and expectations associated with the gathering. The parent's target outcome is for the family to dress formally. The child can explain that the new dress is itchy, while the old T-shirt is soft. The child's target outcome is to not be itchy all day. With some brainstorming, the parent and child can decide that the old T-shirt is to be worn underneath the dress. This solution allows for the formality of the event to be respected without causing the child to be itchy.

A parent and child may deadlock over a snack. The child screams for a chocolate bar after the parent has brought her a plate of cheese and crackers. Some investigation may reveal that the child wants to be given something sweet while the parent wants to give something healthy. It might not take too long before a banana is found in the overlapping territory.

A parent is finished sled riding for the day, but the child wants to continue. An extended argument in the freezing cold is the last thing either one wants. It might turn out that the parent is too tired to climb the hill one more time, while the child just wants to stay on the sled a little bit longer. If the parent pulls the child to the car on the sled, they will both get they want. A little communication and cooperation is all that is needed for this mutually beneficial solution to be reached.

A dress, a banana, and a sled ride don't seem like very impactful outcomes, and in fact they are not. The impactful part is in finding the way there. A child taught how to take time to understand her counterparty and what their motivation is and how flexible their position is, while simultaneously understanding herself and her own motivation and how flexible her position is, will be able to find mutually beneficial arrangements throughout life. She will be able to create alignment between the best of herself and those who take enjoyment from her being the best of herself. She will be able to create resonance.

But it is a long road to resonance. Despite your efforts showing your children how to understand others, understand problems, and decide upon solutions, you will see crude and counterproductive methods being used. Your children may attempt to resolve problems with other children by fighting, delivering cruel remarks, making mean faces, getting the last word, focusing on being right, withholding toys, and being manipulative. They will make many mistakes.

They will need to experience the consequences of their mistakes. It will be helpful to discuss your feelings about those mistakes as well as your child's feelings about what transpired, and to offer some objective commentary, but most direct interventions should be unnecessary. Your child will need to live her social failures.

Unless you have witnessed everything, your interventions may make things worse anyway. A child making an appeal to you for justice to be served may not give an accurate account of what happened. The most articulate child, or the most imaginative, or the best at playing victim, may be best equipped to get what she wants from her parents, even if it is not deserved. The child that was wronged by the parental intervention will then be left feeling misunderstood, alone, and betrayed.

Even when you think you have witnessed everything, it is still easy to get the facts wrong. One time I saw my son running away with my daughter's new bag, being chased by her as she cried and screamed. I wanted to stop him right there and reprimand him for picking on his sister by taking her things away from her. But I didn't. Eventually it was revealed that my daughter had hidden one of my son's new toys in her bag and he wanted it back. When he first reached for it she gave chase. That is the part that I saw. The children worked it out for themselves. He got his toy back and she got her bag back.

Children learn to explore their problems and find solutions together by getting practice doing so. Solving problems together with their parents may serve as a model for how to do it, but solving problems together with other children is done when they don't expect an adult's hand to reach from the sky and make things right. Sometimes it is best to stay out of their way. They will learn to solve problems together, through their mistakes.

Each bad result from a mistake is one step closer to a good result from doing it right. Mistakes on the piano, for those who can learn from them, make a better pianist. Similarly, homework mistakes make a better student. Motion mistakes make a better dancer.

When your children have exhausted their tolerance for avoidable mistakes, when they are truly ready to solve problems together, they will remember what they learned from you. That is when you will get to see problem-solving mistakes having made a better problem-solver. That is when you will get to see your child preparing herself for a life of resonance.

KEY POINTS

- Solving problems together requires both awareness and decision-making.
- Understand the people first. Use the traffic light to initiate discussions.
- Understand the reasons for the problem before exploring solutions.
- Find mutually beneficial solutions whenever possible.
- Allow mistakes to be made. Like with decisions, offer objective commentary and discussion of feelings.

REFLECTION EXERCISES

How will you "understand the people"?

The "understanding the people" problem-solving step can be uncomfortable. It requires you to share your thoughts and feelings, which can make you feel vulnerable. Using the traffic light is one of many ways to do this. What ways will be most comfortable for you?

_____

_____

_____

How will you find mutually beneficial solutions?

What have been some recent opportunities for you and your family to build mutually beneficial outcomes? What did you do that worked? What could you have done differently?

_____

_____

_____

They Won't Stay Little Forever

Maintaining responsiveness, structure, and autonomy support at all times is a tall order for any parent. Always serving as a good example, and a cool-tempered one at that, is impossible. Knowing when to encourage exploration, when to recognize preferences, when to explain, when to listen, when to welcome emotions, when to give which type of decision, when to let the consequences play out naturally, and when to solve problems together may seem like an exercise in futility. There are so many ways to do all of these things. So much depends upon your circumstances, your temperament, your child's temperament, your beliefs, and your values. Applying the advice in this book takes effort and creativity.

The truth is that no one knows exactly the right thing to do in any given situation. You may use some of the advice in this book as your bread-and-butter parenting techniques. Other advice may ring hollow to you, and you will disregard it. And you will, no doubt, develop your own practices. By all means, do what you believe is best using the resources available to you. When it all becomes too much to remember, when you are overwhelmed and can't keep the details straight, just keep the thought that your child won't stay little forever.

Show your child that he matters by playing with him, because he won't stay little forever, and show him how to make an impact by working with him, because he won't stay little forever. Go to the beach and watch the waves with your children. Build a sand castle together. Collect shells and classify them. Take a bath afterward. Fill the tub with toys. Show him how to wash himself. Pretend the towel is a superhero cape. Play tic-tac-toe and let him win. Play again and let him lose. Play with flashlights. Make shadow puppets. Make binoculars out of cardboard tubes. Let the children glue the tubes together. Find Africa on a globe. Point the flashlight on the globe to explain day and night. Turn on the television and watch a movie. Turn off the television and just talk. Have the children go outside to retrieve the mail. Play tag while there. Throw a Frisbee back and forth. Blow bubbles. Rake leaves. Jump in the leaves. Go back inside and give piggyback rides. End the rides by tossing the riders on the couch. Go somewhere educational. Buy something from the gift shop. Go somewhere fun. Skip the gift shop. Go home and organize the living room together. Go to the kitchen and learn how to make a new meal. Have a healthy lunch. Have some cookies after dinner. Listen to music. Learn how to make music. Sing, dance, and laugh. Learn how to laugh at yourself. Love your children. Let your children love you back.

REFLECTION EXERCISES

Which practices presented in this book can you adopt into your own parenting repertoire?
List your top three takeaways.

_____

_____

_____

Which practices presented in this book can you adapt to your own circumstances?
Perhaps you tried some techniques and found opportunities to make improvements, or to tailor variations for your situation.

_____

_____

_____

What practices can you add that are uniquely yours?
If you were to revise this book and pass it down to your own children, or write your own book, what would be your top three original pieces of advice?

_____

_____

_____

AFTERWORD

Son and Daughter,

Throughout the course of our existence, we are each able to touch the lives of others. Every hopeful person we offer support to, every eager learner we teach, and every fellow person we let know they matter, like a stone dropped into a pond, begin the significance of our life's actions.

We all leave our imprint on the generations to come. In the end, the only impact that counts is the impact we make on the lives of other people. It is only this that can make our lives meaningful, and make our brief time on this Earth truly matter.

Nowhere but at home are we provided with a better opportunity to set in motion a succession of people living more fulfilled lives, living happier lives, living better lives, because of something we did for them.

I did my best for you, and I know you'll do your best for your children.

Love you and God Bless.
Dad

GLOSSARY OF TERMS

Autonomy: The experience of being a causal agent in one's life.

Competence: A basic human need that, when fulfilled, engenders a sense of confidence, curiosity, and effectiveness that leads one to continually seek challenging activities for purposes of skill enhancement and expression of capacities.

Coupled Choice Decision: A decision characterized by a level of autonomy explicitly coupled to responsibility.

Demandingness: Parental control, supervision, and maturity demands.

Emotional Intelligence: The abilities to manage emotions inclusive of self-awareness, self-regulation, empathy, social skills, and motivation.

Impact: An assessment of whether one can make an impact is the belief in one's competence to develop the capabilities to meet challenges and deal with adversity. The belief that one can make an impact may apply to specific circumstances, and also includes the general sense of confidence, curiosity, and effectiveness that defines competence.

Integrity: The quality of having consistent motivations and behaviors regardless of circumstances.

Limited Choice Decision: A decision characterized by a menu of offered options.

Matter: An assessment of whether one matters is the belief in one's competence to have positive interactions with others, to form healthy relationships, and to manage negative interactions. It may apply to specific circumstances, and also includes the general sense of belongingness that defines relatedness.

Open Choice Decision: A decision in which only the basic structure is given but not the specific options within that structure.

Parenting Goals: Concrete actions that one takes in an effort to move toward one's parenting vision.

Parenting Philosophy: A concise guidance statement that integrates one's parenting purpose, vision, and goals.

Parenting Purpose: A personally defined reason for filling the role of parent. A thoughtfully constructed parenting purpose helps to keep one focused on priorities.

Parenting Vision: The aspirational result of one's parenting endeavors. A parenting vision should be the natural outcome of having adhered to the parenting purpose.

Preferences: Innate inclinations such as those described by the Myers–Briggs Type Indicator.

Relatedness: A basic human need that, when fulfilled, engenders a sense of belongingness derived from feelings of connectedness to others and feelings of caring for and being cared for by others.

Resonance: The state of continually becoming one's best self, for purposes beyond oneself, while fostering closeness with other people who are enriched by that best self.

Responsiveness: Parental warmth, involvement, and benevolence with respect to a child's needs, emotions, and interests.

Self-Esteem: The attitude toward whether one matters and whether one can make an impact.

Structure: An environment set by a parent conducive to a child's competence development, consisting of clearly communicated expectations, explanations of contingencies, and observations on the child's efforts.

Virtue, or Virtuous Character, or Virtuous Behavior: Behavior patterns that facilitate others-oriented relationship growth (resulting in relatedness fulfillment) and self-oriented personal growth (resulting in competence fulfillment).

FURTHER READING

There are lots of great resources in the reference section (pages 301–311). I would recommend each one, but I couldn't expect you to track down and read them all. Here are my top four choices, along with some commentary. These are all well-known resources from widely respected authors. The list is arranged as a continuum of theoretical to practical, starting with theoretical.

Ryan, Richard M., and Edward L. Deci. *Self-Determination Theory: Basic Psychological Needs in Motivation, Development, and Wellness.* Guilford Publications, 2017. Written in an academic style, this book canvasses over thirty years of research. In addition to parenting, there are chapters on many other facets of life. Context is provided by covering concepts, models, and theories that preceded, and some that compete with, self-determination theory. I have never encountered such an expansive and comprehensive volume on what it means to be human. An unequivocal masterpiece.

Goleman, Daniel P. *Emotional Intelligence: Why It Can Matter More than IQ.* Bantam Books, 1995. This book contains some parenting examples, but it is definitely not a parenting book. The real value parents can gain from this book is an understanding of the impact of emotions on human development. I read it for the first time in 2005, and it changed the way I think about everything. Daniel Goleman has several good titles, but I would suggest starting here.

Gottman, John. *Raising an Emotionally Intelligent Child*. Simon and Schuster, 1997. This book reduces the theories of emotional intelligence to a practical level directly applicable to family living. Incidentally, Gottman is a key influence of Daniel Goleman. Much of Gottman's work is featured in *Emotional Intelligence*. Perhaps I was primed from having just read *Emotional Intelligence* when I first picked up *Raising an Emotionally Intelligent Child*. I have internalized more practices from *Raising an Emotionally Intelligent Child* than I have from any other resource.

Faber, Adele, and Elaine Mazlish. *How to Talk So Kids Will Listen & Listen So Kids Will Talk*. Simon and Schuster, 1980. While Gottman was strongly influenced by famed child psychologist and parent educator Haim Ginott, Faber and Mazlish were actually Ginott's students. As a result, Faber and Mazlish seem to have a lot of the same underlying motives as Gottman. *How to Talk So Kids Will Listen & Listen So Kids Will Talk* is therefore a great complement to *Raising an Emotionally Intelligent Child*. There are more approaches covered in *How to Talk So Kids Will Listen & Listen So Kids Will Talk*. This book goes deep into the practical aspects of parenting. It is filled with examples, instructions, and exercises. I have personally found a lot of the tactics to be useful and powerful.

FOLLOW-UP

As a natural continuation to the post-chapter reflection exercises, a *The Kind of Parent You Are* journal was designed for you to:

- Record your responses to key reflection exercises in a logically organized format.
- Log your progress daily through customizable journal entries.
- Monitor your progress monthly with tracking templates.
- Document your development annually with an end-of-year review.

The journal is available everywhere *The Kind of Parent You Are* is sold.

Printable versions of the different journal pages may be downloaded for free by visiting TheKindOfParentYouAre.com.

REFERENCES

1   Michaels, Gerald Y. *The transition to parenthood: Current theory and research.* Cambridge University Press, 1988: 5.

2   Deci, Edward L., and Richard M. Ryan. *Handbook of self-determination research.* University Rochester Press, 2002: 6–8.

3   Baumrind, Diana. "Child care practices anteceding three patterns of preschool behavior." *Genetic psychology monographs* (1967): 43–88.

4   Maccoby, Eleanor E., and John A. Martin. "Socialization in the context of the family: Parent–child interaction." *Handbook of child psychology*: formerly *Carmichael's Manual of Child Psychology*/Paul H. Mussen, editor (1983): 1–101.

5   Driscoll, Lucy C. "Parenting styles and self-esteem." (2013).

6   Lamborn, Susie D., Nina S. Mounts, Laurence Steinberg, and Sanford M. Dornbusch. "Patterns of competence and adjustment among adolescents from authoritative, authoritarian, indulgent, and neglectful families." *Child development* 62, no. 5 (1991): 1049–1065.

7   Ibid.

8   Ibid.

9   Ibid.

10   Soenens, Bart, and Maarten Vansteenkiste. "A theoretical upgrade of the concept of parental psychological control: Proposing new insights on the basis of self-determination theory." *Developmental review* 30, no. 1 (2010): 86.

11   Baumrind, Diana. "The discipline controversy revisited." *Family relations* (1996): 412.

12   Kernis, Michael H., Anita C. Brown, and Gene H. Brody. "Fragile self-esteem in children and its associations with perceived patterns of parent-child communication." *Journal of personality* 68, no. 2 (2000): 225–252.

13   Finkenauer, Catrin, Rutger Engels, and Roy Baumeister. "Parenting behaviour and adolescent behavioural and emotional problems: The role of self-control." *International journal of behavioral development* 29, no. 1 (2005): 58–69.

14   Barber, Brian K. "Parental psychological control: Revisiting a neglected construct." *Child development* 67, no. 6 (1996): 3296–3319.

15   Finkenauer, Catrin, Rutger Engels, and Roy Baumeister. "Parenting behaviour and adolescent behavioural and emotional problems: The role of self-control." *International journal of behavioral development* 29, no. 1 (2005): 58–69.

16   Barber, Brian K. "Parental psychological control: Revisiting a neglected construct." *Child development* 67, no. 6 (1996): 3296–3319.

17   Soucy, Nathalie, and Simon Larose. "Attachment and control in family and mentoring contexts as determinants of adolescent adjustment at college." *Journal of family psychology* 14, no. 1 (2000): 125–143.

18   Society for Research in Child Development. "Teens whose parents exert more psychological control have trouble with closeness, independence." ScienceDaily. Accessed May 7, 2017. www.sciencedaily.com/releases/2014/10/141023091944.htm.

19   Soucy, Nathalie, and Simon Larose. "Attachment and control in family and mentoring contexts as determinants of adolescent adjustment at college." *Journal of family psychology* 14, no. 1 (2000): 125–143.

20 Baumrind, Diana. "The discipline controversy revisited." *Family relations* (1996): 405–414.

21 Larzelere, Robert E., D. Baumrind, and P. Cowan. "Ordinary physical punishment: Is it harmful? Comment on Gershoff (2002)." *Psychological Bulletin* 128, no. 4 (2002): 580–589.

22 Ryan, Richard M., and Edward L. Deci. *Self-determination theory: Basic psychological needs in motivation, development, and wellness.* The Guilford Press, 2017: 319–350.

23 Bowlby, John. *Attachment and loss.* Pimlico, 1969.

24 Booth, Cathryn L. "Predicting social adjustment in middle childhood: The role of preschool attachment security and maternal style." *Social development* 3, no. 3 (1994): 189–204.

25 Grolnick, Wendy S., Richard M. Ryan, and Edward L. Deci. "Inner resources for school achievement: Motivational mediators of children's perceptions of their parents." *Journal of educational psychology* 83, no. 4 (1991): 508–517.

26 Eisenberg, Nancy, Qing Zhou, Tracy L. Spinrad, Carlos Valiente, Richard A. Fabes, and Jeffrey Liew. "Relations among positive parenting, children's effortful control, and externalizing problems: A three-wave longitudinal study." *Child development* 76, no. 5 (2005): 1055–1071.

27 Hatfield, John S., Lucy Rau Ferguson, and Richard Alpert. "Mother-child interaction and the socialization process." *Child development* (1967): 365–414.

28 Grolnick, Wendy S., Richard M. Ryan, and Edward L. Deci. "Inner resources for school achievement: Motivational mediators of children's perceptions of their parents." *Journal of educational psychology* 83, no. 4 (1991): 508–517.

29 Farkas, Melanie S., and Wendy S. Grolnick. "Examining the components and concomitants of parental structure in the academic domain." *Motivation and emotion* 34, no. 3 (2010): 266–279.

30 Vasquez, Ariana C., Erika A. Patall, Carlton J. Fong, Andrew S. Corrigan, and Lisa Pine. "Parent autonomy support, academic achievement, and psychosocial functioning: A meta-analysis of research." *Educational psychology review* 28 (2015): 605–644.

31 Grolnick, Wendy S., Carolyn O. Kurowski, Jannette M. McMenamy, Inna Rivkin, and Lisa J. Bridges. "Mothers' strategies for regulating their toddlers' distress." *Infant behavior and development* 21, no. 3 (1998): 437–450.

32 Bindman, Samantha W., Eva M. Pomerantz, and Glenn I. Roisman. "Do children's executive functions account for associations between early autonomy-supportive parenting and achievement through high school?" *Journal of educational psychology* 107, no. 3 (2015): 756–770.

33 Marbell, Kristine N., and Wendy S. Grolnick. "Correlates of parental control and autonomy support in an interdependent culture: A look at Ghana." *Motivation and emotion* 37, no. 1 (2013): 79–92.

34 Ryan, Richard M., and Edward L. Deci. *Self-determination theory: Basic psychological needs in motivation, development, and wellness.* The Guilford Press, 2017: 179–215.

35 Ibid., 334–340.

36 Ibid., 349.

37 Gottman, John. *Raising an emotionally intelligent child: The heart of parenting.* Simon and Schuster, 1997: 50–52.

38 Gottman, John. *Raising an emotionally intelligent child: The heart of parenting.* Simon and Schuster, 1997: 16–17, 30, 52.

39 Ibid., 17.

40 Branden, Nathaniel. *The psychology of self-esteem: A revolutionary approach to self-understanding that launched a new era in modern psychology.* Jossey-Bass, 2001: 143–144. [Citations refer to the Jossey-Bass 32nd anniversary paperback edition.]

41 Shavelson, Richard J., Judith J. Hubner, and George C. Stanton. "Self-concept: Validation of construct interpretations." *Review of educational research* 46, no. 3 (1976): 407–441.

42 Hosogi, Mizuho, Ayumi Okada, Chikako Fujii, Keizou Noguchi, and Kumi Watanabe. "Importance and usefulness of evaluating self-esteem in children." *BioPsychoSocial medicine* 6, no. 9 (2012).

43 Coopersmith, Stanley. *The antecedents of self-esteem*. W.H. Freeman, 1967.

44 Harter, Susan. "Developmental perspective on the self system." In *Handbook of child psychology, volume IV: Socialization, personality, and social development*, ed. E. Mavis Hetherington. Wiley, 1983: 275–385.

45 Gottman, John. *Raising an emotionally intelligent child: The heart of parenting*. Simon and Schuster, 1997: 103–104.

46 Chadwick, Ian. "The unknown monk meme." Ian Chadwick. Accessed July 12, 2015. http://ianchadwick.com/blog/the-unknown-monk-meme/.

47 Rizzolatti, Giacomo, and Laila Craighero. "The mirror-neuron system." *Annual review of neuroscience* 27, no. 1 (2004): 169–192.

48 Goleman, Daniel. *Social intelligence: The revolutionary new science of human relationships*. Bantam Dell, 2006: 156–157.

49 Erickson, Milton H., Ernest Lawrence Rossi, and Sheila I. Rossi. *Hypnotic realities: the induction of clinical hypnosis and forms of indirect suggestion*. Irvington, 1976: 15.

50 Bowlby, John. "Forty-four juvenile thieves: Their characters and home-life." *The international journal of psycho-analysis* 25 (1944): 107–128.

51 Gottman, John. *Raising an emotionally intelligent child: The heart of parenting*. Simon and Schuster, 1997: 104.

52 Zeis, Patrick. "Quote 20: Abraham Maslow Quotes," Balanced Achievement. Accessed August 17, 2017. https://balancedachievement.com/grow-more/abraham-maslow-quotes/.

53 Bowlby, John. *A secure base: Parent-child attachment and healthy human development*. Routledge, 1988: 118–136.

54 Field, Tiffany, Brian Healy, and William G. LeBlanc. "Sharing and synchrony of behavior states and heart rate in nondepressed versus depressed mother-infant interactions." *Infant behavior and development* 12, no. 3 (1989): 357–376.

55 Goleman, Daniel. *Social intelligence: The revolutionary new science of human relationships*. Bantam Dell, 2006: 4.

56 Ibid., 15–16.

57   Matt 7:12 (New Testament, World English Bible).

58   Goleman, Daniel. *Social intelligence: The revolutionary new science of human relationships.* Bantam Dell, 2006: 164.

59   Ryan, Richard M., and Edward L. Deci. "Self-determination theory and the facilitation of intrinsic motivation, social development, and well-being." *American psychologist* 55, no. 1 (2000): 68–78.

60   Ibid.

61   Duckworth, Angela L., Christopher Peterson, Michael D. Matthews, and Dennis R. Kelly. "Grit: perseverance and passion for long-term goals." *Journal of personality and social psychology* 92, no. 6 (2007): 1087.

62   "Avon values and principles." Avon Company. Accessed May 15, 2016. http://www.avoncompany.com/aboutavon/history/values.html.

63   Karp, Harvey. *The happiest toddler on the block.* Bantam Dell, 2004.

64   Goleman, Daniel. *Emotional intelligence: Why it can matter more than IQ.* Bantam Dell, [1995] 2005 (reprint): 13–29.

65   Gottman, John. *Raising an emotionally intelligent child: The heart of parenting.* Simon and Schuster, 1997: 111.

66   Ibid., 112.

67   Navarette, Sergio. "Setting up your leasing office for success." EzineArticles. Accessed July 28, 2015. http://ezinearticles.com/?Setting-Up-Your-Leasing-Office-For-Successandid=3011216.

68   "Abigail Van Buren, Quotes." GoodReads. Accessed August 18, 2017. https://www.goodreads.com/author/quotes/812826.Abigail_Van_Buren

69   Gottman, John. *Raising an emotionally intelligent child: The heart of parenting.* Simon and Schuster, 1997: 170–171.

70   "10 reasons why you should read to your kids." Early Moments. Accessed August 21, 2015. https://www.early-moments.com/promoting-literacy-and-a-love-of-reading/why-reading-to-children-is-important/.

71   Sagan, Carl. *Cosmos.* Random House, 1980.

72   Dayton, Tian. "Creating a false self: Learning to live a lie." Huffington Post. Accessed June 8, 2016. http://www.huffingtonpost.com/dr-tian-dayton/creating-a-false-self-lea_b_269096.html.

73   Robinson, Ken. "Do schools kill creativity?" TED. Accessed July 30, 2015. http://www.ted.com/talks/ken_robinson_says_schools_kill_creativity?language=en.

74   Myers, Isabel, and Peter B. Myers. *Gifts differing: Understanding personality type.* Mountain View: Davies-Black, [1980] 1995.

75   "Big five personality traits." Wikipedia. Accessed November 4, 2016. https://en.wikipedia.org/wiki/Big_Five_personality_traits.

76   Nowack, K. "Is the Myers Briggs Type Indicator the right tool to use? Performance in practice." *American society of training and development,* Fall 6 (1996).

77   Myers, Isabel, and Peter B. Myers. *Gifts differing: Understanding personality type.* Mountain View: Davies-Black, [1980] 1995: 7. [Citations refer to the 1995 paperback edition.]

78   Ibid., 2.

79   Ibid., 3.

80   Ibid., 8.

81   Ibid., 182–183.

82   Rath, Tom. *StrengthsFinder 2.0.* Gallup Press, 2007: 8.

83   Myers, Isabel, and Peter B. Myers. *Gifts differing: Understanding personality type.* Mountain View: Davies-Black, [1980] 1995: 183.

84   Nadia, Steve. "Kids' brain power." The Riggs Institute. Accessed August 1, 2015. http://www.riggsinst.org/brainpower.aspx.

85   "Child development fact sheet: Stages of brain development." Child, Youth and Family. Accessed August 1, 2015. http://www.cyf.govt.nz/documents/info-for-caregivers/fds-cd-stages-of-brain-dec11-hu.pdf.

86   Nadia, Steve. "Kids' brain power." The Riggs Institute. Accessed August 1, 2015. http://www.riggsinst.org/brainpower.aspx.

87 Ibid.

88 "The role of questions in teaching, thinking and learning." The Critical Thinking Community. Accessed August 21, 2014. http://www.criticalthinking.org/pages/the-role-of-questions-in-teaching-thinking-and-learning/524.

89 Hawking, Stephen. *A brief history of time.* Bantam Books, [1988] 1998. [Citations refer to the trade paperback edition.]

90 Faber, Adele, and Elaine Mazlish. *How to talk so kids will listen & listen so kids will talk.* Scribner [1980] 2012: 269. [Citations refer to the 2012 paperback edition.]

91 Covey, Stephen R. *The 7 habits of highly successful people: Powerful lessons in personal change.* Fireside [1989] 1990: 239–241. [Citations refer to the paperback edition.]

92 Faber, Adele, and Elaine Mazlish. *How to talk so kids will listen & listen so kids will talk.* Scribner [1980] 2012: 9.

93 Karp, Harvey. *The happiest toddler on the block.* Bantam Dell, 2004: 112–120.

94 Gottman, John. *Raising an emotionally intelligent child: The heart of parenting.* Simon and Schuster, 1997: 101–102.

95 Shaver, Phillip, Judith Schwartz, Donald Kirson, and Cary O'connor. "Emotion knowledge: Further exploration of a prototype approach." *Journal of personality and social psychology* 52, no. 6 (1987): 1067.

96 "What is emotion? 4 ways of manifestation, part 3." Experiencing Architecture. Accessed August 6, 2015. http://experiencingarchitecture.com/2010/01/31/what-is-emotion-part-3-4-ways-of-manifestation/.

97 Ekman, Paul, and Dacher Keltner. "Universal facial expressions of emotion." *California mental health research digest* 8, no. 4 (1970): 151–158.

98 The translations for anger, sadness, and fear were inspired by Cornelia Maude Spelman's *The way I feel* books: *When I feel angry.* Albert Whitman and Company, 2000. *When I feel sad.* Albert Whitman and Company, 2002. *When I feel scared.* Albert Whitman and Company, 2002.

99   Moglen, Laurel. "The science of parental love." The Mother Company. Accessed August 9, 2015. http://www.themotherco.com/2011/02/the-science-of-parental-love/.

100 Ibid.

101 "The seven basic emotions: Do you know them?" Humanintell. Accessed August 6, 2015. http://www.humintell.com/2010/06/the-seven-basic-emotions-do-you-know-them/.

102 Santangelo, Paolo. *From skin to heart: Perceptions of emotions and bodily sensations in traditional Chinese culture.* Harrassowitz Verlag, 2006: 35.

103 "Surprise (emotion)." Wikipedia. Accessed August 9, 2015. https://en.m.wikipedia.org/wiki/Surprise_(emotion).

104 "The seven basic emotions: Do you know them?" Humanintell. Accessed August 6, 2015. http://www.humintell.com/2010/06/the-seven-basic-emotions-do-you-know-them/.

105 "Surprise (emotion)." Wikipedia. Accessed August 9, 2015. https://en.m.wikipedia.org/wiki/Surprise_(emotion).

106 Mills, Harry Mills. "Physiology of anger." Mental Help. Accessed June 10, 2016. https://www.mentalhelp.net/articles/physiology-of-anger/.

107 "Anger." Wikipedia. Accessed August 6, 2015. https://en.wikipedia.org/wiki/Anger.

108 "The seven basic emotions: Do you know them?" Humanintell. Accessed August 6, 2015. http://www.humintell.com/2010/06/the-seven-basic-emotions-do-you-know-them/.

109 "Affect theory." Wikipedia. Accessed August 6, 2015. https://en.m.wikipedia.org/wiki/Affect_theory.

110 Mills, Harry Mills. "Physiology of anger." Mental Help. Accessed June 10, 2016. https://www.mentalhelp.net/articles/physiology-of-anger/.

111 "Sadness." Wikipedia. Accessed August 9, 2015. https://en.wikipedia.org/wiki/Sadness.

112 "The seven basic emotions: Do you know them?" Humanintell. Accessed August 6, 2015. http://www.humintell.com/2010/06/the-seven-basic-emotions-do-you-know-them/.

113 Ibid.

114   "Fear." Wikipedia. Accessed August 9, 2015. https://en.wikipedia.org/wiki/Fear.

115   "Disgust." Wikipedia. Accessed August 10, 2015. https://en.wikipedia.org/wiki/Disgust.

116   Green, James A., Pamela G. Whitney, and Michael Potegal. "Screaming, yelling, whining, and crying: categorical and intensity differences in vocal expressions of anger and sadness in children's tantrums." *Emotion* 11, no. 5 (2011): 1124–1133.

117   Goleman, Daniel. *Emotional intelligence: Why it can matter more than IQ.* Bantam Dell, [1995] 2005 (reprint): 99.

118   Ibid.

119   Deci, Edward L., and Richard M. Ryan. *Handbook of self-determination research.* University Rochester Press, 2002: 6–8.

120   Branden, Nathaniel. *The psychology of self-esteem: A revolutionary approach to self-understanding that launched a new era in modern psychology.* Jossey-Bass, 2001: 113.

121   Ibid., 111.

122   Gottman, John. *Raising an emotionally intelligent child: The heart of parenting.* Simon and Schuster, 1997: 121.

123   Ibid., 120–121.

124   Wansink, Brian, and Jeffery Sobal. "Mindless eating: the 200 daily food decisions we overlook." *Environment and behavior* 39, no. 1 (2007): 106–123.

125   Kahneman, Daniel. *Thinking, fast and slow.* Farrar, Straus and Giroux, 2011: ch. 1. [Citations refer to the EPUB edition.]

126   Ibid.

127   "Recognition Primed Decision." Wikipedia. Accessed October 23, 2015. https://en.wikipedia.org/wiki/Recognition_primed_decision.

128   Mehl, Matthias R., Simine Vazire, Nairán Ramírez-Esparza, Richard B. Slatcher, and James W. Pennebaker. "Are women really more talkative than men?" *Science* 317, no. 82 (2007).

129   Hart, Betty, and Todd R. Risley. "The Early Catastrophe: The 30 Million Word Gap by Age 3." *American Educator* 27, no. 1 (2003): 4–9.

130 Kohn, Alfie. "The Risk of Rewards." Alfie Kohn. Accessed December 10, 2015. http://www.alfiekohn.org/article/risks-rewards/.

131 Ibid.

132 Ibid.

133 "Math Class Squared." *The Wonder Years*. Season 3, episode 9. American Broadcasting Company: December 12, 1989.

134 Owen, David. *The first national bank of Dad: The best way to teach kids about money*. Simon and Schuster, 2003.

135 Gottman, John. *Raising an emotionally intelligent child: The heart of parenting*. Simon and Schuster, 1997: 24.

136 Faber, Adele, and Elaine Mazlish. *How to talk so kids will listen & listen so kids will talk*. Scribner [1980] 2012: 103.

137 Goleman, Daniel. *Emotional intelligence: Why it can matter more than IQ*. Bantam Dell, [1995] 2005 (reprint): 276.

138 "Alfie Kohn Questions Our Basic Assumptions About Raising Children." Leading Edge Parenting. May 27, 2009. Apple podcast app.

139 Myers, Isabel, and Peter B. Myers. *Gifts differing: Understanding personality type*. Davies-Black, [1980] 1995: 116.

INDEX

Locators in *italics* are used for figures and those in **bold** for tables.

ABOUT THE AUTHOR

Brian Vondruska is the author of *The Optimal Life Experience*. He is also the founder and author of the website TheKindofParentYouAre.com, a portal for parents to help their children, and themselves, become their best selves. Brian realized that to help his children grow, he needed to stretch his own limits. He was disappointed in the lack of resources available to help him direct his self-development as a parent. Now he creates those resources for other parents.

Made in the USA
Lexington, KY
24 October 2018